"I needed this type of information when I started my coaching career many years ago… This should be in the hands of all persons who will be dealing with the young ladies who are playing basketball."

Carroll Graham
National Chairman
AAU Girls' Basketball

"Mike has come up with a real winner…and I recommend it strongly…A must-read for any coach or player who wants to improve."

Morgan Wootten
All-time winningest high school
boys' basketball coach

"*The Complete Guide to Girls' Basketball* is one of the most thorough and comprehensive books on basketball that I have ever come across. Mullaney touches on all aspects of the game: from general philosophies, to offensive and defensive strategy, to specific drills… this book covers it all. It would be a valuable companion for any coach who wants to take his or her team to the next level."

Joanne Boyle
Head Women's Basketball Coach
University of Richmond

"*The Complete Guide* is an encyclopedia of basketball. It is a valuable guide for coaches since it includes many useful drills and diagrams that help demonstrate how the drills should be executed. I recommend the book to coaches and players at any level."

Bill Finney
Head Women's Basketball Coach
Marymount University

"This book is the most complete guide to girls' basketball that I have ever seen! Whether you are a player, coach, or fan and regardless of what level of development you are at, this book is a must-have for everyone. You should be so fortunate to run across a book like this in your lifetime!"

Brenda Frese
Head Women's Basketball Coach
University of Maryland

"*The Complete Guide to Girls' Basketball* is a tremendous resource! This book provides thorough explanations for young coaches, multiple defensive and offensive drills for all coaches, and quotes to inspire and challenge even the most experienced coaches. Mullaney's vision for the growth of girls' and women's basketball is put into action through the pages of this book."

Sue Semrau
Head Women's Basketball Coach
Florida State University

D1299441

The Complete Guide to Girls' Basketball

MICHAEL D. MULLANEY

WILLIAMSBURG REGIONAL LIBRARY
7770 CROAKER ROAD
WILLIAMSBURG, VIRGINIA 23188

MAY   2007

The Complete Guide to Girls' Basketball

Library of Congress Cataloging-in-Publication Data

Mullaney, Michael D.
   The complete guide to girls' basketball
Includes index
   ISBN 0-9761005-0-9 (soft cover)

Copyright © 2004 by Michael D. Mullaney

All rights reserved. No part of this book may be reproduced or transmitted in any form or by any means, electronic or mechanical, including photocopying, recording or by any information storage and retrieval system without written permission from the author.

Editor: Katherine Day
Designer and Diagram Templates: Christine Marsh
Cover Design and Typesetting: Julie Phinney, BookMasters, Inc.
Cover and Interior Photographs: Greg Fiume
Printer: BookMasters, Inc.
Printed in the United States of America

The schools and/or organizations whose names and/or logos may be visible in photographs found in this book have not collaborated with the author in the writing of this book. Action photographs were taken at high school games in Maryland, a game played in Boyds, Maryland that was coached by the author, and of AAU teams playing in Boyds. Any names or logos that may be visible in these photographs are not intended to imply association with, or endorsement or sponsorship by, any of the respective schools and/or organizations pursuant to Section 43 of the Lanham Act (15 U.S.C. Section 1125). Use of the names or logos is nominative and all trademark rights are the exclusive property of their respective owners.

*This book is dedicated
to the parents who make the girls'
game possible through their
tremendous support and enthusiasm.*

Contents at a Glance

PART FIVE: DRILLS

PART SIX: APPENDICES

Contents

PART TWO: OFFENSE

Table of Contents

Table of Contents

ACKNOWLEDGMENTS

I want to thank everyone who contributed to this book. Without their help, *The Complete Guide to Girls' Basketball* would never have been written.

I want to thank my wife, Sue, for all of her love and support; my daughters, Melissa and Michele, and the players on my basketball teams and their parents (they are wonderful young women with supportive families); and Bruce Goldin and Rick Herald for their time and input. I also want to acknowledge the positive influence of my high school coach, John Baldwin.

Katherine Day performed the skillful job of editing. She was a pleasure to work with and I am lucky to have found her. Greg Fiume took the top quality action photos. Julie Phinney created the cover design and typeset the complicated layout. My wife, Sue, assisted greatly with computer and software issues, and provided many valuable suggestions as well. It was a well-executed team effort.

KEY TO DIAGRAMS

Path of player   ⟶
Path of ball   - - - - ⟶
Dribble   ∿∿∿⟶
Screen   ⊢
Ball   ⊕
Offensive player   ❶ ❷ ❸ ❹ ❺ ●
Player with ball   ✹❶ ✹❷ ✹❸ ✹❹ ✹❺ ✹●
Defensive player   **X1 X2 X3 X4 X5 X**
Coach   ℂ
Assistant Coach   𝔸ℂ

Solid black circles represent additional offensive players
X with no numbers are additional defensive players

The right and left sides are determined when facing the basket. This may confuse you at first: for instance, the right wing is on the right side of the court but on the left side of the page.

The "elbow" refers to the point where the free-throw line intersects with the line coming from the baseline, also known as the lane line. The right elbow is where the lines meet on the right side of the court (facing the basket) and the left elbow is where they meet on the left side.

Court dimensions:
The court is 50 feet wide and 94 feet long (47 feet to half-court).
The free-throw line is 15 feet from the point directly under the backboard.
The outside of the three-point line is 19 feet 9 inches from the point directly under the rim.

INTRODUCTION

I decided to write this book because I love basketball, have a passion for teaching the game and see a real need for a resource to help coaches and parents teach basketball properly to young women. Girls' basketball has become enormously popular, and now more than ever, coaches, parents and players want and need guidance. This book is designed to be understood by every individual who wants to learn and enjoy the game.

I have coached hundreds of basketball games. In this book, I want to share my thoughts on how basketball should be taught and played, and, just as important, how individuals can appreciate and value basketball as a sport and as a way of life. Basketball can play a major role in a young woman's development; coaches shouldn't underestimate how great of an influence (positive or negative) they can have! Have you ever noticed that many players seem to remember their coaches for the rest of their lives? These basketball experiences *do* stand out in players' minds. That's why it's so important that coaches and parents, together, make those experiences positive!

When I was growing up in Jacksonville, Florida, I didn't live near an indoor gym. I spent many hours on an outdoor basketball court shooting. On windy days, I would modify my shot to "play the wind." (Don't worry—there aren't any plays or drills in this book that take blustery weather conditions into account.) I was determined to become the best basketball player I could be. In my first game in 8th grade, I scored 42 points; that year I averaged 25 points a game. I went on to start in high school as a point guard. During my high school years, I made the All-City team, was named the team's Most Valuable Player, was All-State in the mile and two-mile runs, and won the John Burke Award for being the top student-athlete in school. I'm especially proud of that because I'm only 5 feet 9 inches tall (if I round up). I learned that success comes from hard work and playing together as a team.

This book is intended to benefit girls at all skill levels, from elementary school through high school (including AAU players), and is a great resource for any young woman wanting to play in college. It explains and analyzes basic fundamentals, advanced skills, and game strategies, and also provides practice plans. Many explanations are supplemented with diagrams and photos that try to capture the game.

Part One of the book provides an overview, tips on how to develop a plan for the season and some suggestions on how to communicate with players and parents. Part Two covers offensive fundamentals like shooting and the fast break. Part Three covers defensive fundamentals and man-to-man and zone defenses. Part Four explains special situations, such as the press and out-of-bounds plays, and includes tips on developing strategies and effective practice plans. Part Five contains drills. Finally, Part Six consists of appendices that include the all-important rules of the game, basketball definitions, and references to other basketball books and web sites.

Part Five is a particularly important section. Teams tend to play like they practice. So, *The Complete Guide to Girls' Basketball* provides over 200 drills, broken down to target specific skills. Some drills are basic plays that can be used directly in games; some drills focus on single basketball skills; others incorporate more than one fundamental concept. I've also included suggestions for drill variations; typically these variations describe a more advanced or more competitive alternative. As an additional teaching tool, I've included state-of-the-art illustrative diagrams to assist coaches and players alike.

The quotations in this book, sports-related or otherwise, serve as a reminder that, whether coaching, playing or spectating (for that matter, in life in general!), we all need to keep our sense of humor and enjoy the game.

I feel fortunate to have written this book. The reality is, I have made more friends through my basketball associations than through any other activity. I hope readers will experience the same excitement and reap the same benefits from the sport that I have. After you finish *The Complete Guide to Girls' Basketball*, you will see just how far the girls' game has progressed.

Have fun with this book. I hope you enjoy reading it as much as I enjoyed writing it!

Mike Mullaney

NOTES

In this book, the male pronoun "he" and the adjective "his" are used to describe and refer to coaches (since it provided a natural way to differentiate between coaches and the female players). This does not mean to imply that there aren't hundreds of great women basketball coaches. There certainly are! I also use the term "man-to-man" to describe certain defensive sets; it is a common basketball term and is intended to be viewed as gender-neutral.

PART ONE
Coaching Philosophy

CHAPTER 1
The Popularity and Growth of Girls' Basketball

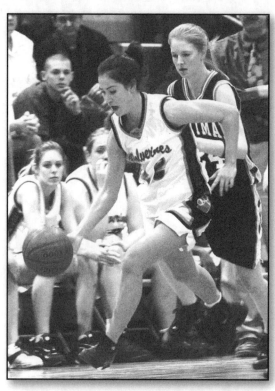

Surprise! Basketball isn't just for boys anymore. Thirty years ago, it was rare for schools to field a girls' basketball team, and it was even more unusual for there to be girls' basketball leagues outside of school…but a lot has changed since then. The game is now enormously popular among girls and women of all ages, from elementary school age up to professionals. What's more, it's no longer *just* a winter sport; now, with the advent of organized fall, spring, and summer leagues, basketball is a year-round activity.

Millions of girls play basketball each year on high school, middle school, elementary school, recreational, and AAU (Amateur Athletic Union) teams combined. Basketball is the most popular girls' high school sport; more than 500,000 young women participate across the country in a given year. It is played at almost 20,000 high schools in all 50 states and in the District of Columbia. That's a lot of athletic young women!

TEAMS AND LEAGUES AVAILABLE

SCHOOL TEAMS

According to a National Federation of State High School Associations (NFHS) 2002–2003 Athletics Participation Survey, the top ten most popular high school girls' sports programs (in order of participation) are:

1. Basketball
2. Outdoor Track and Field
3. Volleyball
4. Fast-Pitch Softball
5. Soccer
6. Cross-Country
7. Tennis
8. Swimming and Diving
9. Competitive Spirit Squads
10. Golf

Most schools have varsity and junior varsity teams, and some have a freshman squad as well. A typical high school team plays about 20 games during the winter season, beginning in early December and ending in late February (and possibly later if they qualify for the playoffs). In some localities, varsity and junior varsity coaches are prohibited from coaching their school teams outside of certain specified dates in the winter months. Volunteer parents or other individuals coach during the spring, summer, and fall seasons, thus enabling the girls to play varsity or junior varsity-level basketball with their school teammates practically all year long.

The growth of girls' basketball has been proportional to the overall growth in high school girls' sports. According to the NFHS survey, for the schools responding, participation by girls in all high school sports increased from 1.3 million in the school year ending in 1974 to 2.8 million in the school year ending in 2003. (By comparison, boys' participation was slightly above 4 million in the 1974 school year and slightly below 4 million in the 2003 school year.) Equally as impressive is the fact that the number of girls participating on middle school, elementary school and recreational teams actually exceeds the number of girls participating on high school teams. In other words, a lot of young women are getting out there and playing, even if they aren't able to join their school teams.

RECREATION, CYO AND OTHER LEAGUES

Recreational, CYO (Catholic Youth Organization), and city/county leagues have also become very popular. Many girls who play on their school basketball teams also play on at least one other team in an outside league. These teams provide opportunities for players at all skill levels to be on a team and to enjoy the game. In many recreational leagues there are no tryouts, and players are assigned to a team based on where they live. CYO leagues start as early as the third grade and end in twelfth grade. New leagues and tourna-

"Now that I'm here, we'll turn this program around 360 degrees."

—Jason Kidd

ments are being formed each year to meet the growing demand of youth girls' basketball.

AAU

The AAU is one of the largest, nonprofit athletic associations in the United States. It is dedicated to the promotion and development of amateur sports and physical fitness programs. Basketball is now the number one AAU girls' sport and continues to grow each year. AAU girls' basketball has doubled in size over the last 10 years!

AAU has sponsored the formation of hundreds of basketball clubs around the nation. Under the AAU umbrella, athletes are able to play basketball practically year-round on the same team. AAU teams fill the void left by school-sponsored squads that only play serious basketball during the regular winter season, but disband afterward. Perhaps most importantly, AAU teams give players the opportunity to compete at a high level with players at or above their own skill levels (something that a high school team doesn't always guarantee).

The national AAU organization does not decide how tryouts are conducted or how teams are formed. Instead, these issues are left to the local individual clubs to decide. As a result, there can be wide variations in the manner that players are selected and the level of play. The national AAU organization sponsors tournaments throughout the year at both Division I and Division II levels. These tournaments have become important for college recruiting. In fact, many consider AAU basketball to be the center of highly skilled youth play in the United States.

COLLEGE BASKETBALL

Do the high participation numbers for women's basketball hold at the college level? Yes. There are approximately 14,500 women playing on 1,000 NCAA varsity basketball teams, according to an NCAA 2001–2002 Sports Sponsorship and Participation Report. Divisions

"Sports is the only profession I know that when you retire, you have to go to work."

—Earl Monroe

I, II, and III have 4,800, 3,900, and 5,800 women's basketball participants, respectively. Basketball is the only sport with over 1,000 teams, but is not the number one college sport for women in terms of participation. It ranks behind soccer, outdoor track, indoor track, and softball. Part of the reason that basketball drops to number five in college is that most other sports have more players on each team. For instance, the average soccer squad consists of 22 players in contrast to only 14 players for basketball.

In addition to the NCAA, there are also more than 150 colleges that compete as part of the National Association for Intercollegiate Athletics (NAIA) and over 200 two-year colleges that are members of the National Junior College Athletic Association (NJCAA). Many young women also play on college intramural or club teams.

Taking into account players, families and fans, tens of millions of people follow girls' and women's basketball, and the sport is growing. Now you can see why this book is necessary!

"I wanted to have a career in sports when I was young, but I had to give it up. I'm only six feet tall, so I couldn't play basketball. I'm only 190 pounds, so I couldn't play football. And I have 20-20 vision, so I couldn't be a referee."

—Jay Leno

CHAPTER 2
Developing a Plan

Coaching girls' basketball is different than coaching boys' basketball. This may partly be because girls and boys develop at different ages, or because girls tend, in general, to value friendships more. But boys and girls also differ in the way that they approach physical activity in general, how they respond to making physical contact with other players, how they react to various forms of criticism and praise, how they relate to their teammates and coaches, what they want to accomplish by playing on a team, and what they believe is fun and rewarding.

"I like to take all the shots in tough situations. As a matter of fact, I like taking all the shots."

—Mike Mitchell

Coaches also need to factor in basic skill differences based on age. For example, younger girls tend to score close to the basket. A coach working with young players should develop strategies that attempt to get the ball down low, run the fast break at every opportunity, and encourage players to drive to the basket to shoot high percentage layups and draw fouls. Coaches should determine which teaching points to emphasize in order to maximize both learning and enjoyment.

BECOMING A GREAT COACH

Below I have listed the top ten characteristics (besides having read this book, of course!) needed to be an outstanding girls' basketball coach:

1. Understand the game.
2. Be organized and plan all practices and games (make sure that all administrative matters are handled effectively).
3. Be patient.
4. Treat people with respect (eliminate rudeness, do not allow disrespect, and coach for the benefit of the girls).
5. Be enthusiastic.
6. Know that it is okay to yell instructions to players, but not to yell at them.
7. Work hard, insist on hustle, and play to win (within reason, of course).
8. Set a good example and surround yourself with good people.
9. Teach the game in a way that improves play and makes it enjoyable.
10. Be a great teacher by communicating clearly and being consistent.

Many coaches never played basketball in high school—or at any organized level, for that matter. Other coaches were stars in their college programs or as professional players. When it comes down to it, it's more about a coach's ability to learn and adjust to the game and connect with players than it is about personal athletic experience.

BASKETBALL PHILOSOPHY

What follows are important issues that a girls' basketball coach should consider when he develops his plan.

PLAN CHECKLIST

SELF-ESTEEM

A coach's primary goal should be to improve the self-esteem of his players. Every time a coach notices a player doing things right, he should communicate a sense of acceptance and approval. This doesn't mean he should mislead players by giving them false praise purely in the hopes of boosting their self-esteem. To do so would be to make excuses for them to protect their egos. However, every basketball player on the team should feel good about herself. For a player to suffer from low self-esteem while playing basketball means that the coach and player are not a successful match.

Coaches should teach their players to accept responsibility for their actions and to critically examine both their strengths and their shortcomings. It is through this realistic approach of setting expectations, being honest with constructive criticism, and providing encouragement that coaches help players learn.

ENJOYMENT

Playing on a basketball team should be fun, but in a different way than a sleepover or birthday party. The enjoyment of playing basketball is knowing that the individuals and the team have done their very best. Many people confuse "recreational fun" with "basketball fun." The former is the joy of leisure, the latter is the joy of accomplishment.

"They say that nobody is perfect. Then they tell you practice makes perfect. I wish they'd make up their minds."

—Wilt Chamberlain

When I say, "The joy of accomplishment," I mean the enjoyment that stems from doing one's best, progressing toward a goal, and successfully playing together as a team. In basketball, fun does not mean goofing off or clowning around and laughing with friends at practice; fun is working hard and getting better. (Players will learn on their own sooner or later—it's just no fun to play badly, game after game.)

WINNING AND LOSING

Coaches are responsible for determining the role that winning and losing will play for their team. Some coaches assert that winning isn't truly important, that simply playing and improving should be the ultimate goal. Other coaches try to win every game. The best option for youth coaches is to create a winning program while providing playing time for every player. Each team member has a role, and every role is integral to the team.

I have found that coaching to win provides the team with a purpose. In no way does that mean that a team's goal should be to win at all costs (for example, by forcing some players to consistently sit the bench). Rather, winning should provide a focal point for the team as a whole; the goal should be to win as a team and to have fun in the process.

TEAMWORK

It is important that a coach establish an ethic of teamwork. You might be surprised to realize that the concept of teamwork is foreign to many youth players when they first join a competitive basketball team. At home they may be pampered with every convenience. Only through basketball are they taught the valuable lesson that the team is greater than any one individual player. One of the most rewarding parts of coaching basketball is teaching young players to work as a cohesive unit.

PRACTICE AND PREPARATION

High school teams typically practice every weekday during the winter season except for game days, and in some cases, also on the weekends. A coach should plan practices in advance; they should be used for conditioning as well as the development of fundamental skills. (Sample practice plans and drills are included later in this book.)

> "We're the only team in history that could lose nine games in a row and then go into a slump."
>
> —Bill Fitch, on a losing Cleveland Cavaliers team

> "If you're not going to play, you might as well not play for the best."
>
> —Jack Mansell, bench-warmer on fourth ranked Georgia Tech team

DISCIPLINE

Without discipline, a team has no direction. Rules and discipline help create winning programs by developing focused players. As difficult as it may be to instill, in the long run, discipline serves the best interests of the players and the team as a whole.

PATIENCE

Being a successful basketball coach requires a lot of patience. Patience is a quality that contributes to the quality of a player's experience.

LUCK

Lucky teams avoid serious injuries and are blessed with supportive parents. Even the greatest coaches need a little bit of luck on their side!

ENTHUSIASM

Enthusiasm is important, even to the most disciplined teams. Practices, in particular, are fueled by the passion of players and coaches. Enthusiasm makes great practices, and great practices win games.

CONSISTENCY

Consistency provides both coaches and players with the means to develop a safe and stable environment. Players will likely perform better if they trust their coach; trust begins with consistent coaching.

FAITH

Coaches, players, and parents—in short, the team as a whole—must have faith in themselves and in each other. It's as simple as that.

MOTIVATION

A coach can motivate players by setting rules, establishing high but realistic expectations, challenging players to do their best and letting them know that he cares about them individually—as human beings and as team members.

> *"I'm not stupid. I just talk stupid."*
>
> —Lefty Driesell

> *"Girls just wanna have fun."*
>
> —Cyndi Lauper

FEAR

Fear can be a motivator—most players (and coaches) hate to lose. But it is important that fear doesn't enter into a player's psyche when she's on the court. At that point, she should have only positive thoughts.

COMPETITIVE ATMOSPHERE

The game of basketball is highly competitive. Basketball is a fast-paced game played indoors in a very close environment. In many games, parents and other fans sit directly behind the bench—so close that their shouts and instructions can easily be heard on the court. Even at a very early age, girl basketball players will have to learn to cope with this unique competitive environment.

PHYSICAL CONDITIONING

Physical conditioning is an important aspect of a successful basketball team. High school teams that play 5 days a week should be in great shape, but it can be difficult for teams to maintain a high level of conditioning if they meet for no more than two practices a week. Fortunately, many youth players play other sports that keep them active throughout the week.

WINNING AND PLAYING TIME

It can be a difficult decision—whether to play games solely to win, or to give each team member playing time in the attempt to develop their skills. Of course, it's natural for some players to play more than others; for example, a team may have only one outstanding point guard. But coaches can take advantage of non-championship (and blowout) games to give nonstarters playing experience.

In close games, a coach faces difficult decisions—should the substitute players, who may not be as skilled but need additional playing time, be put into the game? It's like having a little devil on one shoulder telling you that you need to win, while on the other shoulder, an angel whispers in your ear to do the right thing by putting reserve players in the game. There's no good answer to this difficult question. In fact, deciding whether or not to listen to the "angel whispers" is one of the toughest parts of coaching. Varsity high school teams tend to emphasize winning more than others. It's something a coach has to determine on a game-to-game basis.

TEAM CULTURE

The overall atmosphere at practice can be an important factor in determining whether or not players progress. For example, if a coach shows up late to practice, he sends a signal that it is acceptable to be unreliable. In the same way, if he lets players get away with slacking off during drills, he sends a message that it's acceptable not to give 100 percent.

Coaches and players contribute to the team culture. All team members need to understand that playing on the team is a commitment; they need to be dedicated to improving as individuals; and finally, they should always know that their coach cares about them as people.

ATTENTION SPAN

It's important that youth coaches recognize that the attention span of many players is less than 5 minutes for any given practice segment.

SPEED OF THE GAME

What separates good teams from great teams is quickness. On the better teams, everything from ballhandling to passing happens faster. As players progress, they become more decisive; as reaction time decreases, game speed increases.

WHERE POINTS ARE SCORED

It's useful to analyze where on the court the opposing team is likely to score most of its points. In youth basketball, a disproportionate number of points are scored by layups, shots within five to seven feet of the basket, and foul shots. But as players develop their skills, they start to make shots from outside the foul line and the three-point circle. Generally, girls are able to shoot comfortably from three-point range beginning between the ages of 13 and 14. In structuring a defense, a coach should be aware of the number of points the opponent is likely to score and where on the court those points are likely to be achieved.

> "Coaches are always under the gun. I'd like to see the won-lost records of doctors out front where people could see for themselves. Won 10, lost 3, tied 2."
>
> —Abe Lemons

> "I want to be on God's squad—He's my kind of head coach."
>
> —Bobby Bowden

> "Every time I see my mother I say, 'Why didn't you wait?'"
>
> —Hot Rod Hundley, on only signing for $10,000 after being a first-round draft choice in 1957

EFFORT

A good team will be fundamentally strong, well conditioned, and cooperative; a great team will be all of these things, but most importantly, it will be hard working. There's nothing wrong with throwing a few incentives into practice to encourage effort and competition. A coach might offer a soft drink to the player who can grab a certain number of rebounds in a practice drill. The increase in intensity in going after the ball will be easy to see!

COMMUNICATING WITH PLAYERS AND PARENTS

At the beginning of the season, a coach should hold meetings with parents and players. Parents should be made aware of team expectations and their own roles within the team's goals. With players, coaches should discuss expectations. (This is discussed more fully in Chapter 3.)

DEVELOPING A PLAN

Chapter 16 covers practice and game strategies, but I want to emphasize here the importance of developing a plan. One important element of any game plan is to make sure that all players know their assignments, both on offense and defense. Players must know the team offenses by heart; for example, when running out-of-bounds plays, all players must immediately know where to set up and how to precisely execute their cuts.

An effective way to communicate assignments is to have a walk-through practice before a game. Coaches should remind their players of:

- The positions they will be playing in the game
- Their position on defense and who they will be guarding
- If the opponent is likely to press, and the corresponding assignments for the press offense
- General offensive and defensive schemes
- Offensive and defensive assignments for fast-break situations
- Out-of-bounds plays and assignments
- How substitutions will be made

> *"I slept like a baby— I woke up and cried every two hours."*
>
> —Fred Taylor, after losing a close football game

> *"I learned a long time ago that minor surgery is when they do the operation on someone else, not you."*
>
> —Bill Walton

The more precise a coach is in describing offensive and defensive assignments before a game, the less likely it is his players will make mistakes during the game.

A coach must be clear when making assignments. To simplify, he might consider having players stay on the same side of the court when playing both offense and defense. For example, he can assign players to the right side of the team's basket (the right wing) on offense to a defensive position on the same side of the court and vice versa for players on the left. Early in the season, it is advisable to have players play the same position until they really learn it.

POINTS OF EMPHASIS BEFORE A GAME

Sometimes, players have a difficult time remembering all of the teaching points made during practice. Therefore, during pre-game meetings, it is a good idea to summarize certain points that players should remember. Points that I've found to be important follow:

1. **Rebound** by gaining the inside position. As the ball is in the air, block out by making contact with opposing players. Make a quick outlet pass after every defensive rebound.
2. **Run the fast break** at every opportunity. Take the ball all the way to the basket to force the defender to make a great play. The keys to the fast break are a strong rebound, quick **outlet pass**, and players sprinting down the court.
3. **Drive** the ball to the basket as much as possible to put pressure on the defense. The goal is to score a layup or to get fouled—ideally, make the basket and draw the foul.
4. Take **high percentage shots**—layups and shots from the foul line.
5. Run **out-of-bounds** plays effectively, as most games are decided by four points or less. Out-of-bounds plays can make the difference in the game.
6. **Don't foul.** Getting into a foul shooting contest with the other team is a losing strategy.
7. **Pressure the ball** on defense—challenge all shots. Play team defense.

"I asked him to spell Mississippi. He said, 'the state or the river?'"

—George Raveling

"Half this game is 90 percent mental."

—Danny Ozark

"Go to bed early, get up early—this is wise."

—Mark Twain (obviously not a teenager at the time)

8. Make sure of your **assignments** before entering the game.
9. Always **hustle**! The team that puts out more effort and stays focused has a better chance to win.

(Chapter 16 more fully covers strategies.)

GOALS

> "The taste of defeat has a richness of experience all its own."
>
> —Bill Bradley

It is also a good idea to establish statistical goals prior to each game, such as having more rebounds than the other team, committing less than seven fouls in each half, committing less than five turnovers per half, or holding the opponent to less than 20 points in each half. Statistics can be used to monitor the performances of individual players and the team as a whole. Statistics can include:

- Points
- Rebounds
- Number of steals
- Assists
- Fouls
- Turnovers

Statistics kept during intrasquad scrimmages can also be used to help motivate players to improve. Even in an informal setting, it is important for both teams on the court to have specific goals, such as improving man-to-man defense, rebounding, and running the fast break.

> "The best way to have good health is not to get sick in the first place."
>
> —Michael D. Mullaney (I always wanted to be quoted in a book)

Goals are also important for developing individual skills. Below is a checklist of goals and qualities of successful basketball players. It includes both physical and mental components of the game.

- Great effort
- Defensive skills
- Ballhandling skills
- Shooting ability
- Passing ability
- Athleticism
- Conditioning, strength, quickness, and speed
- Footwork, coordination, and jumping ability
- Aggressiveness, work ethic, and motivation
- Court sense and initiative

- Teamwork and leadership
- Ability to anticipate
- Unselfishness and dedication
- Competitive attitude and desire
- Concentration and ability to learn quickly

Mental aspects and attitude:
- Ability to follow instructions
- Instinct and ability to anticipate
- Aggressiveness
- Desire for the game
- Alertness
- Attention to details
- Unselfishness
- Ability to get along with teammates
- Work ethic

Physical skills:
- Physical condition
- Straight away speed
- Ability to change direction quickly
- Jumping
- Quickness
- Footwork

Game performance goals:
- Individual defense
- Team defense
- Individual offense
- Team offense
- Rebounding
- Shooting
- Shot selection
- Ability to penetrate
- Ballhandling
- Passing
- Catching

"I told one player, 'Son, I can't understand it with you. Is it ignorance or apathy?' He said, 'Coach, I don't know and I don't care.'"

—Frank Layden

According to John Wooden, success is defined as trying one's very best. Success should not be measured in terms of wins and losses, but rather in the effort put forth.

CHAPTER 3
Communicating with Players and Parents

Perhaps the most important part of coaching is effectively communicating with players and parents. How will your team conduct itself on the floor? How will you handle problems both on and off the court? Players, parents, and coaches need to share realistic expectations. That is, it is important that a coach establish rules and goals up front, and that he communicates these to the players and parents.

Unfortunately, some children are led to believe that because they can shoot a seven-foot shot at age 6, they will be the star player on their AAU, high school, and even college basketball team. The reality is that the majority of youth basketball players do not play college ball; many do not even make their high school teams. These inflated expectations hurt children in the long run. There's nothing wrong with setting goals and striving to achieve them; but coaches and parents have a responsibility to keep their players' expectations within the realm of reality.

COMMUNICATING WITH PLAYERS

PLAYING TIME

Coaches need to be very sensitive to the issue of playing time. Many players (and parents) take personal offense if they don't play as much as they think they should. Unfortunately, basketball only allows five players from each team to be on the court at one time. This means that a team of 12 will have more than one-half of its players sitting on the bench at any given moment. On average, a player will play less than one-half of the game. These are challenging circumstances for coaches! I believe that only in the most important championship contests should there be a scenario where a youth player has to sit on the bench for the entire game.

THE NUMBER OF PLAYERS ON A TEAM

Having eight players on a nonschool team is one way to accommodate the playing time issue. However, with so few players, it's a problem when someone misses a game. The other drawback to having eight players is that the team cannot practice five-on-five unless coaches, parents, brothers or sisters help out.

"A team should be an extension of the coach's personality. My teams are arrogant and obnoxious."

—Al McGuire

"I want to gain 1,500 or 2,000 yards, whichever comes first."

—George Rogers

"I told Zollie Volchok we needed an ultrasound machine and he asked me why we needed music in the locker room."

—Lenny Wilkens

Having ten dedicated players is a happy medium. True, individual playing time might be reduced, but overall, the team will be able to have more effective practices.

INSTILL SOME DISCIPLINE

Players do not always appreciate how important it is to listen to their coach and follow his instructions. They may have a dozen or more coaches from grade school to high school, and the sheer number of successive authority figures may make it difficult for them to appreciate their current coach (particularly if a player only stays with the team for one season). But it's important that they *try* to give every coach the respect he deserves.

> "The secret of managing a ball club is to keep the five guys who hate you away from the five who are undecided."
>
> —Casey Stengel

There are different reasons why players refuse to listen to coaches. They may be more interested in the social aspects of the game than learning basketball skills and being part of the team. Some players learn more quickly the others; some are just plain defiant. One of a coach's hardest jobs is making sure that one player's negative attitude doesn't affect the other players. Parents can help by telling their child to listen to her coach.

Playing on a competitive basketball team may be the first opportunity that young athletes have to learn how to share with and sacrifice for others. This means a youth coach has a responsibility of overseeing not only the physical, but also the emotional development of young women. Exciting, huh?

HOW TO CRITICIZE

> "If we were supposed to talk more than we listen, we would have two mouths and one ear."
>
> —Mark Twain

An effective method of constructively criticizing a player is the "sandwich" technique. This approach is a great way to inform a player that she made a mistake while simultaneously building her confidence. It involves positioning two positive comments around a negative comment or correction. The first positive comment softens the blow of the correction, while the second ensures that the player walks away with a sense of encouragement. An example—"Cathy, it was great that you ran over to guard the player, but make sure to take away the baseline so she can't drive by you again. That was great effort."

When making any sort of correction, coaches should sincerely acknowledge the effort and not just the result (whether good or bad). In the end, players should be focused on the solution rather than the problem.

Constructive feedback creates a positive and productive team environment. Coach John Wooden determined that over the course of a typical practice, he gave three positive instructional messages for every one negative comment. Comments can range from the general to the specific, such as "good hustle" to "stay low." Like the sandwich technique, the three-to-one approach ensures that players can digest criticism without suffering blows to their confidence.

> "Some teams are so negative they could be sponsored by Kodak."
>
> —Tommy Dockerty

COMMUNICATING WITH PARENTS

Parents can be great assets to a basketball program. It only makes sense that coaches be receptive to their concerns, encourage them to be active participants, and keep them involved with the team. Everyone—coaches, players, and parents—needs to work together for a basketball team to be successful.

I view basketball teams as partnerships between coaches, players, and parents. In this context, the old saying of a chain being only as strong as its weakest link is true. It's difficult to have a successful team if any one part of the triad doesn't perform well—for example, if the coach is poor, if the players are uncommitted, or if the parents are unsupportive. So that means in addition to developing relationships with his players, coaches should embrace the parents as well.

> "It wouldn't have happened if I started."
>
> —Ronnie Seikaly, on getting hurt while getting off the bench to enter a game

Effective communication between coaches, players, and parents is essential, as misunderstandings only lead to dissension. I recommend that coaches send e-mails to parents to keep them informed about practice and game times, and in a broader sense, to keep them abreast of general thoughts regarding the squad. This helps parents know that they are an integral part of the team. A coach should start communicating his expectations for the team early in the season. Holding a parent meeting at a dinner or other informal setting can help set a positive tone and build team unity from the beginning.

It's natural for parents to want their child to play as much as possible and to be included in the starting five. However, the sheer number of players on most teams means that not every child will be able to start games. Part of a coach's job is to make sure that parents, like players, have realistic expectations. The enthusiastic support that parents show for their children's athletic activities should be admired, not downplayed. They are advocates for their daughters, and many of them feel they have an obligation to make sure their daughters are getting fair treatment, but the important thing is for the coaches and parents to treat each other with respect.

Most parents are supportive and well behaved; but the reality is that the behavior of a small number of parents is, at times, harmful. For whatever reason, they let the criticism fly, either at the coach, the referees, or sometimes even at the players. The worst part is that this kind of negativity is contagious; once it starts, it's hard to keep it from spreading. (Some leagues now require all parents to sign conduct statements before allowing their daughters in the league.)

> *"Very well. I just do everything he tells me."*
>
> —Lee Corso, asked how he gets along with a coach

THE ALL-IMPORTANT PARENT MEETING

In some respects, the parent meeting is the most vital meeting of the year. This is when a coach sets the guidelines for parental involvement. There are a number of issues a coach should address up front. These issues depend, in part, on the age of the girls, how competitive the team is, and the attitude of the parents (and the school, if applicable). But at the most basic level, they all have to do with parent/coach boundaries and treating people with respect.

On nonschool teams, parental involvement is especially helpful; it takes a lot of parental sac-

rifice of time (and money) to get the girls to practices and games. But there should still be some rules. For example, one time when I was coaching a youth recreational team, I noticed that one girl was playing a zone defense while the rest of the team was playing man-to-man defense. When I asked her why, the girl replied that her dad had told her to play a zone. At the time, all I could do was laugh, but the reality is that many girls are heavily coached by family members (with or without the coach's knowledge).

Here is a checklist of some key issues that coaches may want to address in the parent meeting:

- The goals of the team.
- The importance of setting realistic expectations.
- Parents are an important and integral part of the team.
- The team values sportsmanship.
- It is important to treat people (coaches, players, and referees) with respect.
- Grades and school work are priorities.
- The role of the parents is to support the team.
- How playing time will be decided and whether or not the coach will discuss complaints about playing time.
- Consequences for a player missing or being late to practices and games.
- How complaints by players or parents should be handled.
- Financial requirements (for nonschool teams).

Special note to coaches—remember not to take parental criticisms personally, particularly those said in the heat of an unpleasant moment. It's natural for parents to defend and support their daughters.

> *"Where you stand on something depends in large part on where you sit."*
>
> —Unknown

> *"It was the most difficult year I've had since puberty."*
>
> —Dave Bliss, on a losing season

PART TWO
Offense

CHAPTER 4
Basic Offensive Skills

Learning how to play basketball (or any sport for that matter) begins with understanding and mastering the fundamentals. "Fundamentals" are the essential tools and skills needed for consistent success.

Basketball fundamentals include such skills as how to hold a basketball, dribbling, passing, catching, footwork, pivoting, faking, jumping, running, rebounding, and shooting. Communication (i.e., talking) is also an important and underrated fundamental. Without the development of strong fundamentals, players will never achieve their maximum potential. What follows is a compilation of fundamental skills that every coach should attempt to instill in his players.

FUNDAMENTALS

HOW TO GRIP AND HOLD A BASKETBALL

It has been my experience that the majority of players simply don't know how to grip a basketball. The proper grip just doesn't come naturally to most young women!

Learning the proper grip is the first step in learning how to play basketball. If they have the proper grip, players can feel the ball and guide its motion in the air. A good grip maximizes a player's flexibility and strength and enables her to shoot, dribble, and pass effectively.

To grip the ball properly, a player should balance the ball on her fingers and the outside of her palm while applying light (but firm) pressure to it. This grip will give her feel, control, and flexibility. Rolling the ball too far onto her fingertips or sinking the ball into her palm will weaken her range and ballhandling skills.

Another part of gripping the ball is utilizing the seams that run around the basketball. Placing the fingers across (perpendicular to) the seams helps a player grip the ball solidly, which leads to consistent shooting and passing.

DRIBBLING

In order to dribble effectively, a player should keep her head and eyes up and the ball on the same side of her body as her dribbling hand. The ball should not stray toward her center (a problem that

> *"I stand by all my misstatements."*
>
> —Dan Quayle

many youth players have). Instead, it should be slightly to her side and away from her body. Her elbow should stick comfortably out, but should be close enough to her torso to power the dribble.

Good ball-handlers receive the ball on the rise. A player should adjust the height of her hand (in most cases, slightly away from the court) in order to make contact with the ball as it rises up from the floor; she should cushion the bounce lightly with her palm. She should cup the ball with her spread fingers for a brief moment before releasing it toward the floor. The elbow of her dribbling arm should still be slightly away from her body in order to maximize her flexibility, control, and power; her legs should be flexed and her back should be held straight.

Some players slap the ball down as it is still on the rise. This patting motion will only result in a loss of control. By contrast, the dribble should be a fluid motion, brought about by smoothly flicking the fingers, hand and wrist down. A player shouldn't have to push down hard on the ball; rather she should only apply light (but firm) pressure to keep her dribble going.

A player should keep her dribble as low as possible—usually below waist level—in order to protect the ball.

Players should learn to dribble well with both hands—this will help prevent them from being too predictable and easy to defend and will, generally, add flexibility to the team offense. It is important for guards, forwards, and centers alike to be good ball-handlers.

Developing the proper footwork is a critical component of becoming a good dribbler. Footwork is often underemphasized in ball-handling drills. When guarded, players should spread their feet to at least shoulder-width apart; their knees should be bent and hips lowered; and their bodies should be turned to protect the ball. Balance becomes more and more important as players' dribbling skills improve (as they attempt to execute advanced dribbling moves).

Good dribbling leads to good passing. A player can use her dribble to create better passing angles and to open up passing lanes. (Another component of good passing is the ball-handler's ability to ball fake and pivot effectively. Both skills will be discussed later in this book.)

> *"The one thing about this game is that it makes fools of us all."*
>
> —Judd Heathcote

Good dribbling skills have indirect effects, as well; experienced dribblers maintain better poise under pressure, a fact that makes them more alert passers. A good rule of thumb for players is to not pick up the dribble until they have identified a player to whom they can successfully pass.

Players should dribble with a purpose! One of the plagues of youth basketball players is the "aimless dribble"; intentionally or unintentionally, players end up hogging the ball, leaving teammates to stand by and watch. Often this aimless dribble is the result of a player's poor ballhandling skills (and indecisiveness).

If a player constantly looks at the ball or at the court in order to keep her dribble under control, she loses sight of her teammates and defender. A good dribbler shouldn't have to look at the ball; she should feel everything with her hands. This will allow her to keep her head up at all times, with her eyes focused on her teammates, opponents, and the basket.

Ballhandling is an important component of any overall offensive scheme. Good ballhandling makes good shooting possible. By extension, the player that becomes an expert ball-handler is likely to be an offensive threat.

It is essential that young players practice dribbling in their spare time! The first step is to develop a good feel for the ball. The more a player can handle the ball, the better she will recognize its sensation. Some players may go so far as to carry a basketball around with them wherever they go. That's an extreme example—the important thing is to not go too long without touching a basketball.

The following is a list of dribbles that players can practice both on their own time and with their teams.

TYPES OF DRIBBLES

Low Dribble
A player should use this dribble when she's being closely guarded. The technique is to keep the ball low by extending the dribbling arm down as much as possible (and bending the knees). The dribbler should keep the elbow of her dribbling hand close to her side. She

> *"Enthusiasm is the greatest asset in the world. It beats money, power and influence."*
>
> —Henry Chester

should rotate her shoulders to keep the ball further away from her defender, and she should raise her other forearm to act as a shield.

Speed Dribble

Players use the speed dribble when they're running at a full sprint. The dribbler should push the ball out in front of her, and then "run after it." Because she's sprinting, the dribbler has to make sure that her dribble bounces a good distance in front of her. The faster she runs, the further she should push the ball out. Her hand should make contact with the ball at a 45 degree angle. Her head should be up so that she can see the entire court, complete with teammates and defenders.

The speed dribble is a high dribble, but the ball should not rise higher than chest level.

Change-of-Pace (or Hesitation) Dribble

This dribble is used to fake out defenders; a player should slow to almost a dead stop, hesitate, and then explode quickly by her opponent.

Crossover Dribble

The crossover dribble involves changing dribbling hands. A player should use one quick dribble to transfer the ball from her right hand to her left (or vice versa). The ball should bounce around the midpoint of the player's stance. To be effective, the crossover dribble should rise no higher than the knees and should be executed as quickly as possible. (Because she dribbles the ball in front of her, the player exposes it momentarily to the defender, which is why her crossover dribble must be fast and low!)

The crossover is a means of changing directions. For example, if a player driving to the right (and dribbling with her right hand) wants to cut back over the middle, she might use a crossover dribble to change directions and start heading to her left.

The key to changing directions quickly is proper footwork. Just as a player transfers the ball from one hand to the other, she should also transfer her weight. She should push off from the foot on the same side as her dribbling hand and use the momentum to explode in the new direction.

The keys to a good crossover dribble are:

- Keeping the ball low
- Positioning the dribbling hand on the side of the ball before crossing it over
- Preparing the opposite hand to receive the ball by holding it perpendicular to the court

A great move is to combine a crossover dribble with a change-of-pace dribble.

Between-the-Legs Dribble

The between-the-legs dribble can be a safer way to transfer the ball from one hand to the other when a player finds herself closely guarded or overplayed.

If the ball is in her right hand, the player should dribble low and, putting her right hand on the outside of the ball, push it between her legs. Her left hand should be close to her legs on the opposite side; her fingers should be spread and pointing toward the floor, ready to receive the ball. Players should be able to execute the between-the-legs dribble in either direction.

Spin Dribble

The spin dribble is a more advanced move than the crossover and can be a potent weapon in a player's ballhandling arsenal. The spin is another method of changing directions (as well as dribbling hands), but it protects the ball better than the crossover dribble. It starts when the player plants the foot on her nondribbling side (for example, if she's dribbling with her right hand, she should plant her left foot). She should then execute a reverse pivot (to be discussed more fully later). She should spin her shoulders, and in so doing, turn her back to the defender. Her legs and shoulders, together, should perform what you might call a "sit spin," and she should bring the ball around with her. To properly execute the spin, a player's legs and shoulders should

not begin to turn until the pivot foot is planted. As a whole, you might describe the spin dribble as a pivot, spin, and pull movement. Ideally the ball should stay in the same hand until the spin is complete. (Although a player might come close to palming the ball, referees hardly ever make that call.)

Coming out of the spin, the player should reach out with her non-pivot foot in order to pull her body past the defender. The non-pivot foot should be pointed in the direction that the player plans to attack. She shouldn't transfer the ball to her opposite hand until she has turned completely.

The benefit of the spin dribble is the fact that, when changing directions, a player can use her body to protect the ball from her defender. However, if she telegraphs the move too much, its effectiveness can be compromised.

Half-Spin Dribble

The half-spin starts like a spin dribble, except for that, after turning halfway around, the ball-handler makes a turn back to her original position and keeps dribbling in the same direction. (This move is particularly effective when paired with the spin. After a few spin moves, defenders might start to overplay the ball-handler's nondribbling hand. The half-spin takes advantage of their adjustment.) Like the full spin, this move must be executed quickly.

In-and-Out (Hockey) Dribble

The in-and-out (hockey) dribble is a staggered dribble move that combines a head-and-shoulder fake and a change-of-pace dribble. Unlike the spin and the crossover, the in-and-out dribble is a move that fakes a direction change.

Staying low and keeping the ball at her side, the player should execute small stutter steps (short, quick steps, also known as hockey steps). As she stutters, the player should throw a head-and-shoulder fake in the opposite direction that she plans to dribble. Then she should explode past her defender, pushing the ball out in front of her in the same direction that she was originally traveling.

Behind-the-Back Dribble

The behind-the-back dribble is mechanically similar to the between-the-legs dribble. It begins when a player slides her palm to the outside of the ball. Cupping the ball slightly with her hand, she should swing it behind and across her lower back, depositing it on her nondribbling side (in this example, from right to left). When she releases the ball, her right hand should be as close to her left hip as possible. The player should push the ball out so that it lands in front and to the side of her left foot. It's important that she not leave the ball behind—ideally, she shouldn't have to slow down at all in order to retrieve it.

Retreat (Backup) Dribble

The backup dribble is also called the retreat dribble and is used to create space between a player and her defender. This dribble looks exactly how it sounds; the player literally backs up while dribbling the ball. She should turn her dribbling side slightly away from her defender, using her "off" (nondribbling) hand, arm and shoulder as a shield. The backup dribble requires that the player plant the foot opposite to her dribbling hand, and that she use it to change the direction of her momentum. This dribble can be especially useful when a player is trying to escape a trap.

PASSING

The quickest way to move the ball on offense is to pass, not to dribble; passing is also the most effective method of creating scoring opportunities. A player with the ball should be aware of the location of the other four players on her team and be prepared to pass to them. This kind of court awareness is what can separate good players from great ones.

TYPES OF PASSES

Two-Handed Chest Pass

The two-handed chest pass begins when a player places a hand on either side of the ball with her fingers spread. She should hold the ball so that she has maximum use of her fingers and finger pads and the upper palm area of each hand.

Before passing, the player should be in a balanced position. Once she has established her pivot foot, she should step toward her intended target (with her elbows still bent). The chest pass is, in essence, an arm-snapping motion that releases the ball toward the receiver. The snap release begins in the arms but ends in the wrists and hands in a follow-through. After a good release, a player's elbows will be locked straight with the back of her hands facing each other; her fingers will be spread and her thumbs will point toward the floor. Although often underemphasized, this "snap" or quick release contributes as much speed and power to the pass as a player's upper arm strength. In addition, holding the follow-through for a moment after making the pass helps players concentrate on their target, which leads to more accurate passing.

One-Handed Chest Pass

Many coaches are teaching the one-handed chest pass in lieu of the two-handed chest pass. The advantage of the one-handed pass lies in its similarity to proper shooting form; that is, in this case, the passing and shooting motions are the same. A player that uses the one-handed chest pass will be less likely to develop the habit of shooting with both hands. She will never have to change her grip on the ball, whether she is attempting to shoot, dribble, or pass.

The fingers on the passing hand should be across (perpendicular to) the seams of the basketball; the opposite hand should rest lightly on the side of the ball. All ten fingers should be spread. The one-handed release should be identical to that of the two-handed pass, except this time, only one hand does the snapping. (This one-handed horizontal "snap" mirrors the vertical "snap" of a player's shot release.) The player should hold her one-handed follow-through just as she would hold it for a two-handed pass.

Bounce pass

The bounce pass can be made as a two-handed or one-handed pass. It is identical to a chest pass but for the path that the ball takes; it should bounce once on the floor before reaching the intended receiver. The pass should hit the court approximately two-thirds or three-quarters of the way to the target. Any further, and the pass will bounce too low; the receiver will have to stoop to catch it. A pass that bounces before that point most likely won't make it to the receiver on the first hop. If it does, it will be too high. The bounce pass is a useful method of creating different passing angles and is particularly useful in certain offensive situations—for example, on the backdoor play or when a player is guarded from behind in the low post.

Overhead Pass

The overhead pass, like the two-handed chest pass, begins when a player places a hand on either side of the ball with her fingers spread. The ball's starting position should be directly above (not behind) the player's head; she should space her hands evenly on either side. Having established a pivot foot, she should step forward with the other leg toward the intended target. She should release the ball directly from the overhead position—the passer shouldn't bring it down to eye level before letting it go. As with every other type of pass, it is important that she snap the ball away and hold the follow-through.

The overhead pass is especially useful when a player needs to swing the ball from one side of the court to another against a zone defense.

Step (or Lateral) Pass

The step pass is a derivative of the one-handed chest pass, but rather than passing to a teammate directly in front of her, the passer "steps through" and delivers the ball to someone to her left or right. The two starting positions are identical. The offensive player should then step through her defender by bringing her nonpivot foot across her body (in the direction that she wants to pass). To protect the ball as she carries it across her torso, the player should lower her shoulder in order to shield it from her defender. As she plants her foot, she should cock her wrist, drop her helping hand, and snap the ball to the receiver. The step bounce pass is also an option.

Baseball Pass

The baseball pass covers the most distance—strong players can use it to pass the ball from one baseline to the opposite end of

> *"Baseball is 90 percent mental. The other half is physical."*
>
> —Yogi Berra

the court. The mechanics are just as the name suggests; players should pretend that they are center fielders throwing the ball to home plate. To make a good baseball pass, players should keep their nonthrowing hand on the ball as long as possible for maximum control. They should bring the basketball back behind their head with their throwing hand and lean back. A right-handed player should step with her left foot toward the intended target (vice versa for lefties). She should release the ball in a controlled fashion with her throwing arm coming up and over her head; she should hold her follow-through.

Off-the-Dribble (or Push) Pass

The push pass, which should be made with only one hand, happens off the dribble. This pass requires a high degree of finesse, because, from the onset, the passer has less control of the ball. The push is quick and can be either a straight or a lob pass, depending on the defensive alignment.

Behind-the-Back Pass

The behind-the-back is another finesse pass. As she starts to bring the ball around her hips, the passer should grip it with both hands. Her helping hand should stay on the ball until the last possible moment (until her inside arm can't go any farther behind her back); at that point, she should release the ball. A good pass ends with a good follow-through—with the passing hand near the opposite hip and the fingers pointing to the target.

Handoff

The handoff is a safe way to get the ball to a teammate who is either cutting next to or circling behind the passer. It is a direct transfer between two teammates. But the handoff isn't totally foolproof; even though her receiver is nearby, the passer needs to protect the ball. Her passing elbow should be tucked into her body; her opposite hand should be resting on top of the ball as she offers it to her teammate. (As players become more skilled, they can be less careful with the ball; the handoff can become more of a toss or a flip.) Much of the success of the handoff hinges on good timing between passer and receiver. It's surprising how often players fumble seemingly straightforward handoff passes.

"Son, it looks to me like you're spending too much time on one subject."

—Shelby Metcalf, to a student who made four F's and a D

CATCHING THE BALL

To properly catch a pass, a receiver should:

1. Get open and call for the ball.
2. Provide a good target. The receivers should show the passer her raised, open palms in order to signal that she is ready to catch the pass.
3. Keep her hands out in front of her chest.
4. Keep her fingers pointed up and spread comfortably with her palms almost touching. Her fingers and fingertips should be the first parts of her hands to touch the ball.
5. Extend her elbows to meet the ball.
6. Keep her eyes on the ball until it is in her hands.
7. Step toward the ball to prevent the defense from stepping in for a steal (aggressively go after the pass!).
8. Cushion the impact of the ball by bringing it into her chest after it touches her fingers.
9. Catch the ball in the ready (or "triple threat") position; from this stance, she can shoot, dribble or pass (more on this in the "Footwork" section).

The passer is not completely to blame for intercepted passes; many receivers don't do a very good job of moving toward the ball, of providing a target with both palms facing the ball, and of calling for the pass. I've also noticed that some players flinch as they receive passes; this leads to dropped balls (and jammed fingers!). By keeping her eyes on the ball, not catching the ball with the palms, and providing a slight cushion with her hands, a player can ensure that it won't bounce off of her fingertips.

Both passer and receiver can improve their accuracy by faking. The former can pretend to pass in one direction before whipping the ball in another; the latter can fake away from the passer before cutting back to receive the ball.

> *"Most games are lost, not won."*
>
> —Casey Stengel

FOOTWORK

The term "footwork" is an umbrella concept that describes both stationary positions and dynamic movements, like the pivot. To say that a player has good footwork is to say that she has good balance and the capability to move agilely. Throughout this book, I emphasize the importance of good footwork for both offense and defense.

Good offensive footwork enables players to change direction efficiently and to protect the ball. Forwards and centers must use footwork to get open in congested post areas and to move around other players in confined spaces without traveling. For their part, guards need good footwork, for example, in order to make quick moves to the basket. Footwork also comes into play on defense, as players need to be able to slide their feet at the proper angles and to change directions quickly in order to put pressure on offensive players.

> *"If you can't keep quiet, shut up!"*
>
> —Gregory Ratoff

TRIPLE-THREAT POSITION

Good footwork on offense usually begins with establishing the "triple-threat" position. As I said earlier, the triple-threat refers to a player's ability to shoot, pass, or dribble from a single stance. A player in triple-threat position is square to the basket and has established her pivot foot. Her knees are bent, her hips are lowered into a near sitting position. She has positioned the ball to the side of her strong-hand hip. She is ready to be an athletic basketball player.

The following eight sections—"The Fundamental Basketball Position," "Pivoting," "Moving Backward," "Faking," "Stopping," "Jumping," "Running," and "Rebounding"—all have to do with developing good footwork. (That is to say, none of those skills are possible without it.)

THE FUNDAMENTAL BASKETBALL POSITION

A player without the ball should be in the "fundamental basketball position." This position enables a player to quickly start, stop, pivot, and change pace; it also helps her eliminate wasted movement. Her feet should be at least shoulder-width apart. Her knees should be flexed so that she is ready to move in any direction with power and quickness. She should hold her arms close to her chest with her elbows flexed so that her hands are ready to receive the ball. Her fingers should be spread.

PIVOTING

When a player steps in any direction with one foot while keeping the other foot planted on the court, she makes a pivot.

A proper pivot isn't a travel; while in possession of the basketball, a player can move one foot, provided the other (the pivot foot) remains in contact with the court. Pivoting is an important fundamental skill because it is useful in so many situations—for example, protecting the basketball, getting one's body in position to shoot, getting ready to pass, moving one's feet in the post area, and even playing defense.

It's easier for players to pivot when their weight is on the balls of their feet. Their knees should be slightly bent and their hips should be lowered. (In other words, they should be in a balanced, athletic position.) A mistake that many young basketball players make is to pivot with the heel of the pivot foot on the court. Not only does this restrict their ability to move, it makes it harder for them to maintain their balance.

The pivot itself is a swiveling motion; youth coaches might describe it as a "squish the bug" movement. Players can pivot in any direction, for any magnitude—45 degrees, 90 degrees, or in some cases, all the way around. Pivoting can occur with or without the ball.

I believe that pivoting is one of the most underemphasized areas of the game at the youth level. Not being able to pivot properly severely limits a player's ability to protect the ball, to get off good shots, and to pass. Pivoting is especially important because it is the basis for more advanced offensive and defensive skills. A lot of turnovers could be avoided if youth players knew how to pivot properly.

> *"Considering their leaping ability, a face-off would have been more appropriate."*
>
> —Paul Westphal, on a jump ball between two players

REVERSE PIVOT

When making a reverse pivot, a player moves her free foot backward instead of forward—in effect, turning her back to what's in front of her. The reverse pivot is a useful tool that can help players protect the ball against tight defensive pressure and execute various moves in the low post.

WHICH FOOT TO USE

There's a little bit of the controversy regarding which pivot foot is better to use. It's my opinion a beginning right-handed player positioned away from the basket should use her left foot as her pivot foot. This will allow her to protect the ball with her right (strong) hand. Once the player becomes more skilled, the less it matters which pivot foot she uses.

"To be a coach today you must be a teacher, father, mother, psychologist, counselor, disciplinarian, and Lord-knows-what-else. If all we had to do was coach, they have to cut our salaries because coaching is the easiest part of the job. "

—Bobby Bowden

MOVING BACKWARD

Although moving forward and sideways comes naturally to most players, moving backward doesn't. And it's a skill that needs to be developed; players must be able to move backward in order to: reverse pivot, execute a spin or reverse dribble, make moves in the low post, block out for rebounds, defend players with the ball, slide effectively on defense (perhaps in an attempt to turn a dribbler at an angle), and defend the fast break.

Backward running has a distinct form. Players should bend at the waist more than they would if they were running forward; this is to ensure that their weight stays in front of them (so that they don't topple over). They should pump their arms even more vigorously than they ordinarily would. Good arm movement will help them maintain their momentum. Most importantly, they should pick their feet up high as they extend them backward. Players will stumble and fall if they let their feet get tangled!

Moving backward is a skill and only improves with practice. In addition to simply running in reverse, players can practice executing slides at different angles and moving back to box out for rebounds.

PLAYING WITH YOUR BACK TO THE BASKET

It is particularly vital for low-post players to be comfortable with receiving the ball with their backs to the basket. Forwards must learn how to read the defender by feel and to move backward to the basket without traveling or fouling.

FAKING

Many youth players tend to telegraph their passes and the direction of their dribbles by looking directly at their intended targets. As a result, their moves are predictable and easy to defend. Below are two standard fakes that both guards and forwards can use to shake off their defenders.

JAB STEP

When an offensive player moves her nonpivot foot in a short quick step (usually a few inches) in order to move her defender out of position, she makes a jab step. A good jab will force a defender to adjust her position, either backward or from side to side. In order to jab step effectively, the attacker should first establish her triple-threat position. Her weight should be on the balls of her feet, her knees bent, and her hips lowered. Most of the fake consists of the movement of the player's foot—the ball should move quickly in the same direction, as a fake dribble or pass.

The jab is most effective when used on the perimeter; guards can use this fake to create an open lane to the basket. It can also be executed without the ball; a player can fake going one direction before making a cut in another.

PUMP FAKE

A good pump fake (also known as a shot fake) will make a defender believe that a player is about to shoot. The pump consists of a head, shoulder, and ball fake upward in the direction of the hoop. (To be convincing, it should be a short, abrupt movement.) As the defender moves out of position to block the shot, the offensive player can drive to the basket or shoot if the defender has jumped and returned to the floor. The pump fake is especially effective in the low post, when an offensive player needs to clear space to the basket in a confined area, but can be used anywhere within shooting range.

> "Coaching is easy. Winning is the hard part."
>
> —Elgin Baylor

STOPPING

Stopping is an important concept to teach young players, as many of them have a tendency to travel. Two types of "stops" are particularly effective.

JUMP STOP

In a jump stop, a player's two feet land on the floor at the same time, spread slightly more than shoulder-width apart. This stop enables a player to use either foot as her pivot foot; having immediately established her triple-threat position, she can move in any direction. The jump stop is a forceful stop that usually happens at the end of a run. In one sense, it can help a player quickly gain balance and control; however, if she doesn't manage to stop her momentum, the jump stop can easily turn into a travel or even a charge. The key to avoiding a violation is to bend the knees and to make sure that both feet land on the floor at the same time. If a player tries to stand up too soon, she'll fall forward out of her stop. (A good rule of thumb—the faster a player is traveling before the stop, the lower her center of gravity must be.)

STRIDE STOP

The stride stop is a more common stop. A right-handed dribbler stops by putting her left foot down first—the right comes down just behind it (in a heel-to-toe alignment). The faster a player is traveling before she stops, the lower her center of gravity must be. As with the jump stop, her back should be straight and leaning slightly forward. Her knees should be bent to at least 90 degrees; from that crouched position, she can explode upward into her jump shot.

Good footwork and good balance have one ingredient in common— flexed knees. For one reason or another, youth players don't bend their knees as much as they should. Coaches should impress this point on their players; bent knees bring about agility and control!

JUMPING

In general, youth players have a difficult time jumping. Part of the problem is that many don't know how to begin their jumps. In the proper starting position, the entire body should be "cocked": the elbows and knees should be flexed; the feet should be slightly more than shoulder-width apart; the hips should be lowered; the elbows should be held slightly away from the body; and the hands and arms should be poised below the chin. (By contrast, when they should be preparing to leap, many young women lock their knees and let their arms hang down by their sides.)

The jump itself begins when a player quickly transfers all her weight to the balls of her feet. From there, she should jump upward from the floor. All parts of her body should be synchronized so that they move upward at the same time. The jumping movement should start in the lower parts of the body and move upward. (That's another mistake that a young player might make—her jump might be disjointed and unsynchronized, or she might make it into predominantly upper body movement.)

RUNNING

As strange as it may seem, running is a fundamental skill. (When I say "running," I mean the ability to move quickly and efficiently up and down the court.) Coaches shouldn't assume that incoming players have proper running form and should address the issue early on in the season.

When running, players should:

- Pump their arms vigorously in a coordinated and smooth fashion, with their elbows swinging forward in the direction they are running.
- Keep their elbows in close to their body.
- Land on the balls of their feet, rather than letting their heels touch the surface of the court first.
- Lift their knees aggressively off the floor.
- Make a short and fast initial step.

A common running weakness is the inefficient use of the arms and hands. When used properly, a player's arms should increase her running speed (while, in fact, many players' arms impede their forward progress).

> *"The greatest mistake is to continue to practice a mistake."*
>
> —Bobby Bowden

REBOUNDING

A good rebounder always assumes that the shot will miss. Furthermore, she always wants the ball for herself! Her hands should always be held in a ready position—palms open at shoulder height. Her elbows should be out to prevent other players from entering her rebounding zone. The player should be blocking out with her backside. Her feet should be spread to form a wide, solid base. She should time her jump so that she reaches the ball at the apex of her leap. (Chapter 6 is devoted entirely to rebounding.)

> *"Magic Johnson is the best player who plays on the ground, and Michael Jordan is the best player who plays in the air."*
>
> —John Paxson

SHOOTING

Shooting is a very important fundamental skill and is fully covered in Chapter 5.

In order to become an outstanding shooter, a player needs to learn the proper shooting fundamentals. Proper shooting form is not achieved by accident, but rather by hard work and practice.

Shooting a basketball is fun, but it's always more fun when the shots go in! Having learned the proper mechanics, players need to practice them to perfection. The key is consistency. Having excellent shooting form increases a player's ability to make shots consistently; by contrast, having poor technique most often will produce erratic results.

THE JUMP SHOT

A great way to learn how to shoot is what I call the **SURF** Shooting Method. The SURF jump shot can be broken down into four stages:

Stage 1: Get into proper shooting **S**tance
Stage 2: Jump **U**pward
Stage 3: **R**elease the ball
Stage 4: Hold the **F**ollow-through

STAGE 1: GET INTO PROPER SHOOTING STANCE

The proper stance begins with the proper grip with both the **shooting** and the **nonshooting hands.**

THE SHOOTING HAND

The *fingers* of the shooting hand should be spread for maximum control. The *index finger* should point directly toward the target; the thumb should be at least at a 45 degree angle in relation to it. The ball should be touching the finger pads and the outer portion of the palm; it should not rest in the palm of the hand! The player should position the fingers of her shooting hand so that they are spread across (perpendicular to) the seams of the basketball. This will allow her to grip the ball more effectively.

NONSHOOTING HAND

The *fingers* of the nonshooting hand should be spread, resting on the side of the ball where the seams merge. This hand's only purpose is balance—it shouldn't interfere with the shot in any way.

"Never try to keep more than 300 separate thoughts in your mind during your swing."

—Henry Beard Mulligan's law

HOW TO SET UP THE SHOT

First, a player must focus her eyes on the target—namely, the front of the rim. Even a player in motion, for example, one cutting across the lane on a drive, should first see the rim before she shoots. The longer she can keep it in her sights, the better chance her shot has to go in. In fact, her eyes should see the rim prior to any upward movement and shouldn't leave the basket until she sees the ball hit the rim/target. (A common mistake is to watch the ball in flight. This will make the shooter less accurate.) Focusing on the target involves creating a clear visual line to the rim; neither a player's arms nor the ball itself should obstruct her view of the basket.

The player must assume the proper **shooting stance** prior to actually taking her shot; among other things, this good foundation will make sure that she doesn't rush.

A player in a proper stance will satisfy the following criteria:

- Her *feet* should be shoulder-width apart and positioned under her shoulders. Her shooting *foot* (namely, the foot on the side of her shooting hand) should be established. It should be lined up with the center of the basket, closer to the rim than her opposite foot (forming a heel-to-toe relationship).
- Her *toes* should be pointing toward the rim.
- Her *knees* should be bent to at least a 45 degree angle.
- Her *waist and hips* should be lowered into a crouched position. Her hips should be positioned as if she were getting ready to sit in a chair.
- Her *shoulders and hips* should be "square" to the basket. (There is a lot of confusion regarding what "square" means. Remember that the shooting foot should be closer to the basket than the other foot. The heel-to-toe stance of her feet will probably cause a natural rotation of the shoulders and hips. The shoulder and hip on the same side as the shooting hand will most likely end up slightly closer to the basket.)
- Her *back* should be straight.
- Her weight should be slightly forward, but not totally on the *balls of her feet*—just enough to slip a quarter under her heels.
- The *elbow* of her shooting hand should be underneath the ball and aligned with the basket.

- The ball should be slightly *below her chin,* on the side of her shooting hand.
- Her *hands* should be relaxed.
- The *fingers* of both hands should be spread.
- The fingers of her shooting hand should grip the ball across the *seams*. The *index finger* of her shooting hand should point toward the front of the rim.
- Her *knees, elbow and the index finger* of her shooting hand should all be in direct line with the target.
- The back of her *wrist* should be parallel to the floor, or "cocked." (From that position, the player needs only to push up-and-through the ball to shoot. If her wrist is only half-cocked, she'll tend to throw the ball toward the basket. Cocking her wrist will allow her to loft the ball up so that it comes straight down into the center of the hoop.)
- Her *nonshooting* hand should be on the side of the ball, fingers pointing toward the ceiling.
- Her *eyes* should be looking directly at the basket. (Ideally, she should focus on the target for one second before her jump, and afterward until the ball hits the target.)
- Her *head* should be up.
- She should have come to a *complete stop* for about one second after establishing her shooting position (without dipping or bouncing).

In order to establish her shooting position quickly, a player should practice **pivoting** so that she can get her feet into the appropriate stance. She should practice this preshot maneuvering on different areas of the court, assuming that she will receive the ball at various angles to the basket. A player might be perfectly balanced before she receives a pass, but if her footwork is poor, she will stumble as she attempts to square to the basket.

If a shooter starts with the ball slightly below her chin, she'll be able to **jump** up as high as she possibly can during her shot. It will be difficult for her to elevate if the ball is already above her head when her shot begins. Conversely, if the shooter starts with the ball too low, the extra motion will reduce her control.

I indicated before that the fingers of the shooting hand should be positioned across the seams. Two fingers, in particular, determine

> *"It's so bad that the players are giving each other high fives when they hit the rim."*
>
> —Ron Shumate

> *"The only sure thing about luck is that it will change."*
>
> —Bret Harte

whether the shot will go straight and if the ball will have good rotation. The index and middle fingers of the shooting hand, together, form what's called the **shooting fork.** The shooting fork should be the last thing to touch the ball before it is released—these fingers, formed like a "V," snap through the ball at the very last second.

The shooter should spread the fingers of her shooting hand until the ball begins to fill her hand, but not so much that it touches the flat part or stem of her thumb. Too much contact with the thumb can produce a sideways spin. By contrast, if the ball rests only on the outside quarter of a shooter's thumb, it has a better chance of going straight.

STAGE 2: JUMP UPWARD

Players need to make sure that the various parts of their bodies are all moving in the same direction at the same time. The jumping movement should begin with the feet and the knees. There should never be a rocking or a dipping motion toward the floor after a player gets set. After she has established the shooting position in Stage 1, her body should only move upward.

In one fluid movement just before her jump, the player should shift her weight to her toes, begin to straighten her knees, raise her hips, and start to extend her arms into her shooting position. If the player's **knees, hips, and arms are synchronized,** she will be able to maximize the height of her jump. Furthermore, she will avoid extraneous movements that could throw off her shot.

Many players lift the ball above their head first and jump second. This technique limits a shooter's range. In fact, a shooter's object should be to elevate as high as possible before releasing the ball. In addition to adding both distance and height to her shot, jumping first will help her protect the ball from taller defenders. (On the other hand, a player shooting close to the basket may need to keep the ball above her head before jumping to avoid having her shot blocked.)

When attempting a long shot, some shooters will make the mistake of jumping excessively toward the basket. A shooter's goal should be to jump up as high as possible and land in the same position as she started. But, it is natural (and okay) to land slightly closer to the basket.

STAGE 3: RELEASE THE BALL

THE SHOOTING HAND

The shooter should release the ball as she is moving upward, just before she reaches the top of her jump. The proper basketball shot is an **up-and-out** motion; the shooting arm extends fully, the wrist quickly "snaps" or breaks forward, and the ball rolls off the shooter's fingertips. Hypothetically, if the angle created by a player's two arms (one held out parallel to the floor, the other held upright, perpendicular to the floor) is 90 degrees, then the shooter's arm should extend at around a 45 degree angle at the point of release. A good rule of thumb is that the shooter's elbow should be at least to the level of her eyebrows as she releases the ball.

The ball should last touch the index and middle fingers of the shooting hand (the aforementioned "shooting fork"). It's vital that these two fingers snap through the ball; in fact, the fork makes or breaks the shot. It not only determines the direction that the ball travels, but also its rotation, height/arc, and accuracy. (A good practice drill is to shoot the ball with only those two fingers. That way, players get a feel for the fork and learn just how much power and spin can be generated by the fork alone.)

In order to be able to shoot the ball without getting it blocked, a player needs a quick release. She can develop this by 1) quickly assuming her shooting position, square to the basket, from any point on the court, 2) avoiding dipping the ball or her body after getting set, and 3) consistently shooting with the same form. Another part of a quick release is the ability to feel the ball without having to look at it. Every shot should start with the player's fingers across the seams, but every pass won't enter her hands in that configuration. Players need to practice adjusting the ball in their hands while keeping their eyes on the basket.

A quick shot isn't the same as a hurried shot. A quick shot is a necessary component of a player's arsenal, as it is the most effective means of releasing the ball in the midst of heavy defensive pressure.

> *"I site down my nose to shoot, and now my nose isn't straight since I broke it. That's why my shooting has been off."*
>
> —Barrie Haynie

THE NONSHOOTING HAND

The position and movement of the *nonshooting hand* are critical to consistent and accurate shooting. The nonshooting hand should be positioned on the side of the ball where the seams intersect. This hand acts as a guide and helps the shooter keep control of the ball during the initial part of her jump. It is not responsible for releasing the ball! As the shooting hand engages in the up-and-out motion, the guide hand should stay entirely still, perpendicular to the player's face. (A common problem that young players have is to involve the thumb of the guide hand in the shooting motion. Although she might think that she is keeping her nonshooting hand still, a player might twist her guide thumb forward in order to give the ball a little extra oomph. All this does is create sidespin and send the shot to the right or left of the basket.)

If the player properly executes her shot, the ball should be directly in line with the target; she might miss short or long, but not to the right or left.

> *"He has the shooting range. What he doesn't have is the making range."*
>
> —Pete Carril

STAGE 4: HOLD THE FOLLOW-THROUGH

The term "follow-through" refers to the position of a player's shooting arm, hand and body after she has released the ball. A player with proper follow-through will satisfy the following criteria:

- Her *shooting elbow* will be locked straight, held near the level of her eyebrows.
- The *wrist* of her shooting hand will be "snapped" forward at a 90 degree angle to her forearm.
- The *fingers* of her shooting hand will be spread, her thumb will point to the side, and her other four fingers will point to the ground.
- Her *nonshooting hand* will end up at face level or slightly higher, with her fingers pointing up. The elbow of her nonshooting arm will still be bent.
- Her *knees* will be flexed.
- Her *shoulders and hips* will be square to the basket.

A player should hold her follow-through until the ball hits the rim. Among other things, this will force the shooter to concentrate on the shot taken and to analyze if she needs to adjust her next shot; she might be able to tell what caused her to miss.

Analyzing the follow-through can be instructive. For example, if a shooter's elbow ends up below head-level, it's likely that her ball had a low trajectory.

ANALYZE EVERY SHOT

A shooter's best tool is her own ability to analyze her shots after she takes them. Two important components that she should focus on are height and backspin.

Putting arc on the ball—that is, increasing the height of its flight path—maximizes a shooter's chance of making the basket. Unfortunately, most players don't put enough arc on their shots. A telling indicator for coaches and players alike is whether or not the ball passes through the basket with a "swish." Regardless of whether the shot goes in, the general rule is if the ball bounces on the front of the rim before dropping in, its trajectory is too low. A shooter's goal in practice should be to make every shot without touching the rim. In addition to forcing her to shoot higher, this will also force concentration.

A player should also take note of the backspin that she puts on the ball; this will help her determine if she's gripping the ball properly (across the seams) and if she is truly shooting with one hand. If she grips and releases the ball well, she should see "pure" backspin on her shot; the horizontal seams will rotate backward toward her. If her backspin is irregular, then she knows that something is amiss. She might be gripping the ball improperly or shooting the ball off the side of her hand; her non-shooting hand might be interfering with her release. If that's the case, she might have sidespin, or no backspin at all. Players who shoot with two hands, rather than with the shooting fork, tend to push the ball to the basket.

FOUL SHOTS

The four-stage **SURF** Shooting Method can be used to shoot foul shots. There are, however, some differences; for example, the shooter might want to dribble the ball a couple of times to relax before she shoots. The most important difference is that she shouldn't jump during her free throw.

> "We're good at shooting threes. We're just not good at making them."
>
> —Sonny Smith

> "They throw up enough bricks during warm-ups to build a condominium."
>
> —Bill Foster

Stage 1: Get into proper shooting stance: A shooter that makes a high percentage of her foul shots is relaxed at the line. Her feet should be shoulder-width apart, with her toes pointing toward the middle of the rim. Her "shooting foot" should be about one inch behind the free throw line—slightly closer to the basket than her other foot (heel-to-toe position). As with the jump shot, her shoulders and hips should be square to the target, and her weight should be on the **balls of her feet.**

Many players develop a dribbling routine at the line to help them calm their nerves and focus on the upcoming shot. After that, though, their setup should be identical to their jump shot preparation.

Stage 2: Move upward: After the shooter has established her shooting position, her entire body should move in a synchronized manner upward and slightly toward the rim. Her power and distance will still come from her legs and hips, even though she won't actually leave the ground. All at once, her knees should straighten, her hips should rise, her heels should lift off the floor, and she should release the ball.

Stage 3: Release the ball: The shooting and nonshooting hands should move in an up-and-out motion identical to that described in the jump shot section.

Stage 4: Follow-through: Holding the follow-through until the ball hits the rim is especially important on a free throw. A hard wrist snap will give the shot good rotation. Balls with good height and backspin usually hit the rim "softly"—instead of bouncing right off, they roll around the basket and (maybe) eventually drop in. There's no reason why a player with a sound release and a good follow-through shouldn't make a high percentage of her free throws.

Even though a player might have a routine that involves dribbling and rocking, she should avoid dipping or bouncing right before she shoots. It's important that a player release every shot in the same way, but the foul shot, in particular, relies on muscle memory. In fact, a player shouldn't even have to think about her release when she steps up to the line. Her eyes should stay on the rim from the time she takes her first dribble to the time the ball hits the basket.

"It ties the school record for highest free-throw percentage in a game."

—John Justus, positive spin on shooting only one-for-one from the free throw line for an entire game

HOW TO SHOOT A LAYUP

Shooting form for a layup differs from that of a jump shot or free throw. For one thing, players are often driving to the basket as they go up to shoot.

As she's driving to the basket from the wing, the shooter should pick up her dribble just inside the foul line. From there, she should take two long, powerful strides toward the basket, and explode up for the layup. The ball itself should be released just like a normal shot—soft and high, but this time, off the backboard. Generally, if the shooter aims for the upper corner of the box on the side that she's shooting, her ball will pass through the basket unimpeded. If she doesn't put the ball up high on the backboard, it may not make it past the bottom of the rim. It's important to briefly hold the follow-through when shooting layups.

The player should plant her foot opposite her shooting hand—as she's driving toward the basket, her inside foot. Specifically, if she's shooting a right-handed layup, she should plant her left foot; if it's a left-handed layup, she should plant her right foot. From there, she should drive her shooting knee (the knee on the same side as her shooting hand) up to help her explode upward from the floor. (Her thigh should reach a point at least parallel to the floor.) The shooter should try to pick up her dribble with as little excess motion as possible. The ball should travel straight from the floor into her shot pocket (just beneath her chin, on the side of her shooting hand).

Layups should be simple, high-percentage shots, but in fact, players miss them too often. Easy baskets make a big difference down the stretch of a close game. Coaches should not allow sloppy layup drills in practice or in warmups. The fact is, making a layup requires concentration.

Many youth basketball players who have a problem with making layups do not take advantage of the fact that the rules allow two full steps before the shot. Many players try to take short, quick stutter steps, which usually put them too far underneath the basket. Taking long steps allows a player to gain control and jump as high as possible.

THE HOOK SHOT

The hook shot is a difficult shot to make, but it's effective because it's so hard to defend. Being able to use the hook shot effectively is well worth the time it takes to learn it. Very few girls shoot the hook shot; nevertheless I believe that it is underutilized and should be emphasized more. Some points to remember are listed below.

- Start with both hands on the ball
- Protect the ball by moving it away from the defender
- Keep the eyes on the target
- Keep the shooting elbow straight
- Use the opposite arm to protect the ball
- Drive the shooting knee up strong
- Point the index finger of shooting hand to the target
- Jump as high as possible
- Flick the ball with the shooting wrist and fingers
- Shoot the ball softly

Players should practice using the backboard, but as their skills increase, they can try to flip the ball just over the front of the rim.

SHOOTING TIPS

HOW TO WARM UP

Every player should have a shooting practice program. Girls that show up to the gym with no plan tend not to warm up properly, nor to practice their shots at game speed. For example, they might come in to practice and start launching balls from all over the court before they've warmed up.

Players should begin practice with the 2-4-6-8 drill described in the Drills 5 section later in this book. Standing directly in front of the hoop, about 2 feet away, the shooter should snap the ball up and out with only her shooting hand. The shot should be perfect, complete with a good follow-through, sharp rotation, and plenty of arc. After two shots from two feet, she should move back to 4 feet, then 6, then 8. Shooting **close to the basket** will not only warm up her shot and loosen her arms and wrists, but it will also give her confidence in her shooting ability. (In general, players should always start close to the basket, and move outward). Another good drill for players on their own at the beginning of practice is the perfect shooting form drill described in Drills 5.

> "If one of our guys misses a layup and the next guy tips it in, I say to the first guy, 'nice assist.'"
>
> –Norm Stewart, on getting a better perspective on life after battling cancer

Once she's warmed up, the shooter should take several shots from single spots on the floor, before starting to move around the hoop. Ideally, these spots would be the locations from which the player shoots most during games. Post players should focus on practicing their skills around the basket; guards should work on their outside shots and moves to the hoop. Everyone should practice free throws.

That being said, every player should develop her outside shot, including her three-point range. Just because a young woman is tall doesn't mean that she should be confined to shooting near the basket.

> "We have a great bunch of outside shooters. Unfortunately, all of our games are played indoors."
>
> —Weldon Drew

MUSCLE MEMORY

It is important that young players develop good shooting habits; it's more difficult to change bad technique than it is to do things right the first time. What's more, the body has a remarkable way of remembering how a specific physical action was performed. Many refer to this habit of repeating certain actions as **muscle memory.** Ideally, a player's muscle memory will be of proper shooting form!

VISUALIZATION

Prior to shooting, players should visualize the ball going into the basket with a swish. Visualizing will help boost a shooter's confidence. If she does it enough in practice, it will become second nature to her during games.

> "I could hear groans from the crowd when we were getting ready to shoot."
>
> —Andy Russo

CONSISTENT RELEASE

Players should strive to shoot with the same motion every time, whether the shot is from close range or from a distance. The only difference should lie in how much she uses her legs (how much distance she puts on the shot).

SIMPLER THE BETTER

Consistent shooters have compact forms and they don't waste any motion. In practice, players should work on eliminating excess motion. As I said before, a player's toes, knees, hips, waist, shoulders, elbows, and hands should all work together. That's how the best shooters make even difficult shots look simple.

> "We're shooting 100 percent—60 percent from the field and 40 percent from the free throw line."
>
> —Norm Stewart

CHAPTER 6
Rebounding

You might be surprised that height isn't the most important factor in rebounding. It certainly helps, but when it comes down to it, rebounding is the result of effort. Position matters more than height. Rebounding also requires a certain attitude and tenacity. Great rebounders always, *always* want the ball for themselves.

Defensive rebounding can control the tempo of a game and wear down opposing offenses; good offensive rebounding can lead to scoring from close range and inject a team with confident energy, while providing the added bonus of deflating opponents.

REBOUNDING MECHANICS

First, a couple of terms: "defensive rebound" refers to a rebound obtained by a defensive player off of an opponent's missed shot; "offensive rebound" refers to a ball grabbed by an offensive player off of another offensive player's missed shot or her own shot. A defensive rebound signals a change of possession; after an offensive rebound, the attacking team has another chance to score (which is why offensive boards are so valuable).

POSITIONING

If players are standing around, the rebound usually goes to the tallest player near the basket; but if players are rebounding properly, it will usually go to the quickest jumper with the best position. A player in good rebounding position will be able to corral the ball quickly and efficiently.

Rebounding is a pitfall at the youth level for several reasons. Players stand too far away from the basket and spend too much time watching the ball in flight rather than fighting for position near the basket. If they do move in toward the hoop (or "crash the boards"), they are content to stand in a clump, waiting for the ball to bounce to the player with the longest outstretched arms.

To have the advantage, a rebounder should gain the **inside position,** in which her body is between the opposing player and the rim. If she stands behind her opponent, the only rebound she has a chance of getting is a long carom off the rim.

ESTABLISH POSITION EARLY

When the shot goes up, there's no time to act like a deer in head-lights. Part of establishing good position is getting into the lane quickly. (In a perfect world, players wouldn't even have to wait until the ball leaves the shooter's hand before crashing—they would be able to anticipate the shot itself. That kind of anticipation only comes with years of playing experience.) Rebounders should always assume that the shot will miss and should be firmly entrenched in their positions before the ball hits the rim. This will not only increase their chances of getting the rebound, but also decrease the likelihood that they will commit a foul (more on fouling in a later section).

PLAY THE ODDS

In many situations there are one or more open spaces near the basket that can easily be filled by a hustling forward or guard. Great rebounders position themselves in order to maximize their chances of obtaining the ball when it comes off the rim.

The cardinal rule is to gain inside position. Generally, the player **closest** to the basket has the inside track and thus a built-in advantage. An exception to this rule is if the shot is taken from three-point range, in which case, the ball will likely bounce far off the rim. More advanced players should be familiar with rebounding **probabilities**—where shots are likely to bounce, depending on the distance and angle of the shot. I usually assume the ball will bounce to the opposite side of the court as the shooter. This is especially the case for long shots.

In their effort to get close to the basket, players must be careful not to let themselves get pushed underneath the rim. Players who are too far under the basket are taken out of the play—they will usually not get the rebound. Coaches must teach their players to establish a medium—to find a position close enough to the basket to be effective rebounders, but not so close that they get taken out of the play.

STANCE

Finding and getting to a position on the court is only half of the battle. Once having gotten there, players need to assume the rebounding **stance.** This stance gives the rebounder several advantages:

> *"Offense wins fans, defense wins games and rebounding wins championships."*
>
> —Unknown

> *"I never thought I'd lead the NBA in rebounding, but I got a lot of help from my teammates— they did a lot of missing."*
>
> —Moses Malone

"I believe in higher education. You know, 6'8", 6'9", 6'10"."

—David "Smoky" Gaines

she will be balanced; she will occupy as much space as possible and be able to withstand pushing and shoving from other would-be rebounders; she will be in an athletic position, ready to jump explosively; and most importantly, the stance will allow her to box out effectively (see the next section).

The rebounding stance is similar to the shooting stance. A player's weight should be shifted to the balls of her feet, her knees should be bent, her hips lowered, her back straight, her head up and looking at the basket. A rebounder's feet, however, should be wider apart, and her knees should be bent more than a shooter's. A stance breakdown follows:

Feet: The rebounder's feet should be at least shoulder width apart, but she can spread them as far as she needs to in order to stay wide, keep her balance, and hold her opponent on her back (that is, prevent her from getting to the rim). Her weight should be distributed so that she can move quickly in any direction: equally balanced between the balls of both feet.

Knees, Hips and Torso: A rebounder's knees should be bent at all times, to varying degrees. Flexing her knees will give her leverage against the opponent that she is blocking out and also get her ready to jump up for the rebound. Her hips should be lowered slightly. The trunk of her body should lean slightly forward to the basket.

Elbows: Her elbows should be up and pointed away from her body. Her arms should be raised up in a "rebounding frame." Together, her elbows and arms (along with her rear end) should prevent opponents from encroaching on her rebounding area.

Hands: A rebounder's hands should not drop below shoulder level. She should be prepared for the ball to come off the rim at any angle, and at any speed. Her fingers should be spread apart and her palms should face the basket.

A fact often forgotten is that players can get a lot of loose rebounds by hustling to fill an open space near the basket as other players are fighting each other for the ball. In some cases, getting into the position will mean running from the strong to the weak-side of the court (if the rebounder anticipates the shot will bounce long).

Rebounding isn't an easy task—it is both physically and mentally demanding. The benefits, however, are well worth the effort.

Coaches should be on the lookout for the four mistakes most common among youth players: watching the ball or resting during the shot, not getting close enough to the basket, letting the hands drop below the shoulders, and standing up out of the stance.

In scrimmages, I like to make it a requirement that every player move toward the basket after a shot goes up—a minimum of one step. If they stand still, they run a suicide.

BOXING OUT

Boxing, or blocking out, is making contact with and screening an opponent from the basket in anticipation of a rebound. In other words, to box out, a player uses her back and rear end to keep her opponent at bay as she establishes her rebounding position. A box out can start with a pivot: as the player turns to face the basket, she should drive her rear end back into the opposing player. In the end, a box out is essentially the completion of the rebounding stance that I described earlier: it is the rebounder's squat position, with the added component of physical contact from behind. The goal of the box out is to put the opponent at a disadvantage relative to the basket.

The initial contact that a rebounder makes with her opponent should ideally be outside the lane—if she finds herself too close to the basket, she should literally move her opponent slightly backward with her legs and rear end. Boxing out can be a matter of holding ground: or a player can use her body to clear some space in front of the rim. That's why having a wide, strong stance is so important. Many coaches will use the term "push back" to describe the box out movement to signify that very idea. Another common phrase is, "keep her on your back"; this saying is useful because it involves motion. No matter where the opponent travels, it is the rebounder's responsibility to keep her on her back, to maintain constant contact.

Blocking out is a particularly important component of defensive rebounding. Defenders naturally have the inside position when

> *"If I ask a kid how he did on the boards, and he says, '12 a game,' I know he's not going to Harvard."*
>
> —Coach Peter Roby, Harvard

the shot goes up (they should be between their players and the basket, in good defensive position.) But many make the mistake of running to the basket as soon as the ball is shot—in so doing, they lose sight of their opponent, giving them a free lane to the hoop. Boxing out should be a defensive rebounder's first priority. Her first movement, then, should really be sideways or backward, to make contact with her opponent. After boxing out, she should go to the basket to grab the rebound (all the while, making sure that her defender stays behind her). A box out can fail if a player holds it for too long. She must "release" from her opponent and go after the rebound.

The box out should be a defender's first option. There are some cases, though, in which a full box out isn't a good idea. Getting the ball is the primary goal. If a player doesn't have time to find her opponent, pivot, box out, release and proactively go after the ball, she should cut her movement down to minimum. In those cases, the key is to force the offensive player to adjust her position as she goes for the board.

Great defensive teams work together to get rebounds. Getting in good rebounding position takes into account where the other players are on the court. For example, if there are three defenders on the left side of the basket and none on the right side when a shot is taken, a player might consider making a quick move to the right side to get in position for the long rebound. Furthermore, it's not always necessary for a player to box out her matched opponent.

ANTICIPATE THE REBOUND

A shot can miss any manner of ways: it can be long or short, off to one side or another, or any combination thereof. As rebounders become more experienced, they will start to learn where rebounds will likely come off the rim. Developing that sort of innate anticipation is difficult for younger players, though. Coaches should teach them a few simple guidelines for reading the rebound:

- Most shots miss long, so the rebound will often bounce to the opposite side of the rim. For example, if the shot comes from the right wing, the rebound will usually fall on the left side of the hoop. (This is called a "weak-side" rebound.) By contrast, if a shot has a flat trajectory, there's a good chance it will bounce off the front of the iron (rim) and come back out on the same side as the shooter.

- The angle of the shot makes a difference. Shots taken within 45 degrees of the baseline (on either side) are more likely to bounce long or to the side of the hoop. Shots taken in the middle of the court are generally more likely to bounce into the lane.

- The distance of the bounce off the rim is usually proportional to the distance the shot travels. That is, three-point shots will bounce harder and further than, for example, a shot from inside the key. Players should position themselves accordingly—further from the basket for threes, closer for twos and layups.

- The quality of the rebound bounce has to do with the ball's rotation in the air. A well-shot ball will normally hit the rim softly.

> *"If you come to a fork in the road, take it."*
>
> —Yogi Berra

Another factor that affects how the ball will carom off the basket is the rim's flexibility. A tight or firm rim will result in harder, longer bounces; a loose or flexible rim will be more forgiving. A player should be able to determine what kind of rim she is dealing with during warmups.

JUMP!

Some players rebound by standing on the tips of their toes and reaching up for the ball. Taller players seem especially prone to this mistake. However, great rebounders—particularly ones that want to be successful at a higher level—jump!

The jump starts from a crouched stance. Players can't elevate off the floor if their knees are locked. Getting into the stance is equivalent to coiling a spring before letting it go.

The rebounder should jump as high as she possibly can while keeping control of her body. The important thing is that she time her leap so that she jumps prior to her opponent and can catch the ball at the height of her elevation, when her arms are fully extended. At that point, her hands should take over: flexible, but strong, they should be ready to corral the ball as it caroms off the rim.

JUMP QUICKLY

Quickness is an essential element of the rebounding jump. The player with the highest vertical leap doesn't always get the rebound—more often than not, it goes to the player that is quickest off the floor. Having a quick jump starts with balance. As she maintains her box out, a player's weight should stay on the balls of her feet. That way, she doesn't have to waste time transferring her weight before she leaps.

The rebounder should be sure to grab the ball with both hands when she reaches the peak of her jump. A bobbling rebound around the basket is available to the opposing team. The moral of the story is: secure possession of the ball as quickly as possible (by jumping quickly and catching it with both hands).

AFTER THE REBOUND

PROTECTING THE BALL

One of the more frustrating events in basketball is to lose the rebound after working so hard to get it. There are several steps that a rebounder on defense should take to protect the ball: the first is to assume the so-called **chin position.** The player's lower body should be in a sturdy athletic stance, with her feet at least shoulder-width apart, her weight distributed evenly across the balls of her feet, and her knees bent. Her hands should tightly grip both sides of the basketball. (Players should squeeze the ball—that kind of iron grip will prevent opponents from slapping it away.) Her elbows should be up and pointed out, held at right angles to her forearms; her forearms should be parallel to the floor. She should firmly hold the ball near her chest, slightly under her chin.

Assuming the chin position after a defensive rebound is an effective way of keeping opponents from swarming, in the hopes of getting a steal. As an added bonus, players will be in good position to quickly dribble or pass. An offensive rebounder can also use the chin position before putting the ball back up, or making a pump fake.

The **pivot** is another means of protecting the ball after a rebound, but works best in conjunction with the "chin." After her jump, a player is free to choose either foot as her pivot foot (assuming that she lands on both feet at the same time). If she holds the ball in a strong chin position, and uses her pivot to quickly rotate away

from her opponent, she shouldn't have any trouble maintaining possession of the ball after a rebound.

LANDING

Offensive and defensive players rebound for different purposes. An offensive rebounder's goal is to immediately put up a shot, to try to put the ball back in the basket. Therefore, when she lands, she should think about gathering her strength and momentum in order to power up to the hoop. She should make her base as wide as possible (by landing with her feet apart and bending her knees). Her eyes should stay focused on the basket. She should hold the ball in the chin position. One of the biggest problems in youth basketball is the tendency to bring the ball down too low after an offensive rebound. Players may think that it helps them maintain their balance, but really, all it does is expose the ball to speedy opponents' hands.

Out of her strong landing position (which is a combination of a box out and a chin position), she should drive up to the basket, holding the ball with two hands for added protection. A well-executed pump fake before the shot can be very effective. Her first look should always be to the basket; only after that option has failed should she pivot away from the basket to look for a kick-out pass (a pass from the post to the perimeter).

It's also important for defensive rebounders to land with a wide and balanced (and therefore strong) base; but they use that strength in a different way. Their first priority is to turn and make a quick **outlet pass** to a guard, in the hopes of starting a fast break. From the chin position, the rebounder's first movement should be to look to the wing for an open guard. She should make a strong pivot in her direction, and pass to her. The pass could be an overhead, chest, or bounce pass, depending on where the guard is located, the strength of the rebounder, and the passing angle. More advanced rebounders can work on turning toward the outside wing as they are still in the air (eliminating the need to pivot speeds up the outlet pass and the possible fast break).

If an opponent manages to put herself between the rebounder and the outlet guard or if the rebounder is guarded, she can take one or two dribbles to get herself free. These dribbles should be powerful and quick, and should lead directly into a pass to the outlet guard.

OFFENSIVE REBOUNDING

I've devoted an entire section to offensive rebounding because it is such an important part of the game. Rebounding is the best and simplest addition to a set offense and an effective method of scoring in itself. In fact, offensive rebounding can be as much or more an offensive strategy as a drawn play!

Offensive rebounding involves a slightly different strategy—since defensive rebounders naturally have the inside position, offensive rebounders rely more heavily on movement. Often, offensive rebounds are obtained by making a quick spin or slashing cut to the basket.

HOW TO GO AFTER OFFENSIVE REBOUNDS

If boxed out: Assume that the defensive player has inside position and has effectively blocked out the offensive player. The offensive rebounder can run around the side of the defender, or fake one way and go the other. Alternatively, the attacker can use the defender's own body weight against her. Leaning on the defender's back for support, she should stick out one foot and plant it to the side of her opponent. Then she can roll around her, bringing herself even with the defender on a horizontal plane. If she moves quickly enough, she might even be able to swing her body in front of her defender, thus gaining the coveted inside position. Arms can be a valuable rebounding tool; offensive players shouldn't be shy about using their elbows and biceps to move their defenders' arms out of the way.

If not blocked out: If, by chance, the offensive player is not boxed out, she should find the clearest lane to the basket and fill it. If the defender is still facing her when the shot goes up, she should make a head-and-shoulder fake and quickly move by her opponent. This move is especially effective for guards who want to crash the boards from the wing (particularly because guard defenders generally don't box out as well as forwards).

Tip the ball: If the offensive rebounder isn't in position to grab the ball with both hands, she might try to tip it out to an alert teammate. But, she should be careful not to commit a foul by going over the back of another player.

Rebounding is hard work; players have to do whatever they need in order to get in good position for the board. Great rebounding sometimes looks like reckless abandon, with players using cuts, spins, and fakes to get into position. When executed properly, rebounding is one of the most exhausting parts of the game of basketball.

QUALITIES OF A GOOD REBOUNDER

HAVE NO FEAR

Good rebounders can't be afraid of making contact with other players. A rebounder's rear end, back, legs or arms should touch at least one opponent on most shots. It's important to practice rebounding because many girls are naturally reluctant to be physical. Coaches need to practice drills that make female players comfortable with using their bodies in this manner.

WANT THE BALL

Rebounding is a matter of hard work and desire. The player who hustles and is willing to pay the price of that hustle, in the form of bodily contact, will get the most rebounds. A great rebounder never expects her teammate to get the ball for her. She will go to the ball, instead of waiting for it to come to her.

ANTICIPATE

Every player should assume that every shot will miss, but those who are able to determine where the ball will come off the rim will be better rebounders. This sort of knowledge only comes with playing experience.

COMMUNICATE

Rebounding should be a team effort. If a player finds herself near another opponent (other then her matchup) when the shot goes up, she should box her out.

RELEASE

Once the play is over, it's over. The rebounder should usually either hustle back on defense or get right back into the fast-break offense.

"The athlete who says that something cannot be done should never interrupt the one who is doing it."

—John Wooden

TEAM REBOUNDING

Usually, a coach can send four of his defenders to the defensive boards—sending the fifth rebounder is optional. Ideally, three should be positioned near each block and in the middle of the lane in front of the basket; the fourth player should hover just below the foul line. (It's best to have a guard or small forward play this long position. If she doesn't get the ball, she's still in a position to run the fast break.)

The coach of a fast-break team generally won't commit all of his players to the rebound. He would want to ensure that at least one player would be on the wing, ready to receive the outlet pass and start the break.

If the defensive team is a fast-break team, then a coach might only send three of his offensive players to the boards; the other two would linger back as safeties. On the other hand, if the opponent always runs a set offense (and rarely the break), a coach can afford to put four or even all five of his players on the offensive boards.

COMMON REBOUNDING FOULS

The most common rebounding foul is called "over-the-back" and occurs when one player encroaches on her opponent's rebounding space from behind. (The NCAA calls the over-the-back foul a violation of the "principle of verticality.") When two players are in the same horizontal plane, they both have equal right to the ball. However, when one rebounder has established position in front of another, the player that is behind cannot violate her space. Over-the-back fouls occur when the disadvantaged player reaches over her opponent's head or shoulders with her arms and makes physical contact.

Another possible rebounding infraction occurs if a player uses her arms to displace her opponent. This is not the same thing as using your arms to jockey for position; nor is it the same as using your rear end to clear space in front of the basket. Using your body or arms to displace is a foul!

The NCAA definition of a rebound and a rebounding foul follow:

"A rebound is an attempt by any player to secure possession of the ball after a try for a goal. To attain or maintain legal rebounding position, a player shall not:

- Displace, charge or push an opponent.
- Extend either or both shoulders, hips, knees or extend either or both arms or elbows fully or partially in a position other than vertical so that the freedom of movement of an opponent is hindered when contact with any of these body parts occurs.
- Bend the body in an abnormal position to hold or displace an opponent.
- Violate the principle of verticality.

Every player shall be entitled to a spot on the playing court, provided that the player gets there first without illegally contacting an opponent."

The rules, therefore, allow each player to establish a rebounding position; technically, from that point on, no one is allowed to dislodge her. Contact is allowed when it is a means of holding a position. The truth is, though, a good box out that pushes an opponent slightly back usually won't be penalized.

"I don't believe in boxing out. My idea about rebounding is just to get the ball."

—Charles Barkley

"My nine-year-old daughter could run around out there for 27 minutes, and two rebounds would hit her on the head."

—Gary Williams, on his top rebounder getting only one rebound

CHAPTER 7
Team Offense

An effective offense takes advantage of its strengths and attempts to exploit the weaknesses of the defense. For example, a squad loaded with three-point shooters may gear its offense toward the outside game; by contrast, a taller team will look to work the ball inside as much as possible. A smaller, quicker team may fast break on offense and implement a full-court press. A coach should design his offensive system around his players' abilities, including ball-handling and quickness.

This chapter describes tactics that both individual and groups of players can use to score within the context of a team offense. But first, I'm going to describe the five offensive positions and their various responsibilities.

POSITIONS

POSITIONS BY THE NUMBERS

Number 1: Point guard—the quarterback of the team
Number 2: Shooting guard—can set up on either wing
Number 3: Small forward—spots up on the opposite wing from the shooting guard
Number 4: Power forward—plays the high and low post
Number 5: Center—usually plays the low post from box to box, but also the high post

RESPONSIBILITIES BY POSITION

NUMBER 1
The point guard is a team's leader on the floor and can be considered an active extension of the coach. This player brings the ball up the court, is the team's primary ball-handler, initiates the offense designated by the coach, calls the out-of-bounds plays, and also is usually the first player back to defend the fast break. Her primary skills and responsibilities are:

- Excellent ballhandling skills
- Excellent passing skills
- Speed and quickness
- Ability to run and defend the fast break
- Excellent defensive abilities
- Capacity to be the team leader and quarterback

- Knowledge of the game
- Ability to penetrate and dish (pass to teammates off the drive)

NUMBER 2

The number 2 guard is also called the shooting guard. The main characteristics of a shooting guard are the ability to shoot long-range shots and to run the fast break, and good ballhandling skills. The 2 is often involved in reversing the ball to attack the weak side of a zone defense, and in spotting up for kick-out passes from the post. She must posses:

- Good court sense
- Dribbling skills with both hands
- Good passing skills
- Speed and quickness
- Ability to move without the ball
- Ability to shoot from three-point range
- Ability to run the fast break
- Ability to read defenses

NUMBER 3

The small forward is an all-around player: a shooter, a passer, a driver, and a rebounder. She should possess the following characteristics:

- Accurate shooting range out to the three-point line
- Ability to score from both the wing and the post
- Good passing skills
- Good ballhandling skills
- Rebounding ability
- Speed and quickness
- Defensive skills
- Ability to start and run the fast break

NUMBER 4

The number 4 player, also known as the power forward, should be a hard worker: a tireless rebounder, a hard-nosed defender, and a scorer in and around the lane. The 4 should possess:

- Excellent rebounding skills, on both offense and defense
- Good passing skills
- Reliable ballhandling skills
- Ability to drive hard to the basket
- Ability to start the fast break
- A physical style of play, on both offense and defense

NUMBER 5

Next to the point guard, the center, or 5 player, has the biggest impact on a team. A good center can dominate both offense and defense in the lane. She should be able to score and to keep her opponents from scoring in the paint. The center is usually a team's tallest player. She must have:

- Aggressive rebounding skills
- Good scoring ability from short- to mid-range
- Ability to start the fast break
- Tough defensive skills
- Good passing skills
- Strong hands
- Upper body strength
- Jumping ability
- Quickness
- Good footwork

BASIC MOVES WITHOUT THE BALL

It is estimated that, on average, offensive players have control of the ball for less than 10 percent of the team's total time on the court. That means that most players will have the ball for less than 3 minutes out of a 32-minute game. The point is, that the average player will spend most of her time on offense without the ball. It's easy to see that moving without the ball is important! An offensive player without the ball should be ready to:

1. Set a screen.
2. Keep her defensive player occupied by making cuts.
3. Provide an outlet or kick-out pass opportunity for the player with the ball.
4. Consistently work to get open to receive a pass.
5. Be a threat to score, pass, drive, or rebound.
6. Maintain proper distance and spacing.

COURT BALANCE AND SPACING

A well balanced and spaced offense puts pressure on a defense by increasing the territory that each individual defender must cover. One defender can guard two offensive players that are

"The difference in Namath and me is that when you make the money he makes, they say you're ruggedly handsome. When you make the money I make, they say you have a big nose."

—Jim Valvano

bunched together. By contrast, one defender will have difficulty guarding her player effectively if she also has to worry about another attacker that's properly spaced.

That's the basic concept behind balance and spacing. Players that do not maintain enough distance between themselves and their teammates make the defense's job easier. They also restrict their teammates' ability to move around the court freely. Proper spacing in basketball varies depending on the age and skill of the players. The general rule for many teams is that an offensive player should not be within 12 to 15 feet of any other teammate prior to a shot.

Poor spacing is the plague of youth basketball. Players seem to gravitate toward the ball, wherever it might be. A coach should be sure to address this tendency in practice and make rules concerning the minimum (and maximum) distance between teammates.

By extension, movement on the so-called weak side of the court is an important aspect of the game. (The weak side of the court is the side of the court opposite the ball.) Although they are not directly involved in the action, weak-side players play an important role in the team offense. Their movement keeps weak-side defenders busy, preventing them from playing help defense. Perhaps most importantly, they are in position to receive the ball as it gets "swung" from one side of the court to the other. This sort of ball movement—back and forth from opposite wings—breaks down team defenses. In many ways, it is a player's movement on the weak side of the court that determines her ability to score.

Strong-side and weak-side players can use the following moves to get open for passes and also to score.

THE V-CUT

The principle behind the V-cut is simple: if a defender is situated between an offensive player and the ball, the offensive player isn't open for a direct pass. The potential receiver must force her defender to adjust, to move out of her "deny" position. The V-cut accomplishes this goal.

A V-cut usually starts on the wing. The offensive player should cut into the basket at about three-quarter speed—her goal should be to take her defender as deep as she can (if possible, all the way to the block). By closing the distance between them, the offensive player actually has a better chance of getting away from her defender as she makes her cut back out to the ball.

Before she cuts out, the player should get very close (make physical contact with) to her defender. This involves planting her inside foot (the foot closest to the baseline), making a reverse pivot, and lightly bumping her defender with her backside and back. Then she should turn and sprint out to the wing with her hands up, ready to catch a pass. Her cut out to the ball should be at a shallower angle relative to the passer than her cut toward the basket: it should bring her closer to the ball than she originally was. As she sprints out, the offensive player should call for the ball and provide a target with her outside hand (the hand away from the defender); after receiving the pass, she should pivot into triple-threat position.

THE REVERSE SPIN

If a defender effectively blocks an offensive player as she makes a V-cut to the basket—that is, if she doesn't let her get to the block—she can use a reverse spin to get open for the pass. This without-the-ball move is similar to the spin dribble move, in the sense that it uses the defender's own body weight as a support and pivot point. The attacker should plant her outside leg (leg closest to the ball) between her defender's two feet. As soon as she makes contact with her outside shoulder, she should bring her body around 180 degrees in the direction opposite her pivot foot. (If she plants her left foot, she should spin toward her right shoulder; if she plants with her right, she should spin toward her left shoulder.) As she "spins off" her defender, the player should be sure to use her outside leg to seal off her defender's body. From that position (similar to a rebounding box out), the

> *"That's the one with all the 'no passing' signs."*
>
> —Atlanta disc jockey on Atlanta's proposed Dominique Wilkins Freeway

"That usually means you can't shoot."

—Hosie Grimsley, after being named one of the top five defenders in college basketball

attacker is free to cut out to the ball, using her outside hand as a target. As always, once she has the ball, she should pivot into a triple-threat position.

THE FRONT (MIDDLE) CUT

The front cut is another variation on the V-cut. If the defender is overplaying the wing—that is, not giving the offensive player any space as she moves toward the basket—the attacker can use a front cut to explode by her to the rim. The move starts like a V-cut, with the offensive player jogging at moderate speed toward the defender; as she makes contact with the defender's body, she should plant her outside foot. Until this point, the move has been identical to a reverse spin, but now, instead of swinging her shoulders in a direction opposite to her pivot foot, the player should bring her inside foot through her defender and plant it to her side. She should essentially make a crossover step so that she turns to face the passer with the defender on her back, and then cut directly to the basket. This time, her target should be her inside hand—the hand closest to the hoop. Needless to say, the front cut is a move to score.

THE BACKDOOR

Sometimes, a defender will play what's known as "full-deny defense," which means that she will extend as far out on the wing as she needs to in order to prevent her matchup from catching the ball. The backdoor is a change-of-direction move that exploits a deny defender's overplay position and distance from the basket.

The backdoor consists of a quick fake to the outside (away from the basket), and an explosion past the defender toward the hoop. This move is different than the front cut: players executing the backdoor cut behind their defenders, in a path that takes them on the baseline rather than the lane side of their opponent. In fact, the name "backdoor" stems from the fact that, if executed properly, the offensive player ends up taking the blind or backdoor route to the basket. She should extend her inside hand as a target.

Running the backdoor requires good communication between teammates—this move is essentially a timing play. The moment the receiver passes her defender, the ball should be in the air toward her. Often passers will signal the backdoor call with a closed fist or wave of the hand.

ONE-ON-ONE MOVES

Being able to move without the ball is important—but once a player has the ball in her possession, she has to be able to score. All of the following dribbling one-on-one moves begin from the fundamental triple-threat position. Needless to say, one-on-one moves become more potent when the attacker can handle the ball well with either hand.

THE DRIVE

The drive is the most basic one-on-one move to the basket. It consists of a quick dribbling attack to the hoop. Once the offensive player is side by side with or past her defender, she can drive all the way to the basket for a layup, pull up for a jump shot, or kick (not literally) the ball out to a teammate. The drive is effective because it puts pressure on the defender to move her feet without fouling; it also forces the defense as a whole to rotate and switch, opening up the perimeter for a kick-out pass.

A drive begins when the offensive player pushes off her pivot foot and takes a long first step toward the basket; she should put the ball on the floor just past her defender's hip. (She can use her torso to protect the ball from her defender's roving hands.) This "first step" is a vital part of the drive. If she's not by her defender after her first step, chances are she will have to contend with her opponent all the way to the hoop.

Players should exploit the drive until the defense proves they can guard it effectively. If a defender begins to overplay by backing off her offensive player in an attempt to deny her first step, the offensive player can shoot a jump shot. (Once a player makes a couple of outside shots, her defender will be forced to play up again—then her drive will be open once more.)

An offensive player can set up her drive by using a pump fake—that is, by faking a jump shot to get her defender in the air before driving around her.

THE JAB STEP

The jab step is a foot fake that can be used to set up either a drive or a jump shot. Keeping the ball in her hands, tucked on the same side as her pivot foot, the attacker should take a short, hard step (10 inches or less) toward one side of her defender. Keeping the ball secure, she should fake her dribble by bringing the ball down outside her own knee. If her defender moves toward the ball, the attacker should drive past her in the direction opposite her jab. Alternatively, if the defender jumps back in anticipation of the drive, the offensive player should pull her foot back and take a jump shot. When executing a jab

step, it's important that the first step be quick and not too long, and that the attacker stay in a balanced, crouched position with her knees bent. The attacker may need to perform a series of jab steps to get the defender to move out of position.

THE CROSSOVER STEP

The crossover starts with a jab step toward one of the defender's feet (in this example, with the right foot toward the defender's left). Staying low, the offensive player should cross her right leg over the defender's right foot with one long step; she should then push the ball out with her left hand, almost clipping her defender's shoulder as she goes by her. The dribbler's step should be long enough so that the ball bounces at a point past the defender's right hip.

THE ROCKER STEP

The rocker step starts off like a jab, but involves taking a longer step. The offensive player essentially rocks back and forth by shifting her nonpivot foot. As soon as she sees her opponent move out of position, the offensive player should drive by her to the basket, or shoot a jump shot.

COMBINATION ROCKER OR JAB STEP, SHOT FAKE, AND DRIVE

Adding in a shot fake (pump fake) after a rocker or jab step can put even more pressure on the defender, and open up a wider lane to the basket. The defender will be forced to play the shot (step forward with her hands up) when the offensive player makes a shot fake, which will give her attacker even more of an advantage on the drive.

DEAD-BALL MOVES

Sometimes, after making a one-on-one move to the basket, an attacker has to pick up her dribble before she has time to get off a shot. In most cases, one or more defenders will be positioned between such a player and the basket. Dead-ball moves are designed for exactly that scenario. Both of the moves below begin with a shot fake, and end with a look to the basket.

SHOT FAKE AND JUMP SHOT

The attacker will have stepped out of her drive. She should then execute a shot fake, in the hopes of enticing her defender to leave her feet. As the defender is coming down, the attacker should explode up for her jump shot. If she's a savvy offensive player, she might jump a little bit forward into her opponent, and try to draw a shooting foul.

SHOT FAKE AND STEP THROUGH

This move is the follow-up to the shot fake and jump shot move. If the offensive player notices that her defender overplays the shot fake, she can take one step by her to the basket. This move is often called "up-and-under" because of the path that the ball takes: up on the shot fake, under the defender's outstretched arms, and through to the basket. After her step through, the attacker should explode up to the basket as if she were shooting a regular layup.

BASIC BASKETBALL PLAYS

One-on-one and dead-ball moves are important parts of a player's individual offensive attack. But also important are her skills working in conjunction with one or more teammates—one player can't single-handedly win every game. Players should try to move the basketball by passing instead of dribbling. In my opinion, there is entirely too much dribbling in youth basketball.

Many half-court offenses breakdown into simple two-player and three-player plays to the basket. The ones that I describe below are the fundamental components of most team offenses.

THE GIVE-AND-GO

In a **give-and-go,** an offensive player passes the ball to a teammate and immediately cuts to the basket looking for a quick return pass. Her cut can either be a front or a backdoor cut.

The give-and-go can be effective against both man-to-man and zone defenses. Often, when her player makes a pass, a defender will relax or watch the ball. That moment of weakness is what the give-and-go exploits. Attackers have the advantage of being able to cut at full speed to the basket (without having to handle the ball).

THE BACKDOOR

The **backdoor** play is the scoring continuation of the backdoor cut that I described earlier. A backdoor from the wing can involve a wing player and a player with the ball at the top of the key. As she sees that she is overplayed, the wing attacker should first fake away from the basket and then make a cut to the baseline side of her defender to the hoop; the pass should come in from the guard outside the three-point line near the top of the key.

A backdoor from the post involves a give-and-go cut. The play starts when a wing player (usually, one beyond the three-point line) passes the ball into a post player at the foul line. The wing should then make a hard backdoor to the basket; this time, the pass should come from the post.

The backdoor is effective because it exploits the defender's tendency to overplay the wing and forget about guarding the basket. Furthermore, a good backdoor will force the entire defense to shift over into help—even if the cutter herself doesn't have a shot, chances are there will be an open kickout pass to a wing on the weak side.

THE CLEAR-OUT

A player **clears-out** when she moves out of a certain area of the court in order to give another player room to operate one on one. An effective clear-out play may even involve the entire team shift-

> *"This year we plan to run and shoot. Next season we hope to run and score."*
>
> —Billy Tubbs

ing to the left side of the court so that a player can drive on the right side. The clear-out is really an offensive strategy to create space for a top ball-handler to go one-on-one against a defender—that is, to take advantage of a perceived defensive mismatch.

SET A SCREEN

The screen or "pick" is one of the most common interaction that two offensive players have with one another—it is also one of the most effective. When she sets a screen, a player blocks the movement of her teammate's defender with her own body. The screen can be used in many different settings: for a player that has the ball and that wants a clear lane to the basket; for a guard that needs to get open for a pass; or for a post player trying to get in better position around the hoop. It is, in part, the screen's versatility that makes it such a vital component of team offense.

There are three different types of screens:

Vertical screen: These come in two varieties: the "down" and "up" screens. An example of a down screen is when a player at the high post picks for a teammate in the low post. The screener's movement is down the lane. An up screen works in the reverse fashion: the low post screens for the high (the screener moves up the lane). A blind screen is a type of up screen that is set on the backside of a defensive player.

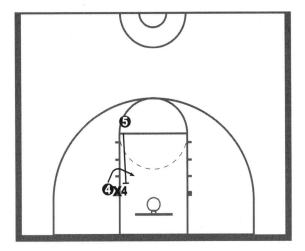

Figure 7.1
Down Screen

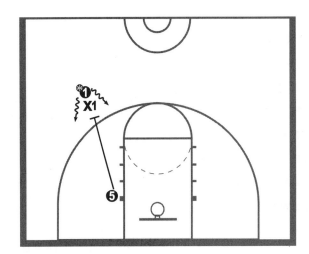

Figure 7.2
Up Screen

Cross screen: A player setting a horizontal or cross screen moves parallel to the baseline. Usually, the recipient of the pick will drive over the top of her screener (around the screener's outside shoulder) to the basket.

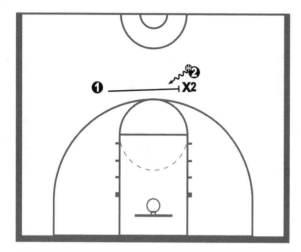

Figure 7.3
Cross Screen

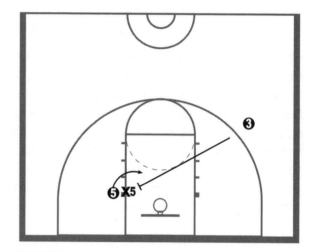

Figure 7.4
Diagonal Screen

"We have a very intelligent team. I've had clubs that when you tell a guy to go back door, he leaves the gym. Or you tell the team you're going to have a closed practice and eight guys don't show up."

—Jim Valvano

Diagonal screen: Diagonal screens have diagonal movement. For example, a player situated on the wing can move down to set a screen at the box for a player cutting to the high or low post.

These three types of screens—vertical, horizontal, and diagonal—are useful in distinct scenarios. A vertical screen can open up a player for an immediate shot in the lane; a blind screen can be a component of a backdoor play; by contrast, a horizontal screen can give a player with the ball an open driving lane to the hoop. A diagonal screen can be used to free up a post player as she cuts across the lane.

HOW TO SET A SCREEN

A screener's most important job is to make herself wide—as large and sturdy of an obstacle as she can possibly be. The wider her base, the further the defender has to go to get around the screen. Usually, the screener should leave about one foot of space between herself and the defender. The opponent's shoulder should line up with the midpoint of the screener's chest (the screener can cross her arms over her chest for protection). A jump stop can be an effective method of establishing the proper screen position.

Once the screener gets set, she cannot move! If she does, contact with her opponent will be considered an offensive foul. This is, in fact, the most common mistake that players make when attempting to set screens—in their effort to block the defender, they move their feet, lean, or stick out their arms or elbows. Referees will call this foul almost every time!

Once the screen is set, the screener must be patient and wait for her teammate to cut off the pick. (If she's setting a blind screen, she must leave the defender enough room to avoid contact or risk drawing an immediate foul.)

A screener's second most important job is to set her screen at the angle and on the side that will be most useful to her teammate. Most likely, the screener's back will be to the offensive team's baseline. Often, players screen on the left side so that right-handed dribblers can drive to their strong side.

Screens are most commonly used against man-to-man defenses, but occasionally they find their way into zone offenses! A screener can screen a player or an area.

HOW TO USE A SCREEN

A screen's effectiveness depends not only on whether it is properly set but also whether the player for whom it is set uses it wisely. That player must "read" her defender in order to determine how she should cut off of her teammate's pick. There are five basic moves off of a screen without the ball:

Straight cut: If the screen seals off her defender, the offensive player can make a straight cut to the basket.

Front cut: If the offensive player notices her defender overplaying the screen to the low side (toward the baseline), she can make a front cut to the basket.

Backdoor: If the offensive player notices her defender overplaying the screen to the high side (toward the ball), she can make a backdoor cut to the basket.

> *"I'll always remember this as the night Michael and I combined to score 70 points."*
>
> —Stacey King after Michael Jordan scored a playoff record 69 points

Pop cut: If, on the other hand, a defender defends a screen by dropping behind it, the attacker can pop out (move directly back from the screen), look to receive a pass and take an open jump shot.

Fade: If a defender defends a screen by moving to the ball side, the attacker can fade to the corner opposite the defender, look to receive a pass and take an open jump shot. (Essentially, the fade cut is a means of creating distance between a wing player and her defender so that she can look for a three-point shot.)

It's vital that a player using a screen set up her defender by faking quickly in the opposite direction. She should be sure to cut off of her pick foot-to-foot and shoulder-to-shoulder with her screener, and to curl tightly around the screen in order to prevent her defender from getting through. She should accelerate the moment she moves by her screener.

A player's first look off of a screen near the basket is usually to score, whether by shooting the ball, making a strong drive to the rim, or executing a post move.

> "I'm often mentioned in the same sentence as Michael Jordan: 'You know that Scott Hastings; he's no Michael Jordan.'"
>
> — Scott Hastings

THE PICK-AND-ROLL

The **pick-and-roll** is the consummate two-player play. It is simple and available to players at all levels of the game, and can be very effective. Beside the obvious benefits of producing points and being difficult to defend, the pick-and-roll teaches young players how to work together as a team. The pick-and-roll consists of three steps:

Step 1: The pick. The screener sets a screen for her teammate with the ball.
Step 2: The drive. The ball-handler drives past her defender and teammate.
Step 3: The roll. As the two defenders focus on the ball-handler, the screener pivots and makes a move ("rolls") to the basket. As she moves down an open lane to the hoop, she can receive the ball off a pass from her driving teammate and score.

The pick-and-roll can create a scoring opportunity out of practically nothing—out of a

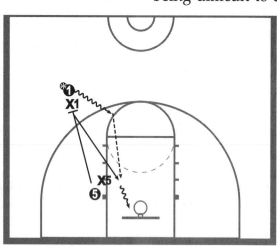

Figure 7.5
Pick-and-Roll

situation in which all five offensive players are closely guarded. Generally, it's most effective when a post player sets a pick for a guard. If a post player is the one to set the screen, she will be able to utilize her wide base and her height as she rolls to the basket. The guard can utilize her ballhandling skills to drive and pass if necessary. That scenario can work especially well if the two defenders call a switch, creating a mismatch.

Another great thing about the pick-and-roll is that it is effective from all over the court. It allows players to take initiative and create their own scoring plays.

It might not seem like it at first, but the player that sets a good pick is as much of a scoring threat as the player for whom she screens. To get around a pick, a defender must adjust—and in that moment of adjustment, there's vulnerability. Many times, both defenders will follow the player cutting to the basket. That leaves an opening for the screener to flash hard to the basket after she sets her pick. Another example is in the post: many times, in the confined area of the blocks, the screener is more open than her teammate if she rolls and pins the defender on her back.

> *"Because that's where the basket is."*
>
> —Anthony "Spud" Webb, 5'7", asked why he likes to drive the lane against taller players

OFFENSES AGAINST A ZONE

The one-on-one and dead-ball moves, as well as the screening plays that I just described, are most effective against a man-to-man defense (in which each defender is matched up to a specific offensive player). The same principles don't work as well against a zone, a defense that forces defenders to guard areas on the court rather than single opponents. However, zones have their own set of weaknesses to be exploited. The principles that I describe next are proven methods of taking advantage of them.

DISTORT THE ZONE

Zones are designed to follow the movement of the ball, and to adjust accordingly. A typical zone's three primary goals are to guard the player with the ball, to prevent penetrating passes into the lane, and to cut off driving lanes through the middle of the key. As the ball moves, though, zones must shift, and open lanes to the basket appear. In fact, the more an offensive team can force a zone to distort, the better its chances to score become.

Conventional wisdom states that quick passing and repeated ball reversals are the best ways to beat a zone. However, dribble penetration is also an effective method. Both styles of attack rely on one basic principle: rapid ball movement.

The formation that an offense uses against a zone usually depends on the type of zone defensive alignment. Normally, it's best to put one player at the top of the key against an even-front (two players, as in a 2-3) zone defense; putting two players up top works better against an odd-front (one player, as in a 1-3-1) zone defense. These alignments help players naturally fill the gaps between defenders, and find open spaces and seams. Basing your offensive setup on the defense's alignment can be problematic, however, if the defense continually changes the zone that it's playing. An alternative is to design the offensive alignment around the strengths and weaknesses of your own personnel.

A two-guard formation works well for teams without a strong point guard. Many youth players benefit from playing with two guards out front, a player in the high post, and two players underneath or at the wings. This formation is helpful because it puts teammates within easy passing distance from each other.

PASSING AGAINST A ZONE

Passing against a zone is achieved by ball reversal and passing to the low and high posts. Reversing the ball—passing it quickly from wing to wing—forces the zone defenders to work and stay in perpetual motion. A defender can't move as fast as the ball as it makes its way from the strong to the weak-side: ball reversal creates gaps for drivers, and open looks for shooters. For just that reason, cross-court or skip passes (passes that go directly from

> *"Fans never fall asleep at our games because they're afraid they might get hit with a pass."*
>
> —George Raveling

wing to wing, without passing through a player in the middle) are particularly effective against zones. The recipient of a skip pass should be ready to immediately shoot or drive before the defense has a chance to recover.

The **pass fake** is another important weapon. Zones are designed to shift with each pass—defenders are often so eager to get a move on the ball that they start moving the second they believe a pass will be made. A great pass fake can send a defender in exactly the opposite direction that she needs to go.

When it comes time to get the ball into the post—when an open lane appears in the zone—the pass should usually be a bounce, rather than a chest pass. There is a good chance that a chest pass, trying to get through a lane clogged with defenders, will be deflected. The post player should be ready to catch the ball, turn and shoot, or make a kick-out pass to the perimeter.

DRIBBLING AGAINST A ZONE

If the principle behind zone passing is ball reversal, the principle behind zone dribbling is to **penetrate the gaps.** Dribble penetration can freeze the defense, create better passing angles, and create two-on-one situations. Consider a zone defender's responsibility: to defend a certain area of the court, and any players that might be in it. As an offensive player drives into the middle of a zone, she forces the defender that she approaches to make a decision. Should she guard the player with the ball, or a player that's already in her zone? If she chooses to guard the ball, the driver has an easy dish pass to her teammate; if she chooses to stay back in her zone, the driver has a clear look at the hoop.

Forwards playing against a zone may not be able to post up as consistently as they might against a man-to-man defense. Instead, they should focus on two principles: finding openings to cut into the middle of the lane, and rebounding. Forwards playing against a zone may float around the paint: they still should make hard cuts to the ball, but they can't stay in any one position for too long.

Post players might consider lining up behind the zone and cutting to the middle via the blind side of the defense. If the offense wants to run a two-post set, the forwards might stack on one side of the lane in order to overload that zone's one defender.

> *"The first thing I learned upon becoming a head coach after 15 years as an assistant was the enormous difference between making a suggestion and making a decision."*
>
> —Rick Majerus

Offensive rebounding is a great way to beat a zone. Often, defenders that aren't matched up to specific players have difficulty boxing everyone out when the shot goes up. (In addition to post players, aggressive guards that crash from the wing can pull down a lot of rebounds.)

The **overload** principle can extend to the entire offensive team. Lining up four or more offensive players on one side of the court creates an instant mismatch: weak-side zone defenders may be reluctant to abandon their areas to help out their teammates on the strong side.

Here are ten coaching points that can be used to help beat a zone:

1. Reversing the ball quickly to the weak side
2. Finding an open area and filling it
3. Penetrating the gaps with the dribble and pass
4. Shooting over the zone
5. Overloading one side of the zone
6. Passing the ball to the low post area or a post player cutting to the foul line area
7. Setting screens
8. Feeding the post and passing the ball back out to the perimeter (kick-out pass)
9. Running a fast break before the zone gets set, and
10. Getting offensive rebounds

Other points of emphasis to beat a zone include:

- Maintaining good spacing and balancing the floor, and forcing the defense to spread out by moving the ball quickly
- Communicating and taking good shots
- Keeping the post players moving around the lane
- Forcing more than one defender to guard one offensive player as she drives to the basket
- Being patient! (Remember, with every pass, the defense works a little harder.)
- Being proactive and aggressive, but playing together as a team

Remember, the most important part of any offense is proper execution.

"I know the guys are out there somewhere: I just don't know where."

—Buck Williams, on averaging less than two assists per game

CHAPTER 8
Fast-Break Offense

The fast break should be an integral part of every team's offense: instead of happening once or twice a game, it should be used as much as possible. The fast break gives players the chance to shoot high percentage shots around the basket; it also can force a change in an opponent's game plan. For example, an opponent may not be able to send as many rebounders to the offensive boards if they are afraid of a fast break developing at the other end. The break also can create opportunities for all players on the team to score (including those that have difficulty getting off shots in the set offensive scheme). The break has the added benefit of being exciting to play, watch and coach.

The basic principle behind the fast break is to take higher percentage shots than in the regular half-court five-on-five offense. This is likely to occur when the offensive team creates a numbers advantage, such as a two-on-one, three-on-two, or perhaps even a three-on-one scenario. Teams may not be able to consistently defend against the fast break and stay out of foul trouble.

RUNNING THE FAST BREAK

The fast break can be a team's primary offense to be run both off of steals and defensive rebounds. It can be challenging to inbound the ball quickly enough to start a break after a made shot, but it can certainly be done (and be effective, since the opposing team may be caught by surprise). Many offensive players relax after their team has scored, providing a brief opportunity to run the fast break after a made basket.

HUSTLE AND TEAMWORK

The window of opportunity to fast break successfully is very brief, so players must act quickly—this is no time to rest or to dawdle! Proper execution requires that all players know their fast-break responsibilities. Here's how I like to teach the start of a fast break after a rebound:

When a rebounder secures the ball, every player except for the point guard should immediately sprint to the other end of the court. The three sprinting players (typically, the 2, 3, and the 4 or 5 player) should *not* wait to see what happens to the outlet pass

"You can say something to popes, kings and presidents, but you can't talk to officials. In the next war they ought to give everyone a whistle."

—Abe Lemons

or spend any time trying to help the rebounder. Instead, their sole focus should be to get down the court as quickly as possible. At that point, it's the point guard's responsibility to get the ball to *them*, not the other way around—they shouldn't slow down for any reason (unless they see that the ball is stolen by the opponent).

The rebounder should immediately make a strong pivot to the outside, with the ball in a secure "chin" position; at the same time, she should be listening and looking for her point guard. The point guard should position herself in an open passing lane on the wing on the same side of the court as the ball. Since the rebounder will most likely be concentrating on holding off swarming defenders, she can't be expected to locate the point guard on her own—that's why it's important that the point guard run to the outlet area, yell "outlet" and provide a target before the rebounder has completed her pivot. The rebounder should make a lead pass to the point guard, who then can advance the ball up the court, whether by dribbling or passing. If the outlet pass is executed to perfection (before the defense has a chance to get set), the point guard might be able to score an easy layup on her own.

As players become more skilled, they should start anticipating fast-break opportunities. For instance, a player might release early to sprint to the other end of the court if she sees that a teammate is about to grab a rebound or a steal. It's not always necessary to wait for a teammate to totally secure the ball before taking off down the court. (The risk in teaching this kind of anticipation, though, is that players might start thinking they can score easy baskets at the expense of playing defense.)

Youth players have several tendencies that work against the fast break: one is trying to receive the outlet pass near the top of the key, which is usually a congested area; another is to linger in the backcourt in an attempt to help the rebounder or the point guard. Worst of all is the tendency to relax momentarily when a change of possession occurs. Coaches need to recognize these habits early on in the season!

The team running the fast break should, in most situations, attempt to score even when they don't have a numbers advantage. The probability of scoring off a fast break is greater because the defense is usually out of position. Furthermore, it can be difficult for players to score in a five-on-five scenario—ten players in one confined area leads to a lot of congestion. Scoring off a four-on-four fast break is easier because players have more space to operate. The odds keep getting better as the number of players goes down: it is even easier to score three-on-three, two-on-two and, of course, one-on-one.

THE OUTLET PASS

Fast breaks often begin with a defensive rebound. After grabbing the ball, a rebounder should make a quick pivot to the outside (away from the basket). Then she should make an aggressive **outlet pass** to her guard. Depending on where the guard is located, this pass might be an overhead, chest, or bounce pass. Whatever kind it is, it should lead the outlet guard down the court toward the opposite basket. The further the rebounder can throw it the better, but she shouldn't sacrifice accuracy for distance. The length of the pass depends on both the strength of the passer and the guard's ability to get open and to catch. The guard should ideally catch the ball while moving toward the other end of the court, with her body turned so that she can run easily.

Another way to speed up the outlet pass, and to create a clearer passing lane, is to have the rebounder immediately pivot, take one or two hard dribbles toward the wing and pass the ball on the run to the guard. This move can be especially effective if players from the other team pause to guard the rebounder or the guard on the wing.

The outlet guard should be alert and quickly position herself on the same side of the court as the rebounder, no lower than the foul line extended. If she catches the ball any closer to the opponent's basket, she will give her opponent too much time to recover on defense. At first, many youth guards want to receive the outlet pass in the middle of the court near the top of the key, but that location can cause problems since the middle of the court is usually very congested. Outletting to a wing (away from the defense) is a more reliable strategy.

I've found that it works best to designate ahead of time which player receives the outlet pass after every rebound. She should be the team's fastest player and best ball-handler (usually, the point guard). The point guard is the natural option because she is the vocal leader on the court: she shouldn't hesitate to yell "outlet!" to jump-start her rebounder. On more advanced teams, the coach can designate different guards on each side of the court to receive outlet passes. (Of course, after a steal, the point guard might not want

"I often quote my-self; it adds spice to my conversation."

—George Bernard Shaw

"A stronger opponent can't hurt you if he can't catch you. There ain't no substitute for speed."

—Bobby Bowden

to wait to get to the ball. In that case, she should just sprint to the basket and look for a layup.)

DRIVING TO THE BASKET AND FILLING THE LANES

Once the outlet guard has the ball in her possession, she should head to the center circle or to the top of the key at the other end of the court. Bringing the ball down the middle makes it difficult for the defense to choose which side of the court it should guard. As she makes her way down the court, the ball-handlers' teammates should **fill the lanes** on the right and left sides. There should be a player running to the left wing; another player should fill the right. The rebounding post should fill the "trail" position. Most likely, a shot will have been taken by the time she gets down the floor—if that's the case, she should cut into the lane to go after the rebound.

The players filling the wing lanes should, in a perfect world, run wide on the court. When they reach the foul line extended, they should cut to the basket at a 45 degree angle. This fast-break spacing forces an already disadvantaged defense to spread out, opening up even wider lanes to the basket. Running the lanes wide gives a breaking team the maximum number of offensive options.

Timing is an important component of the fast break. The moment she sees her teammate grab a defensive rebound (or a turnover), the nonoutlet guard (usually, the 2 guard) should start sprinting down the court in her lane. At the same time, the small forward, who is usually closer to the basket in good rebounding position, should sprint out to the opposite wing. The point guard should be bringing the ball over half-court near the middle of the floor.

On more advanced teams, any player—even a forward—can bring the ball up the court after a rebound or turnover. In that scenario, her teammates are responsible for filling the open lanes, no matter what their positions. That kind of break requires that every offensive player on the floor have strong ballhandling skills.

THE GUARD'S OPTIONS

It is the outlet guard's responsibility to bring the ball all the way down to the top of the key or foul line (provided that she hasn't passed the ball ahead to one of her teammates for an easy layup). She must be under complete control as she surveys her options. If the guard has an open layup—if the defender comes out on her without any defensive help behind her—the guard should drive by her to the rim. Even if there are defenders near the hoop, she should drive and make them commit to playing her. When the defender steps in to stop the ball, the guard should pass (usually a bounce pass) to a player filling a lane on the wing. Ideally, at that point the wing player would already be making a cut to the hoop. The most important thing to remember is, players running the fast break should force the defense to make a play by forcing them to commit, rather than immediately settling for a 15-foot shot or passing too early.

It's also the outlet guard's responsibility to determine when the fast break won't work—when the opponent has hustled back on defense. Trying to force a three-on-four break will likely result in a sloppy shot and a change of possession.

ANTICIPATION

The fast break depends on team hustle, and by extension, anticipation to work effectively. The quicker the outlet guard and other players can start heading down the court, the better. Guards on a fast-break team should learn to anticipate when their teammates are likely to steal the ball or get a defensive rebound, and thus get a better jump down the court. For their part, post players should anticipate where their outlet guards will be, and try to turn in that direction as they are coming down with the board. Running a fast break with defined roles helps a team develop this sort of anticipation: every player should know exactly what to do when there is a turnover, or when a shot goes up.

Three areas of the basketball court are referred to as "the post." The high post is at the foul line, the midpost is halfway between the block and the foul line, and the low post is down on the block. The NCAA rules define a post player as an offensive or defensive player, with or without the ball, that has her back to the basket and that is positioned inside the free-throw line or just outside the lane. **Posting up** is an offensive term used to describe the position assumed by post players in an attempt to receive the ball.

Every player on a team can post up, but not every player is a true post player, like a team's center should be. Because her back is almost always to the basket, a post player's offensive game is very different than a guard's; to be effective, she must learn a special set of techniques. These techniques include using special post foot-work, using one's body to seal a defender, and executing special post moves to the basket.

Effective post play is a necessary component of team offense. Post players can generate high percentage shots; furthermore, they can draw a large number of fouls. Having a post scoring threat can relieve defensive pressure on outside players, as it can force defenders to move or stay in close to the basket (especially if they have to double team). Passing into the post can also be an effective method of reversing the basketball and creating open shots (by having the post player pass the ball to the weak side of the court).

PLAYING THE POST

GETTING OPEN

A good post-up begins with an exaggerated basketball stance. The post player should make herself as wide as possible in order to keep her defender pinned behind her. Her feet should be wider than shoulder-width apart, knees bent, and arms and elbows locked away from her body—this strong frame will prevent her defender from stepping around her or reaching over her back to steal or deflect the ball. One of her hands should be up, presenting a target for her teammates; her other arm should be holding her defender at bay. As a post player becomes more skilled, she can signal to her guard to which side she wants the ball to be passed by raising her palm, spreading her fingers, and turning that hand toward the guard.

When a player posts up, she should be careful not to stay in the lane long enough to be called for a three-second violation. Her post-up normally should start above the block, on either the right or the left side of the basket. (If she starts much lower, she may end up backing too far underneath the hoop.) When a player posts up on one side of the lane rather than in the middle, her angle to the basket ends up being diagonal—the same that it would be on a simple layup. She can post up right in the middle of the lane, but in that scenario, she needs to be careful to avoid a three-second violation. Furthermore, her lack of angle relative to the basket may make it more difficult for her to score.

Often, an advanced post player and her defender will end up leaning heavily on one another, using each other's body mass to support their own positions. Getting and maintaining good position in the post is an important step in playing post offense. How consistently a post player is able to score is, in large part, determined by where she catches the ball, and whether or not she fields it cleanly (without a partial deflection from her defender). A great post player will expend a lot of energy jockeying for position near the basket and attempting to keep her defender behind her. (Maintaining contact with the defender is important because it will alert the post to how and where her opponent moves around the lane.) If she catches the ball cleanly, in good scoring position, and makes a strong move to the hoop, there is very good chance that the post player will make a basket and maybe even draw a foul.

Part of establishing good position is reading the defensive player. An offensive post player can face her opponent as the guard brings the ball up the court. That way, as the ball is passed to the wing, she can see which way her defender is leaning. Then she can make a reverse pivot in the direction that most effectively seals her opponent, and quickly assume her strong post-up position. At that point, her object is to take up as much space around the block as she possibly can.

A defender can defend her opponent in one of a variety of ways. A post player should adjust her position in relation to how the defender sets up:

If the defender sets up low, on the baseline side, the offensive post should angle her position toward the middle of the court—her shoulders should be almost square to the foul line. By sealing her defender to the baseline, the post will open up the middle of the lane for a shot.

If the defender sets up high, the offensive player should seal her opponent to the middle—her shoulders should be parallel with the lane line. A simple turn (roll) to the baseline will give her a clear diagonal lane to the basket.

If the defender tries to deny her opponent the ball by positioning her body between the offensive post player and the passer, the post should turn her shoulders square to the basket and seal the defender outside the lane. One forearm should stay securely in the defender's back; the other hand should be raised, calling for the ball. At that point there should be nothing left between the post and the basket (unless another defender helps out). She can try to score off a lob pass from her teammate.

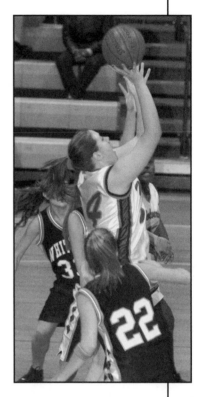

If the defender plays directly behind her opponent, the post should try to get to the high side of the box and pin her defender inside the lane.

Establishing post position isn't an easy job. There's always a defender nearby willing to use her body (and whatever other means necessary) to try to prevent the offensive post from getting position. Often, a post player may have to make flash cuts from one side of the lane to the other (following the ball as it is passed around the outside) before she can get into position to receive a pass. Certain without-the-ball moves, however, can help her lay claim to the position that she wants. These moves help a post player get around a defender that has placed herself between the post and the ball, or one that has put herself in a position to disrupt the entry pass.

The step-through, which resembles a crossover step, is a good way to get open. As the post player faces her defender, she should bring her inside foot (the foot closest to the basket) in front of and past the opponent's legs. As soon as she feels contact on her back, the post player should sit down in a squat position, seal her defender behind her and call for the ball.

The reverse seal resembles the step-through move—in reverse. The post player should plant her outside foot between her opponent's legs. Then she should spin in the direction opposite to her pivot foot (left pivot foot, to the right shoulder; right pivot foot, to the left shoulder). As soon as she feels her opponent on her back, the post should sit down in a squat position, seal her defender behind her and call for the ball.

Post players work hard to establish their positions. But once they have them, they can't be content to stay in them for long. When an entry pass comes in, it's vital that the post move forward to meet the ball.

MAKING A MOVE TO SCORE

Catching the ball in good post position is only half the battle. Next, the player has to make a move to score. But instead of starting facing the basket, as guards do, she must make her initial move with her back to the basket. At some point, a post player may make a pivot to the hoop. But that can happen either at the beginning of her move or at the very end, just before she shoots. Footwork is very important. The post must bend her knees and be strong enough to fend off the physical pressure from her defender, but she also must be quick enough to get past her opponent in a confined space. Below are moves that post players should learn to use when they catch the ball with their backs to the basket.

THE DROP STEP

The drop step can be executed to the baseline or into the middle of the lane. A player's first move should be to reach one foot out (either her right or her left foot, depending on where she wants to move) and to plant it around her defender's leg. Coaches call this "hooking" the opponent. Making one power dribble, she should bring her other foot around and plant it beside her pivot foot. Then she will be in her shooting position, with her shoulders square to the basket.

THE BABY HOOK

The baby hook starts off like a drop step: the post player should hook her defender with her right or left leg. But instead of bringing her other foot around and putting it down on the floor, she should drive her nonpivot knee up and shoot a baby hook shot with her outside hand.

THE FACE-UP

The face-up is a simple pivot to the basket. Without lifting her pivot foot from the floor, the post player should make a turn to the hoop and square her shoulders to the basket. If her left foot is her pivot, she'll turn counterclockwise toward her left shoulder; vice versa if her right foot is the pivot.

THE FACE-UP/CROSSOVER STEP (THE UP-AND-UNDER MOVE)

If her defender adjusts to the face-up move, a post player won't be able to take a direct shot at the basket. But she can take advantage of the move in a different way by adding in a crossover step. After she pivots, the post player should make a pump-fake to force her defender to jump or move forward—then she should bring her nonpivot leg in front of her defender, and explode up to the hoop. If she pivots on her left foot, she should crossover and step-through with her right; as her momentum will be taking her toward her left shoulder, she should shoot the ball with her left hand. If she pivots on her right, she should step-through with her left and shoot the ball with her right hand.

The up-and-under move can be made from anywhere in the lane, either for a layup off the backboard or a flip over the middle of the rim. I prefer that right-handed players use their right pivot foot in the low post so that they end up shooting with their right hand after the crossover.

THE SPIN MOVE

The spin move is a quick, slashing move to the hoop. If a post catches the ball on the left block, she should pivot immediately on her left foot, take a hard dribble with her right hand, take a step and shoot a right-handed layup. The opposite goes for an entry pass on the right block—the player should spin on her right foot, dribble once across the lane, and shoot a left-handed layup.

The pivot is an integral part of many post moves. But when starting with their backs to the basket, many youth players have a tendency not to fully pivot or square themselves to the hoop before taking a shot. Often it's the nonpivot foot that hinders them: if they don't bring that foot all the way around, their bodies never get square to the basket. These players end up being forced to shoot the ball across their bodies. Sometimes advanced posts shoot the ball with their shoulders perpendicular (rather than parallel) to the basket—for example, when shooting a true hook shot. But generally, this technique doesn't work for youth players. Pivoting fully to square to the hoop is a skill that must be developed in practice.

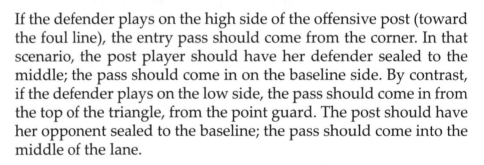

PASSING INTO THE POST

The general rule for passing into the post is simple: pass the ball where the defender isn't. Many teams play a two-post offense, which means that on either side of the court, there is a triangle of offensive players (made up of the point guard, the wing, and a post player). It is up to the two guards to decide not only who should pass the ball into the post, but also what type of pass it should be. The guards should try to keep the ball away from the post defender, and to put their teammate in a good position to score.

If the defender plays on the high side of the offensive post (toward the foul line), the entry pass should come from the corner. In that scenario, the post player should have her defender sealed to the middle; the pass should come in on the baseline side. By contrast, if the defender plays on the low side, the pass should come in from the top of the triangle, from the point guard. The post should have her opponent sealed to the baseline; the pass should come into the middle of the lane.

Often the first look into the post won't be open. Passing the ball back and forth between the point guard and the wing in the corner is the solution to that problem. The defender will have to adjust her position as each pass is made. Typically, she will want to play on the high side when the ball is with the point guard above the foul line extended, and switch to the low side when it gets passed to the corner. Forcing the defender to shift back and forth will create passing lanes and openings to the basket. It's the guards' responsibility to see the proper angle and to get the ball inside.

The two guards have another important decision to make: what kind of pass to throw into the post. Generally, the bounce pass is most effective. Defenders have a harder time reaching around and getting a deflection when the ball is lower to the ground. Furthermore, if the pass needs to lead the post at an angle to the basket, a bounce pass is often easier to handle than a chest pass.

If the passer looks into the post and finds that the defender is playing behind, a good chest pass right into the post player's hands may do the job, but a low bounce pass would be safer.

In the case that the defender is fully fronting the post player, a lob pass is the best option. The post should seal her defender away from the basket; a good lob pass will drop right into the space between the post and the hoop. The offensive player should release, jump to catch the ball, and immediately put up a shot. (But she should be aware of any lurking help defenders that might try to steal the ball as she's watching its flight in the air!)

VIOLATIONS IN THE POST

TRAVELING

The most common offensive violation in the post is the travel. Learning how to avoid the travel involves learning how to establish (and keep!) a pivot foot, and knowing what is legal. Rule 4, Section 65, of the 2004 NCAA Men's and Women's Basketball Rules and Interpretations defines traveling as follows:

SECTION 65. TRAVELING

Art. 1. Traveling occurs when a player holding the ball moves a foot or both feet in any direction in excess of prescribed limits described in this Rule.

Art. 2. A player who catches the ball with both feet on the playing court may pivot, using either foot. When one foot is lifted, the other is the pivot foot.

Art. 3. A player who catches the ball while moving or dribbling may stop and establish a pivot foot as follows:

a. When both feet are off the playing court and the player lands:

　1. Simultaneously on both feet, either may be the pivot foot;

---

2. On one foot followed by the other, the first foot to touch shall be the pivot foot;
3. On one foot, the player may jump off that foot and simultaneously land on both; neither foot can be the pivot foot.

b. When one foot is on the playing court:
1. That foot shall be the pivot foot when the other foot touches in a step;
2. The player may jump off that foot and simultaneously land on both; neither foot can then be the pivot foot.

Art. 4. After coming to a stop and establishing the pivot foot:

a. The pivot foot may be lifted, but not returned to the playing court, before the ball is released on a pass or try for goal;
b. The pivot foot shall not be lifted before the ball is released to start a dribble.

Art. 5. After coming to a stop when neither foot can be the pivot foot:

a. One or both feet may be lifted, but may not be returned to the playing court, before the ball is released on a pass or try for a goal;
b. Neither foot shall be lifted, before the ball is released, to start a dribble.

Reprinted with permission by the NCAA. Rules subject to change annually.

> "To say a good defensive center is more important than a high-scoring forward is like saying that the intestinal tract is more vital then the circulatory system."
>
> —Telford Taylor

It's important that coaches and players understand these rules so that they can intelligently design their low post strategies. Of particular interest is that, having once established her pivot foot, a player may legally lift it off the court to shoot (or pass) without incurring a traveling violation, as long as she doesn't return to the court prior to releasing the ball. Most post players don't realize that a player can take a step with her nonpivot foot without it being a travel. This means that the crossover step is indeed a legal and effective maneuver in the low post!

The travel rule is not as generous if the player is about to dribble. A player can't lift her pivot foot before she releases the ball from her hand to start a dribble. Whether or not this kind of travel gets called is often a matter of individual judgment (on the part of the referees).

Another important point is that, coming off a dribble, a player is allowed one full step after her pivot foot hits the floor. In effect, the shooter is entitled to two steps before she has to shoot her shot. This is an important rule to impress upon youth players. A shooter can plant a foot (the pivot foot) on the floor after picking up her dribble, take a step with the opposite foot, and then lift her pivot foot off the floor. (Of course, she has to shoot before putting that pivot foot down.)

"I've never had major knee surgery on any other part of my body."

—Winston Bennett

FOULING AND OTHER POST GUIDELINES

Chapter 15, "What is a foul," provides all the foul rules that coaches and players (and parents) need to know. Included below is an excerpt from Appendix III of the 2004 NCAA Men's and Women's Basketball Rules and Interpretations. It provides officiating guidelines for female post players that you may find of interest.

SECTION 7. WOMEN'S POST PLAY

The post-play guidelines must be followed by all officials to have consistent foul calls in this important area. A post player is a player with or without the ball with her back to the basket inside the free-throw lane or just outside the lane. Once a player has established her position legally as a defender of an offensive post player, she can neither displace her opponent nor be displaced from that position. When either happens, the official shall call a foul immediately. Officials need to be more aware of offensive post players in the lane for more than three seconds. Making this call will help curtail rough post play.

The following guidelines must be followed by players and called by officials:

a. When an offensive player with or without the ball has her back to the basket, the defensive post player may place a forearm or one hand on the offensive player. The defensive player may place a leg against the offensive player; however, if that leg is raised off the floor, a personal foul shall be called immediately. The defender may not place two hands, two forearms, or a forearm and hand on the offensive post player. A forearm and leg or a hand and leg may be placed on the offensive player as long as there is no displacement.

b. When an offensive post player with the ball has her back to the basket, the defensive post player must have a bend in her elbow if one hand is placed on the offensive player.

c. When a defensive post player places one forearm on the offensive player, she may use this forearm only to maintain position. Neither the offensive post player nor the defensive post player may dislodge her opponent. The official shall call a foul when a player is dislodged from her established position rather than waiting to see if there is an advantage gained.

d. An offensive post player with the ball, facing the basket, may be defended only with a forearm (see hand-checking b-1 in this section) unless she has not dribbled yet. In that situation, the defender may measure up (see hand-checking "a" in Section 7 below). Once the post player with the ball turns and faces the basket, she is no longer a post-player but a ball-handler. When the offensive post player has her back to the basket with the ball and turns suddenly to face the basket, the momentary touching of the hand shall not be called a foul, but if the hand remains for longer than a count of two, a personal foul shall be called.

e. Players may attain a position where their bodies are touching each other but only to maintain position. Any attempt to dislodge an opponent from a position she has legally obtained is a personal foul.

f. The offensive post player cannot "back-down" the defender, once that defender has established a legal guarding position. The offensive post player cannot grab the leg or body of the defender, hook or in any way displace or hold the defender while she is preparing for the entry pass or already has the ball with her back to the basket. Three seconds in the lane is a violation that must be called on the offensive post player. If this violation is not called, the offensive team gains an unfair advantage. CALL THREE SECONDS.

g. The offensive post player with the ball cannot initiate contact and displace the defensive post player who has

> *"Being left-handed is a big advantage. No one knows enough about your swing to mess you up with advice."*
>
> —Bob Charles

established her legal defensive position. This includes a defender with her arms straight up above her shoulders. Once the defender has established this legal position, if contact occurs, the official must decide whether the contact is incidental or a foul has been committed by the offensive post player with the ball. Verbal warnings given to players have proven to be ineffective whether officiating on the ball or off the ball. Officials should not talk to the players to try to prevent a foul but should call a foul when one occurs.

Reprinted with permission by the NCAA. Rules subject to change annually.

"Winning is a habit. Unfortunately, so is losing."

—Vince Lombardi

PART THREE
Defense

CHAPTER 10
Basic Defensive Skills

A good defensive team should be able to employ a number of defensive strategies. A defense might play man-to-man, either in the form of full court pressure or a half-court matchup. It might switch into a zone, and maybe even throw in a zone press. An aggressive defense might try to trap all over the court. This sort of versatility works not only to safeguard teams from specific offensive threats, but also to create defensive unpredictability.

Underlying every defensive strategy, however, are certain principles that apply to man-to-man, zone, and trap defenses alike. In this chapter, I will describe these principles.

INDIVIDUAL DEFENSIVE PRINCIPLES

STANCE

Defensive stance is a basic component of every collective defensive strategy. It forms the primary relationship between a player and the opponent that she is guarding: the quality and angle of the stance often dictates what kind of move an offensive player will likely make.

In a proper defensive stance, the defender should make her feet and arms wide. The defender's feet should be spread slightly further than shoulder-width apart. Her knees should be bent. The more a defender can bend her knees, the more athletic her stance will be. Her torso should lean slightly forward, her back should be straight, and her backside should stick out. Her elbows and arms should be extended to the side and away from her body; her fingers should be spread and ready to follow the ball; and her palms should be facing her opponent. Her eyes should be looking at the stomach area of her opponent (or looking for body language that gives away the opponent's intended next move).

MOVEMENT OF HANDS AND ARMS

Where a defender positions her hands depends both on the abilities of her opponent and her distance from the basket. If the offensive player has the ball and is outside her shooting range, the defender's hands and arms should be extended occasionally. Both palms should face the ball; one of her hands should be extended to the side of the strong dribbling hand. For example, if the attacker is right-handed, the defender should periodically extend her left arm to the side.

If the offensive player is within her shooting range, her defender must take more care not to let her have an unobstructed look at the basket. A hand should be raised to at least at shoulder-height, ready to pop up if the attacker goes up for a shot.

If a player has yet to use her dribble, the defender should stay especially low. It's also important that the defender keep her hands in constant motion, to deter both the dribble and the pass. Once an attacker has picked up her dribble, the defender has more leeway at that point. The only options the offensive player has are to pass or to shoot; therefore, her defender should play much further up on her (to the point of coming out of her defensive stance to "belly up" without making contact).

STAYING LOW

In the battle between defender and offensive player with the ball, the player that stays lower will usually be able to move more quickly. The general rule is, the defender's head should always be lower than her opponent's chin. That way, when the attacker makes a drive to the basket, the defender can keep up with her without committing a blocking foul (impeding the attacker with her arms, hands, or legs).

Many defenders have the tendency to stand up out of their defensive stances. This puts them at a disadvantage! A defender's first responsibility is to crouch down and prevent drives from ever taking place. If the offensive player does happen to drive into the lane, her defender should run to regain position in the hope of pressuring the attacker's shot.

POSITION

UP CLOSE AND PERSONAL

It's important that a defender keep the proper distance from her offensive player. And by that I mean, that she not stand too far away from her! The most common mistake that players make isn't to get too close, but rather, to linger too far away. If she isn't close enough to her, a defender allows the offensive player to relax and take her time. Ideally the defender on the ball should be close enough to put constant pressure on the offensive player, so much that she needs to turn her body to protect the ball. Playing this kind of intensive defense can fluster ball-handlers and make it more difficult for them to see the passing lanes.

A defender guarding the ball should be positioned no more than one arm's length away from her offensive player: she should be able to reach out and touch the offensive player or ball at all times. At the very least, she should be near enough so that if her opponent dribbles, or holds the ball out in front of her, she can get a touch.

That rule holds true for a defender guarding a player in possession of the ball. But what if the defender is guarding a player one pass away from the ball, or if the ball is on the opposite side of the court? In that case, the defender should be in deny or help-defense position (more on deny and help-defense position in Chapter 11). But that doesn't mean that she can lose track of her specific matchup. The closer the ball is to her opponent, the closer the defender must be, too. The offensive player should have to concentrate on her defender, even if she if 30 feet away from the rim. She should never be able to forget about her defender. Great defenders dictate what their opponents can and cannot do by never giving them a moment of peace.

TAKE AWAY THE STRONG HAND

One key defensive principle is taking away the attacker's strong hand dribble. If she's right-handed, for example, the defender should shift her stance toward the offensive player's right side (to the defender's left as she faces her). That way, the defender takes away the attacker's ability to drive to her strong side—if attacker did choose to put the ball on the floor, it would have to be with her left hand. A common mistake in youth basketball is defending the right and left hands equally, even though most players strongly favor one hand over the other.

A defender's object should be to force the dribbler to use her weak hand as much as possible, and then to make her change directions as many times as possible.

> *"The doctors X-rayed my head and found nothing."*
>
> —Dizzy Dean

HEAD-ON-BALL

In terms of on-ball defense, many defenders think about positioning themselves in a direct line between the player they are guarding and the basket. This is a good general rule to follow, but it is usually better for the defender to position her head directly in front of the ball, rather than the dribbler. That way, her body will be on the same side of the dribbler's body as the ball; from that position, she can more effectively force the dribbler to change directions and dribbling hands. This kind of on-ball defense is a great way to pressure ball-handlers by forcing them to repeatedly cut back and forth across the court. More importantly, it puts the defender in control, as she overplays and slides to recover in a zig-zag motion. Playing good head-on-ball defense should force the ball-handler to use her weaker dribbling hand as much as possible.

TEAM DEFENSIVE PRINCIPLES

PRESSURE THE BALL

Applying pressure on the ball creates turnovers. The defender on the ball must be within an arm's length of her opponent.

TAKE AWAY THEIR STRENGTHS

A player with the ball can shoot, pass, or dribble. Defenders can decide which of those options they want to allow. By playing up close, a defender can take away the shot, and force the offensive player to drive or pass. On the other hand, if she gives her opponent space, she can entice the attacker to shoot. By overplaying to the offensive player's right hand, she can invite a dribble to the left, and by positioning herself on the offensive player's left, she can invite a dribble to the right.

But "pressure" extends to pass defense, as well. A player shouldn't be content to sit back and let her opponent catch the ball. In fact, she should play denial defense if she's one pass away. If she's playing a zone, she should start moving toward her opponent as soon as she sees the ball leave the passer's hand. If a defender gets a good enough jump on the ball, she might even be able to get a deflection, or a steal.

RECOVER IF BEATEN

If she allows her opponent to go by her, a defender has two options. The first is to play what's known as position defense. The defender can turn and sprint to the point on the floor that she anticipates the offensive player will reach. For example, if she gets beaten to the baseline from the wing, she can release from her player, turn, and sprint toward the block. If she can cut her opponent off *before* she reaches her intended target, she can still prevent the basket. The other (more daring) option is to try to slap the ball away from behind. The problem with this play is that, if the steal attempt fails, the offensive player has an open lane to basket. The first option is much safer.

The key is, once she's been beaten, a defender can't simply turn her head and watch her opponent go to the basket. She must take some alternative measure to stop the attacker from scoring.

TAKE AWAY THE BASELINE

Most offensive players will try to drive to the baseline, away from the help defense. This means that a defender's first option should be to take away the baseline side by shifting her stance in that direction. (Forcing middle is especially important if the ball starts on the right side of the court, where the strong right hand dribble leads toward the baseline). The defender can go so far as to plant her outside foot on the baseline to make sure that the attacker doesn't slip through. Her goal should be to make the offensive player turn back to the middle, into the help defense that the attacker was initially trying to avoid.

If an offensive player manages to drive baseline, the defender's only thought should be to block her lane to the basket. That means turning and sprinting to a point on the floor where she can cut off the baseline lane.

THE BALL-LINE PRINCIPLE

The ball-line principle describes how defenders (mostly guards) should position themselves when playing off-the-ball defense. In general, defenders are taught to position themselves on the line that connects the ball and the player they are guarding,

> *"I don't like all the TV timeouts. I run out of things to say to my team."*
>
> —Jim Valvano

even if that opponent is above the top of the key (and the ball is in the corner).

The ball-line principle makes an important change to this general rule: it requires that defensive players away from the ball drop down horizontally toward the basket so that at least one of their feet is below an imaginary horizontal line that extends from the ball to the other side of the court. Playing good ball-line defense encourages the team, as a whole, to protect the basket.

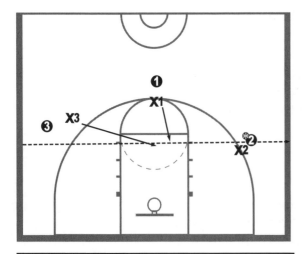

Figure 10.1
Ball-Line Principle: Ball on Wing

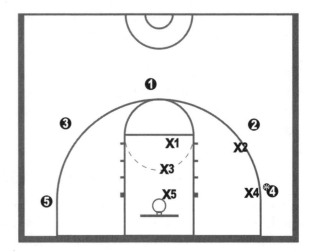

Figure 10.2
Ball-Line Principle: Ball in Corner

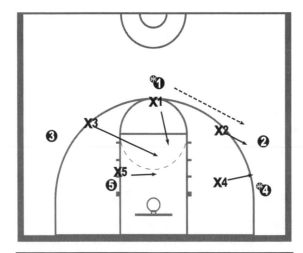

Figure 10.3
Ball-Line Principle: Proper Rotation

Coaching the ball-line principle helps fight the tendency that most guards have to stray away from the basket, in the hopes of staying close to their particular matchups. A player near the basket with the ball is usually a more dangerous threat to score than a player on the outside.

The general rule on my teams is that when the ball is below the foul line extended, all players on defense should be positioned below the foul line. This can change, of course, if the opponent can shoot the three consistently.

THE MID-LINE PRINCIPLE

The mid-line principle is similar to the ball-line principle, but applies vertically instead of horizontally. Under this principle, when the ball is on one side of the court, all defenders should have at least one foot on that same side. This principle forms the foundation of weak-side defense.

The ball-line and mid-line principles apply to both man-to-man and zone defenses.

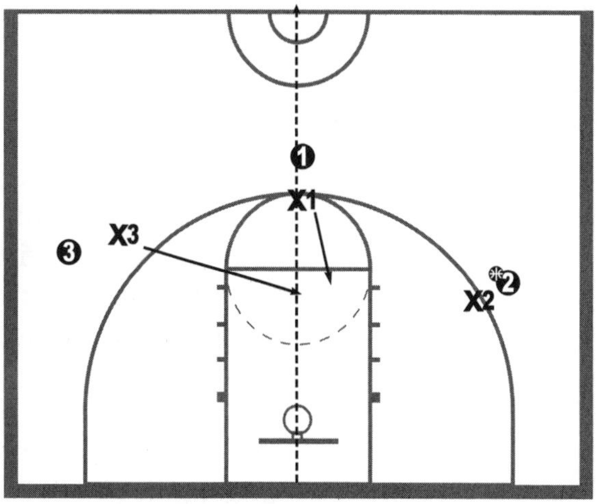

Figure 10.4
Mid-Line Principle: Ball on Wing

AVOID FOOLISH FOULS

Many basketball games are won or lost at the foul line. Players should fully understand what constitutes a foul; more importantly, they should learn how to play defense without committing one! An inferior team can beat its opponent if that opponent lets the game turn into a foul shooting contest. Chapter 15, "What Is a Foul?," provides all the rules that coaches and players (and parents) need to know.

COMMUNICATE

It's imperative that defensive players learn to communicate with one another. Talking on defense lets players know what's going on outside their fields of vision. It also alerts them to defensive shifts and switches. Team defensive talk can include phrases like, "Screen left," "Switch," and "Cutter on the left!"

Talking has the added benefit of increasing team unity. It's not one player's responsibility to stop her opponent from scoring—it's the entire team's. Good communication reinforces that idea by letting a defender know that she has an entire team behind her, waiting to back her up. Unfortunately, team talk doesn't always come naturally. Coaches should make a special point of fostering team talk in practice, and insisting on it.

> *"I'm a defensive coach. I couldn't shoot when I played, so I teach defense."*
>
> —Al McGuire

DEVELOPING DEFENSIVE STRATEGIES

ANALYZE YOUR TEAM

A team's defensive strategy should take into account the strengths and weaknesses of its own personnel. A quick team might pressure its opponent by pressing as much as possible. By contrast, a team loaded with height might play a half-court zone defense in order to exploit its physical advantage. A team that's overmatched might use a trapping defense in order to avoid potential mismatches.

Whatever a team's strategy is, it must attack its opponent intelligently and aggressively. Offense flows out of defense. When a defense makes a couple of stops, the whole team can have a burst of energy that results in points. Steals lead to breaks which lead to layups and fouls. Defensive stops offensively energize even the most half-court-oriented teams.

A good defensive strategy is versatile as well as aggressive. Opponents will try to adjust to whatever defense they encounter. Defenses should be prepared to switch strategies at a moment's notice. As long as its defenders keep adjusting, an offense will never be able to get into a groove.

Together, a team defense should try to:

- Pressure the ball
- Prevent the opponent from penetrating into the lane
- Create turnovers
- Minimize the offense's number of high-percentage shots
- Limit the offense's second shots (offensive rebounds)

As a coach, I try to design effective defensive strategies for my team. Have your players practice changing defenses. Switches can include: lining up in a 2-3 zone, and then changing to man-to-man when the ball crosses half-court; lining up in an apparent passive half-court zone, and jumping into a zone trap; or simply alternating zone press and man-to-man defenses after made and missed shots, respectively.

KNOW YOUR OPPONENT'S STRENGTHS AND WEAKNESSES

Just as important as a defensive team's own capabilities are the strengths and weaknesses of its opponent. Are they likely to score most of their points in the paint? Or are they outside shooters? Are they a quick team with lots of good ball-handlers? Or do they rely on their height? Do they like to run the fast break? Are they dominant on the offensive boards? All of these factors should contribute to a coach's assessment of an opponent and his overall defensive strategy.

CONCENTRATE ON THE TOP SCORER

Part of creating a defensive scheme is determining which offensive player (or players) is likely to score the most points. It might be the case that the overall scoring is spread around the entire team evenly. However, on many teams, there are usually one or two players that dominate on the offensive end. If a defense can stop the two leading scorers, the offensive team will be forced to rely on less reliable players for scoring output. Stopping the leading scorers might involve not only matching them up to the team's best defenders, but also deciding whether they are more effective against a man-to-man or a zone team defense (and then playing the opposite).

MAKE A QUICK STUDY OF EACH PLAYER

Defensive players should be able to quickly determine the strengths and weaknesses of the players that they are guarding. They should be able to figure out which opponents are right- or left-handed, who has three-point range, how fast they are, what kind of moves they like to make to the basket, how well they can pass, etc.

It should only take one or two plays to tell how an offensive player likes to score. For example, as soon as she makes a couple of outside shots, the defender should start guarding her tightly. On the other hand, if she proves she can drive to the basket, the defender should give her some space.

LATE GAME DEFENSE

When a game comes down to the wire, normal defensive strategies simply aren't enough. Basic ball-line defense gives offensive players too much room to catch the ball. In the closing minutes of a close game, a team may want to go into a trap or "full-deny" defense where each player tries to make it impossible for her opponent to catch the ball by playing pressure defense all over the court. The player guarding the ball should, try her hardest to make the attacker pick up her dribble. (Players away from the ball should still step in to stop any drive to the basket).

In this scenario, a coach might consider strategically fouling to stop the clock. If an offensive player misses the front end of a one-in-one, the ball should go back to the defensive team.

> "His reputation preceded him before he got there."
>
> —Don Mattingly, on New York Mets pitcher Dwight Gooden

TRAP TO FORCE TURNOVERS

A **trap,** or double team, is a defensive tactic in which two defensive players put extreme pressure on an offensive player, trying to force a turnover. The typical trap alignment is to have two trappers, two designated stealers (to rotate after the trap has been set), and one player back defending the basket. Ideally, trappers want to pin the dribbler into a difficult position on the court and force her to pick up her dribble. For example, if they trap her in a corner, her only option is to pass: she won't be able to dribble without going out of bounds. Traps are typically components of so-called "press" defenses, in which defenders put pressure on offensive players as they bring the ball up the court. The most common location for traps are in the corners of your front court (just after the ball has been inbounded), along the sidelines, in the topmost corners of your back court, in the corners near the baseline, and in the post area.

A good trap totally disrupts the offensive flow. If it doesn't create an immediate turnover, it might lead to an errant desperation pass, and a steal for another defensive teammate. At the very least, it should get the ball out of the hands of the primary ball-handler or post scorer.

Setting a good trap is a matter of communication and teamwork. As the two defenders converge on the offensive player, they have to make sure that they cut off all of her primary passing and dribbling lanes. One player should plant her foot so that it takes away the sideline or baseline, forcing the offensive player to turn into the second defender, who should approach from the middle. At the same time, the defenders must stay close enough to each other to ensure that the attacker doesn't slip between them. Once the offensive player picks up her dribble, the trappers should both "belly up" to her; their arms and hands should move with the ball, smothering all of her looks out of the trap. If the attacker does manage to pass the ball away, it should be a backward or a sideways pass—a pass down the court should always result in a steal.

After they force the ball-handler into a confined area, the two trappers should seal the trap by getting wide. They should be close enough to each other so that the dribbler can't slip between them,

> *"Make them beat you with their left hand."*
>
> —Morgan Wootten

> *"Basically, what we did is follow them around, watch what they did, and foul them."*
>
> —Rees Johnson, after losing

and they should still be cutting off the primary passing lanes. The trappers inside feet should be close together (or actually touching) as their bodies form a 90-degree angle, or "V" formation relative to one another. The trappers should avoid making any physical contact with the ball-handler with their bodies.

The trap doesn't stop there, though! The defenders' hands should mirror the movement of the ball. It is important that the trappers not reach in since any physical contact is usually called a foul! Reaching in also creates open passing lanes. Remember: the object of the trap is not necessarily for the trappers to steal the ball, but rather to force the ball-handler to make a bad pass or to travel, or to force a 5-second or 10-second violation.

If the offensive player back-dribbles, the trappers have to adjust quickly, step forward and get back into their V position. Their arms and hands should be up and moving. If the dribbler picks up the ball, the trappers should step closer to her, keeping their feet and arms active and cutting off the dribbler's passing lanes even more.

The trap should continue until the attacker passes the ball away (or turns it over). If she back-dribbles or pivots away, the defenders should simply step toward her and trap again. As soon as she breaks the trap, however, the defenders should recover into their regular half-court defense. If the defenders linger in the backcourt after the trap ends, the offense will have a numerical advantage on the basket.

Nontrap defenders also have an important job: to get in position to steal a pass coming out of the trap. The two nontrapping defenders should take away the passing lanes for the two offensive teammates closest to the ball, usually by fronting them. The third nontrap defender should guard the basket. They all should anticipate by reading the eyes and body language of the trapped offensive player.

The trap and the ensuing rotation leaves the offensive player furthest from the ball open. The gamble that the defense is taking is that the ball-handler will be too pressured to see or be able to pass to her open teammate.

Try to let the trappers know that it is not their responsibility to do all of the work. Putting too much pressure on the trappers to steal the ball

> *"I don't know much about psychology. Then again, I don't know much about coaching."*
>
> —Don Donoher, coach, when asked if he tried to influence officials

encourages them to reach in and foul. They should approach the trap with hustle, patience and poise, knowing that their teammates are helping. A well-executed trap is truly a team play.

"That's the same one I broke a couple of years ago."

– Joe C. Meriweather, on breaking his nose

CHAPTER 11
Man-to-Man Defense

In a man-to-man defense, each defensive player is responsible for guarding one opposing player. The name isn't literal, however. Many inexperienced players assume that playing man-to-man defense means that they should guard their matchup exclusively. Man-to-man defense is still a team defensive strategy. It will take a number of practice sessions and a fair amount of convincing to teach youth players that playing man-to-man defense does not involve guarding only one "man"; in fact, the best man defenses employ many zone defensive principles.

There are different man-to-man strategies when defending a player with the ball, a player one pass away, and a player more than one pass away from the ball. Many of the strategies employ the defensive skills described in Chapter 10.

GUARDING A PLAYER WITH THE BALL

STUDY YOUR OPPONENT

A defender on the ball has certain primary responsibilities: to put pressure on the ball-handler and to prevent her from driving to the basket or getting an easy view of the passing lanes, and to prevent her from taking an uncontested shot. She should study her opponent to learn her offensive strengths, weaknesses and tendencies. And that doesn't just mean simply deciding if she is left- or right-handed. Defensive players, in general, should notice where the offensive player looks and in what direction her body faces.

Offensive players may throw any number of fakes before they actually make their move to the basket. If a defender has trouble distinguishing fakes from real moves, she should watch her opponent's stomach. The attacker can fling her arms and legs in whatever direction she wants—her stomach will usually reveal the direction that she plans to go. Many basketball players, however, make unconvincing fakes. Their giveaways are more obvious. These players telegraph where they plan to dribble, who they plan to pass to, and when they plan to shoot. A defender can pick up these signals by watching her opponent's body language, especially her head and eyes.

DEFENSIVE STEPS AND SLIDES

There are certain steps that man-to-man defensive players should use to effectively pressure the ball and defend the basket: the retreat, advance, and swing steps.

RETREAT STEP (AND SLIDE)

The retreat step is a quick backward slide. Out of her defensive stance (in which one foot is slightly in front of the other), the player should push back off of her front foot while taking a step backward with the rear. The front foot should then slide back into a toe-to-heel alignment to maintain good balance. As she's making her retreat step, the defender should stay low, making sure her body and head don't pop up. The retreat is a defender's counter to an offensive player's jab step, or any other type of forward fake or movement.

ADVANCE STEP (AND SLIDE)

The advance step is essentially the opposite of the retreat step. The player should push off her back foot and step forward with the front. Again, she should stay as low as possible. The advance step is a means of putting pressure on opponent when she picks up her dribble or back-dribbles.

SWING STEP (AND SLIDE)

The swing step is the beginning of the lateral slide movement that is used to defend players driving to the basket. It is comprised of a half-reverse pivot and a simultaneous drop step in the direction that the attacker is dribbling. If the offensive player drives to her right, the defender should half-pivot on her right foot, extend her left leg and start to slide alongside her opponent; if the attacker goes left, the defender should pivot on her left foot and extend her right leg. The "lead" foot (the nonpivot foot) should point in the direction of the slide—it should be parallel, rather than perpendicular, to the opponent's dribbling lane.

The defender's goal is to stay between her opponent and the basket, which means that she must react quickly to the offensive player's movement. The first step that a defender takes into her slide is critical. If she allows her opponent to get by her at the beginning of the drive, she won't be able to catch up! For that

> "We have to pursue this subject of fun very seriously if we want to stay competitive in the twenty-first century."
>
> —George Yeo, Singapore Minister of State for Finance and World Affairs

reason, players need to concentrate on moving their feet when they're playing on-ball defense. As she executes a swing step, a player should avoid lunging with her upper body, but instead should concentrate on moving her feet first—specifically, pointing her lead foot in the direction of the slide.

Once the offensive player starts to dribble to the basket (or for that matter, anywhere on the court), her defender should start to slide. The defensive slide is a lateral movement that grows out of the proper defensive stance. After extending her lead foot in the direction that her attacker is dribbling (as described previously), the defender should bring her rear leg in. When a defender strings several of these slide steps together, she's into her full-slide movement.

THE ANGLE OF PURSUIT

The angle that a defender takes as she executes her step, and the angle at which she slides, are important components of on-ball defense. If her step is too deep, she will give the attacker a direct lane to the basket; by contrast, if it is too shallow, she will most likely make contact with her driving opponent (which will be a defensive foul). Many youth defenders have a tendency to underestimate the speed of offensive players driving to the hoop.

The key to remember is that the slide angle should be such that the defender can avoid making contact with her opponent while still making her way to a position on the court that blocks the attacker's lane to the basket.

As I said before, an offensive player is most likely to beat her defender on her initial move to the hoop. Until she learns how quick her opponent is off the dribble, a defender should give her attacker some space. Soon she will be able to gauge her opponent's speed. If the defender knows she is faster on her slide than her opponent is on the dribble, she can afford to put more pressure on the ball.

> *"His gloves, dear. I've never been hit by an eye in my life!"*
>
> —Terry Downes on being asked, by a reporter, if he watched his opponent's eyes or gloves in a boxing match

DEFENDING AWAY FROM THE BALL

A defender away from the ball should be part of a triangle, formed by her opponent, herself, and the ball; she should be able to point at the ball and her player while her back is to the hoop. The defender's head should be in motion: ideally, she should always be able to see her player and the ball in her peripheral vision at the same time. A defender can never lose sight of her matchup! She must adjust to her opponent's every move and every movement of the ball.

Off-the-ball defense should adhere to the ball-line principle that I outlined in Chapter 10. But this principle is particularly important when teaching man-to-man defense—players have a greater tendency to focus on the player they are assigned to guard even if they are away from the basket and the ball when they're playing man-to-man defense than when playing zone.

> "He couldn't play for us. He's too fundamentally sound. We wouldn't have a damn thing to talk about halftime."
>
> —Benny Dees, on opposing player

ONE PASS AWAY FROM THE BALL

DEFEND THE BALL FIRST

The general rule is that a wing defender should have one hand in the passing lane if she is guarding a player one pass away from the ball. However, this defense is most effective if the player defending the ball-handler can single-handedly stop dribble penetration. But since many players have difficulty stopping the ball by themselves, defenders on the wings may need to be ready to first stop any drive by the player with the ball, and then secondarily to defend a pass to the wing player. This is particularly true if their wing player is not an immediate threat to score.

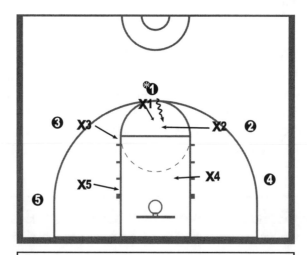

Figure 11.1
One Pass Away: Play Ball and Person

DENY THE WING

If a defensive team decides to employ a more aggressive strategy, it can have its wing defenders play total deny defense. The object of deny defense is to prevent offensive players from even catching the ball at the wing.

A defender in deny stance should position herself differently than a player in a regular defensive stance. Her back should be almost completely to the ball; her feet should be angled more deeply to the basket. The defender's outside hand should be raised in the passing lane; she should be standing a little bit further from her opponent than she ordinarily would. Her eyes should be glued on the offensive player—the only way she should be able to see the ball is by looking over her shoulder out of the corner of her eye. (Alternatively, using a more advanced technique, the defender can rest her chin on her shoulder so that she can see both the ball and her player using her peripheral vision.)

A denial defender should be looking to deny the pass for a deflection, and ideally, a steal. By extension, the danger of deny defense is that the offensive player has a more open lane to the basket; therefore, the defender must be extra wary of the backdoor cut. If she does get beaten backdoor, she should turn and sprint to the block with her inside arm extended (in the hopes of deflecting the entry pass).

> *"He's the most over-rated player since myself."*
>
> —Hot Rod Hundley, on Ralph Sampson

HELP-DEFENSE FROM THE WEAK SIDE

Help- or **weak-side** defense involves defenders more than one pass away from the ball (including on the opposite side of the court). Players in help-defense are responsible for defending the basket, and for helping teammates that have been beaten on a drive. Before committing to help, weak-side defenders should be in the ball-self-opponent triangle that I described earlier—ready to switch but also prepared to close out on their own players if they receive the ball. Help defenders should follow the ball-line and midline principles described in Chapter 10 by making sure that they're close enough to the basket and on the same side of the court as the ball.

Here's an example of good help-defense: a defender on the right wing gets beaten off a baseline drive. At that point, her teammate—the player that was guarding the left wing—should have already dropped down the lane into a good help position. As she sees the right-wing defender get beaten, she should slide across the lane to cut off the driver at the right block (in so doing, blocking the driving player's lane to the basket). When the right-wing (ball) defender recovers and the ball is passed back out, the help defender should recover back into her triangle position on the left wing.

The defense that I just described is called **help-and-recover** defense. The weak-side defender might have to leave her specific matchup—even to the point of completely turning her back and running to the other side of the court—in order to stop a driving player. Once she has stopped the driver, though, and forced her to make an outlet pass, the help defender should find her matchup and recover into good defensive position (or trap along with her teammates).

To play good help-defense, it's vital that defensive players communicate. As soon as a defender gets beaten, she should yell out "Help!" That will alert her teammates that they need to rotate. Communication will allow help defenders to establish position early and to recover quickly (therefore minimizing the effects of the shifts on the defensive team as a whole).

One way to look at this method of man-to-man defense is that the player guarding the ball and players one pass away are playing man-to-man defense, but players more than one pass away are playing zone.

> *"We play a man-to-man defense. Person-to-person sounds like a telephone call."*
>
> —Anonymous coach

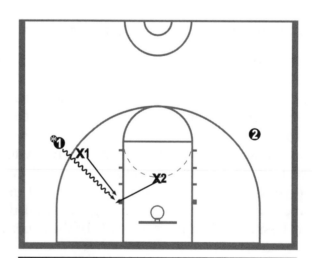

Figure 11.2
Help-Defense

DEFENDING CUTTERS

A defender should not allow a cutter to run in front of her—she should force the attacker to go behind. As the offensive player cuts to the basket, the defender should step toward the ball, turn her body to the cutter, and put a hand in the passing lane (putting her body between the cutter and the ball). The defender can place her chin on her inside shoulder as she's moving in order to see both her player and the ball.

Another way to defend a cutter is to "bump" her: a defender can literally block the defender's cut with her stationary body and force her to go in a different direction.

CLOSING OUT

"Closing out" refers to a defender's movement as she runs out to guard a player with the ball. The close out often applies to players that have dropped into help defense—when the ball swings back to their side of the court, they must recover to their opponents ("close" the distance between them).

The most important part of closing out is maintaining body control. A defender might have to cover a lot of ground to get out to her opponent, but she must be able to break down into her defensive stance quickly as she closes the distance. Even more crucial is her ability to react out of the close out: the defender should be ready to take away the shot or to slide in any direction as soon as she hits her defensive stance. Her weight can't be too forward, nor can it be too far back. She must be perfectly balanced.

As she closes out, a defender should stay low, but at least one of her hands should be up to take away the shot (or just to obstruct her opponent's view of the basket). If the attacker does manage to get a shot off, the defender should turn and box out for the rebound.

DEFENDING SCREENS

Screens are difficult to defend. (That's why they're so effective on offense!) The first and most important step is recognition. Both the defender guarding the screener and the defender guarding the

player screened must be aware of the impending screen. The second step is communication. It's the defender guarding the screener who is responsible for calling it out. (For that matter, even if the ball defender does see the screen, the screening defender should call it, to alert the rest of the defensive team to the play.) In calling the screen, a player should specify to which side the screener is approaching: for example, "Screen right!"

DEFENDING SCREENS ON THE BALL

There are many different kinds of screens, and as such, many different ways to defend them.

- *Defending over the top of the screen* encompasses getting through and running over the top. A defender "gets through" a screen if she manages to get her inside foot (foot closest to the screener) between the screener and the player with the ball. This is accomplished by taking a step toward the player with the ball as the screener approaches; by scooting up, the defender essentially avoids or scoots through the pick. The defender can use her backside to lever herself past the screener as soon as she feels contact.

- *Playing behind the screen* is the opposite of getting though it. Rather than taking a step toward the offensive player she is guarding, the defender takes a step back as she sees the screen approaching. The screened defender goes behind the screen. The defender should then get back into defensive position on the other side of the screen. This technique is most effective if the player with the ball is out of her shooting range (as she will be left unguarded for a brief period of time).

- *Switching on the screen* should be a defender's last option. The defender that had been covering the screener should loudly call "switch" and pick up her teammate's matchup. The ball defender essentially hands her player off to her teammate on the other side of the screen. Switching on picks can be dangerous because it can lead to mismatches, as the player getting screened will be forced to guard the player that set the screen (who might be a lot taller or faster).

The switching screen defense is more effective when the defender guarding the screener calls the switch early and steps in front of the screener (directly in the path of the ball-handler) before she has a chance to drive.

- *Trapping off the screen* occurs when the two screen defenders try to trap immediately off of the pick. As the dribbler comes off the screen, the defender guarding the screener should jump out aggressively and force the dribbler further to the outside. The defender who had been guarding the ball should follow behind and trap the other side of the offensive player. The two trappers' hands should be up—otherwise the ball-handler will have an open look at the screener rolling to the basket (who will have no one on her).

> *"In my prime I could have handled Michael Jordan. Of course, he would be only 12 years old."*
>
> —Jerry Sloan

In general, if the player being screened is out of shooting range, her defender can safely go behind the pick. However, if she's within shooting range, going behind isn't a good option—the offensive player might just step back and shoot a jump shot. Getting through the screen risks a drive, but it's important to remember that there should be help-defense ready to back a defender up.

On a screen away from the ball, the defender guarding the screener should release to give her teammate (the player being screened) room to run behind or in front of the player setting the pick.

DEFENDING THE LOW POST

A post player can defend in four ways: front, 3/4 high, 3/4 low, and behind. These defensive strategies depend not only on the strengths of the offensive post player, but also on the position of the ball on the court.

- *Fronting* is an aggressive post defensive strategy. A fronting defender should position herself between her opponent and the ball (rather than between her opponent and the basket). Her back should be to the basket, and she should lean back slightly so that she makes contact with the offensive post player with her backside and arm. The goal of the front is to deny the entry pass into the post by keeping her body in front of her opponent's, with at least one arm up in the air. Fronting can be a risky strategy, though: if the offensive player seals her defender far enough away from the basket, she can catch an easy lob pass and make a layup. (Of course, a help-defender should be waiting to belly up to the post player after she catches the ball, or even better, to deflect the lob pass.)

- *3/4 high defense* means defending the high side (the side away from the basket) of an offensive post player's body. The defender should form a "T" with her opponent's frame. Her inside foot should be behind the post player's body, her outside foot in front; the middle of her chest should be pushing up against the post player's outside shoulder. The defender's outside arm should be extended in front of and across her opponent's body. A 3/4 high defense prevents a pass from coming in to a post player's outside hand; for that reason, it is effective when the ball is positioned above the foul line extended on the wing. If the pass does happen to come in, this defense will prevent the offensive player from making a move to the inside (from turning in toward the lane on her post move.) Playing 3/4 high defense on the left block is a good way to force an offensive post player to use her left hand: if she can't turn toward the middle and shoot with her right, she has to turn toward the baseline and shoot with her left.

- *3/4 low defense* is identical to 3/4 high defense, only on the opposite side of the offensive post. The defender should play on the baseline rather than the high side of her opponent. Her inside arm should be extended across her opponent's chest. A 3/4 low defense is most effective when the ball is below the foul line extended in the wing or corner. If the ball does come into the post, this defense will take away offensive post moves to the baseline. A 3/4 low defense can also be used to force offensive players to use their left hands, except this time, from the right block (as it compels them to turn into the middle to shoot).

- *Playing behind* is the least aggressive way to defend the post. The defender should simply position herself behind her opponent, between that player and the basket. She

> *"The best zone looks like a man-to-man and the best man-to-man looks like a zone."*
>
> —Unknown

shouldn't try to prevent the entry pass—reaching will almost always be a foul. This defense is most effective when there's a noticeable mismatch in the post (that is, when the defender is much taller than the offensive player). Once the offensive post has the ball, her defender should stand tall with her arms outstretched, making it hard for her opponent to shoot.

The four low post defensive positions are shown in the next diagram: position 1 is in front; position 2 is 3/4 high; position 3 is 3/4 low; and position 4 is behind.

When playing any kind of nonfronting post defense, a defensive player should always be trying to force her opponent off the block with her body. The lower she gets in her defensive position, the more leverage and balance she will have.

Playing post defense isn't a static activity. A good offensive post player should be constantly shifting and reposting, adjusting to her defender's body. Therefore, the defender, too, must be in constant motion—her feet should never stay still for more than a few seconds. On any one play, a defender might go from 3/4 deny high, to a front, to 3/4 deny low, and back again (all based on the movement of her opponent and the ball).

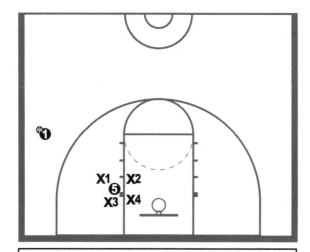

Figure 11.3
Defending the Low Post: Four Positions

DOUBLE TEAMING THE LOW POST

Another post defensive strategy is to double-team after the entry pass has been made. The double can come from two directions: either from the strong-side wing (from the defender guarding the player that made the entry pass) or the opposite wing or post. (If the guard on the same side of the court as the offensive post is a shooting threat, it's best to bring the double-team from the opposite side of the court.) A good double-team sandwiches a post; she should have nowhere to put the ball without contending with swarming hands.

The double-team must come quickly, before the post has a chance to think about what kind of move she wants to make. A player must be ready to shift over and help defend the offensive player whose defender went down to double.

DENYING FLASH CUTS

When guarding a cutter, the mantra of a post defender should be, "Bump, force her to go behind." An offensive post player should not be allowed to flash across the lane with her shoulders square to the ball. As she's coming across, her defender must be *sure* to stay between that player and the ball. Making incidental physical contact with the cutter is perfectly legal.

AVOIDING FOULS IN THE LOW POST

A post defender can play brilliant defense, but if she fouls at the last moment, all her hard works goes to waste. In order to avoid post fouling, it's important to understand the official rules.

VERTICALITY RULE

Much post fouling hinges on the definition of verticality. A defender is entitled to a spot on the floor and all of the space directly above it. As long as she keeps her arms in that space, she won't commit a foul; however, if she reaches forward, out of that sphere, she may. Defenders are not required to maintain any specific distance from their opponents. If contact occurs once a defender has established a legal position, the official must decide whether or not it was incidental. Shown below is an excerpt regarding verticality from the 2004 NCAA Men's and Women's Basketball Rules and Interpretations.

SECTION 69. VERTICALITY

Art. 1. Verticality applies to a legal position. The basic components of the principle of verticality are:

a. Legal guarding position must be established and attained initially, and movement thereafter must be legal.

b. From such position, the defender may rise or jump vertically and occupy the space within his or her vertical plane.

c. The hands and arms of the defender may be raised within his or her vertical plane while the defender is on the playing court or in the air.

d. The defender shall not be penalized for leaving the playing court vertically or having his or her hands and arms extended within the vertical plane.

e. The offensive player, whether on the playing court or airborne, shall not "clear out" or cause contact that is not incidental.

f. The defender may not "belly up" or use the lower part of the body or arms to cause contact outside his or her vertical plane.

g. The player with the ball shall be given no more protection or consideration than the defender in the judging of which, if either, player has violated the principle of verticality.

Reprinted with permission by the NCAA. Rules subject to change annually.

> *"If you ate both pasta and antipasto, would you still be hungry?"*
>
> —Unknown

MAN-TO-MAN DEFENSE VARIATIONS

A team defensive strategy can be tailored to fit the particular offensive threat. For example, a defender that is guarding a team's leading scorer may be told to never leave her player to help a teammate—the help should come from somewhere else. Generally, a defensive player guarding the other team's center may be told not to extend further than the foul line; but if her player is a threat to score from three-point range, she might be told she must get out and play wing defense. The basic point is, man-to-man defense is always fluid, always changing. But the goal is always the same: to prevent the offense from scoring, one player at a time.

"We defend against the free throw very well."

—Lyle Damon, on opponents shooting poorly from the line

Teams should learn different variations of man-to-man defense in order to adapt and confuse the opponent. Below are seven possible variations for team man-to-man defense: traditional, help-and-recover, tight, switching, trapping, run-and-jump, and the combination. These categories can be useful ways to vary the man-to-man defense.

Traditional: Each player guards one opponent with no help from the weak side.

Help-and-Recover: This is the defense described in this chapter and book. Defenders play close to their opponents, and are aggressive when their players have the ball. They force ball-handlers to dribble with their weak hands and go for steals whenever possible. They put a hand in the passing lane when guarding a player one pass away. If the dribbler passes, defenders drop quickly to play ball-line and mid-line defense (help-and-recover principles). Help-and-recover man defense can be used in the full-court, 3/4 court, or half-court.

Tight (closer to the basket): This is played like the help-and-recover defense except that defenders pick up just outside the three-point line, and give their opponents extra space (enticing them to shoot the ball from the outside). This man defense works best against poor shooting teams that rely more on slashing cuts to the basket. This defense is also effective against taller teams, because it allows more players to sag into the middle.

Switching: In a switching man defense, defensive players switch on every offensive screen or cross (with the exception of the players guarding the post). It can look very much like a zone defense.

Trapping: Once she crosses half-court, the person guarding the dribbler forces her opponent to one sideline; another defensive player (usually a guard) sprints toward the ball and attempts to double-team. The defensive player closest to the doubling guard's matchup shifts over to take away one open passing lane; a forward positions herself to take away the other passing lane. The center plays a zone-type defense, drifting around the lane and protecting the basket.

Run-and-Jump: The run-and-jump defense uses switches on drives to the basket. If a defensive player sees her teammates get beaten on the drive, she can leave her own player and "jump" to cover the driver. When the former ball defender hears her call "jump!" she sprints to cover the offensive player that her team-mate left open. If the ball-handler tries to dish to her teammate, the defender should deflect the pass.

Combination: This defense is a special sort of combination defense that takes advantage of man-to-man and zone principles. In this defense, the number 5 player (the center) guards the lane and basket as if she were playing the middle of a zone. The other four defenders match up to whoever is on their side of the court, and then stay with that player. It can be run with two or three players in a zone.

> "The nice thing about egotists: they don't talk about other people."
>
> —Unknown

ILLUSTRATIONS OF MAN-TO-MAN DEFENSE

The following are illustrations of how to rotate and play help-and-recover man-to-man defense when the ball is at the top of the key, the right wing, right corner, and left wing.

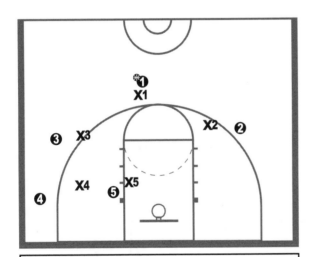

Figure 11.4
Ball at Top of Key

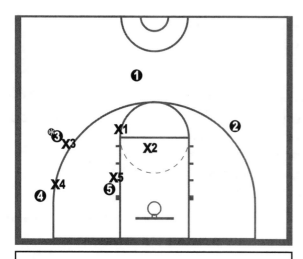

Figure 11.5
Ball at Right Wing: Ball-Line and Mid-Line
Rotations

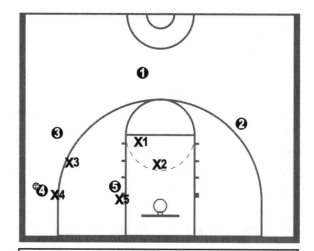

Figure 11.6
Ball in Right Corner: Ball-Line and Mid-Line
Rotations

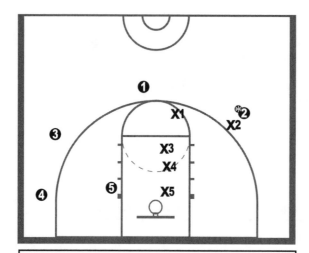

Figure 11.7
Ball at Left Wing: Ball-Line and Mid-Line
Rotations

CHAPTER 12
Zone Defense

There seems to be a lot of confusion among youth teams regarding what it means to play a zone defense. Many players incorrectly assume that in a zone they are responsible for guarding an area of the court even if there is no opposing player in that zone; they hesitate to jump off and guard opposing players driving to the basket (in the same way that they think that man-to-man defense means guarding one player exclusively). An empty space on the floor can't score a basket. If there is no opponent in a particular zone, the defender should shift outside her assigned area and guard a player that is a threat to score, and then shift back to her assigned area at the appropriate time. Some players also tend to assume that playing zone defense means standing still. Players need to realize that zone defense, if executed properly, can be as proactive as man-to-man defense. No defense will be effective if it simply reacts to what the offense dictates!

In many respects, zone defense resembles man-to-man defense. The help-and-recover defense described in Chapter 11 can be thought of as playing man defense on the ball, and zone away from the ball. Of course, once a player starts guarding an opponent with the ball, she must use the fundamentals of man-to-man defense to prevent her from scoring.

ADVANTAGES AND DISADVANTAGES OF A ZONE

ADVANTAGES

There are some advantages to playing a zone. A zone defense is usually designed to force an offense to take outside shots—therefore, zones can be effective defenses against poor outside shooting teams. Playing zone enables a coach to place his players in certain positions on the court, regardless of where the other team places its personnel. Specifically, a defensive team can keep its tallest players near the basket: in a zone, they won't run the risk of being pulled away to defend players on the outside, in so doing losing their rebounding advantage and natural help position. A coach can place his guards in a way that facilitates the fast break (namely, in position for an outlet pass after a rebound).

Often, traps flow out of zone defenses. These traps can be set in the half-court, three-quarter court, or full court.

"Couldn't even win the scrimmage."

—Abe Lemons, team scrimmaging against each other at halftime

Zone defenses are generally easier to teach than man-to-man defenses. They are usually less physically demanding because they require less continuous motion. Playing zone may reduce the number of fouls a defense draws (due to the reduced amount of continuous physical contact).

DISADVANTAGES

In my experience, players aren't as aggressive when they play zone defense. They tend to play looser on-ball defense; they don't deny as many passes. Developing individual rebounding skills can be difficult, too. In a man defense, players are assigned to one opponent—there's little confusion as to who they should box out when the shot goes up. But zone defenders don't have specific matchups. If they can't find a nearby opponent quickly, they often don't box out at all. As a result, opposing players can slip through the gaps and gain rebounding position. Lastly, in a man-to-man defense, players are more likely to take pride in shutting down their defensive matchups. That's one of the big reasons why many coaches believe that teams should play more man -to-man defense than zone defense.

Keys to overcoming these weaknesses are communication and an aggressive mindset. Talking is important in a zone. Good communication leads to good rotation; it can reduce the number of open outside shots as well as increase the number of missed box outs. An aggressive mindset (where players are encouraged to be proactive instead of reactive) will counteract players' natural tendency to be passive in a zone.

PLAYING THE ZONE

ZONE DEFENSE STANCE

Often you'll hear a coach yell to his zone defenders, "Put your hands up!" And he's right: in a zone, every defender's hands should be up. However, arm extension shouldn't come at the expense of foot mobility. You don't want your players to take you too literally or the zone really will look like a stickup, with a bunch of hands straight up in the air. Putting your hands "up" means pushing your elbows away from your body and extending your arms up and to the side. That will make it difficult for offensive players to pass into the middle of the zone.

The zone defender guarding the ball should play exactly as if she were playing man-to-man defense. However, the rest of her teammates shouldn't do the same. Generally, zone defensive stance away from the ball isn't quite as low as the man-to-man stance. In fact, it's most comparable to the stance that man defenders assume in the help position. A player's knees should be slightly bent, legs spread to slightly more than shoulder-width apart; her weight should be on the balls of her feet. The defender's back should be straight; her arms should be extended. She should never lose sight of the offensive player(s) in her zone: her head should move like it is on a swivel to follow both ball and player(s). She should always be aware of players moving behind the defense.

ZONE PRINCIPLES

A zone defense can be modified by playing conservatively, close to the basket (within the three-point circle), or aggressively, away from the basket. Traps fit into in either strategy.

Below are core zone defensive principles.

- Guard the ball as if playing a man-to-man defense.
- Focus on the ball and adjust your position in relationship to the movement of the opposing players.
- Keep your hands extended and moving to eliminate passing lanes through the defense.
- Move quickly with every pass and rotate into position as the ball moves. Close out on a player by taking away her shot, while at the same time overplaying her strong hand.
- Use the ball-line principle to compress the zone as the ball gets closer to the basket. Pack as many defenders as possible into the lane. When the ball goes behind the zone, shift down toward the basket.
- Play weak-side help defense by following the mid-line principle (also explained in Chapter 10). Be quick to recover and close out if the opponent swings the ball to the opposite side of the court.
- Don't let the offense drive or pass into the middle of the zone.
- Move within the zone to find an unguarded player. If there is more than one option, guard the most potent offensive threat. Players are threats to score, not spaces.
- Always have at least one player guarding the basket.

"I hate it. It looks like a stickup at 7-Eleven. Five guys standing there with hands in the air."

—Norm Sloan, on the zone defense

- Box out players when the shot goes up. Try to maintain the rebounding triangle (right box, left box, middle of the lane). Send one player below the foul line to get long rebounds. Emphasize the importance of weak-side rebounding.
- Double-team when the chance arises. (The three remaining defenders won't be matched up to specific opponents—they can be in good position to take away nearby passing lanes and defend the basket.)
- Get into position to run the fast break when a shot goes up.
- Talk on defense.
- Be proactive.
- Always keep an eye on the opposing team's top scorer.
- Hustle!

COMMON TYPES OF ZONES

Some zone defenses emphasize taking away the outside shot, while others stress defending the basket. No matter what type of zone defense a coach chooses, it will not be effective unless players move quickly. Zone defenders should move immediately with every pass; their arms should always be up and moving to create the impression that there are no available passing lanes.

Here are some of the most popular zone defenses at the youth level and beyond.

2-3 ZONE DEFENSE

The 2-3 is a common zone defense. Typically, the point guard and shooting guard line up out front (they represent the "2" of the 2-3). The small forward, power forward and center line up across the lane, stretching from outside one block to just outside the other. Usually the center, the tallest player, will be in the middle of the line, right in front of the basket. The 2-3 can be used to defend the lane, basket, and corners.

The responsibilities of the top two players (guards) include the top of the key (on either side), the foul line area, and the high three-point line. The two box players' zones extend from the mid-post area all the way out to the baseline three-point line (on both sides of the lane). The middle player's zone is the lane itself, below the high post.

The 2-3 defense can be used to force the opposing team to shoot long-range shots. If the opponents can't make threes, they will have a difficult time scoring. (However, if they start to score readily from the three-point line, a coach may need to make adjustments in the zone or pull his team out of the 2-3 alignment.) Playing 2-3 defense can give the defensive team a rebounding advantage. It's a good defense for fast-break teams, as it immediately puts the two ballhandling guards in outlet position.

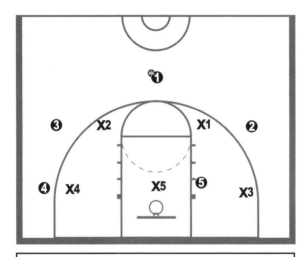

Figure 12.1
2-3 Zone Defense

WEAKNESSES OF THE 2-3 ZONE DEFENSE

One vulnerability of the 2-3 zone is that it leaves the top of the key open. If a player dribbles there, she can force one or both of the defensive guards out of position. Also, the high post area is a vulnerable part of 2-3. It's a no-man's land, between the zones of the high guards and the center and low forwards. Often, the center will have to come out and guard an opponent cutting to the high post, which leaves the basket unguarded.

VARIATIONS OF THE 2-3 ZONE

A tight 2-3 zone is one that is played entirely within the three-point circle. By contrast, defenders playing a loose 2-3 can put tremendous pressure on the ball outside the three-point line. Tight or loose, when the ball is passed to the baseline and the forward on that side goes out to defend it, the guard can come down and trap the ball in the corner with the forward. A coach should decide whether or not to trap based on how aggressively he wishes to pursue the ball.

The following diagrams show zone rotations with and without traps.

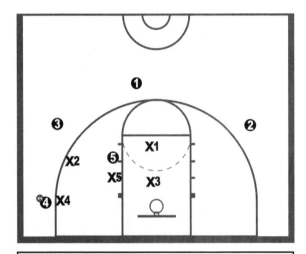

Figure 12.2
2-3 Zone Rotation Without Trap

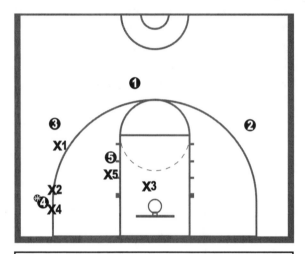

Figure 12.3
2-3 Zone Rotation: Trap in Right Corner

1-3-1 ZONE DEFENSE

In a 1-3-1 zone defense, the point guard sets up at the top of the key, usually outside the three-point line. The shooting guard, center, and small forward line up across the lane, below the foul line extended, with the two wing defenders positioned out wide. The power forward represents the last line of defense—she should be lined up in front of the basket, right in the middle of the lane. Whatever the position of the ball in a 1-3-1, a rule of thumb is that there should always be three defenders between the ball and the basket.

The player at the top of the key defends the ball: her goal is to force the ball to one side of the court. If the ball is passed to a

"I'm tired of breaking all of them. I'd like to get one of our own."

—Cotton Fitzsimmons, on ending three opponents' winning streaks wing player, the strong-side wing defender (on the same side as the ball) should guard the wing zone. The weak-side wing defender should slide into the lane—her zone now includes the weak-side wing and post areas near the basket. The center slides down to defend an offensive player at the block. The power forward is responsible for running the baseline on the strong side of the court. She must run out to guard any offensive player in the strong-side corner; if the ball is reversed, she must sprint to the opposite corner.

> "Most folks are about as happy as they make up their minds to be."
> —Abraham Lincoln

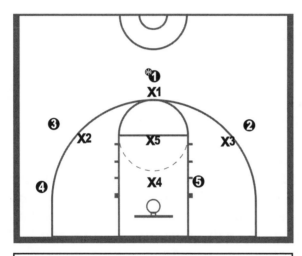

Figure 12.4
1-3-1 Zone Defense

ADVANTAGES AND DISADVANTAGES OF THE 1-3-1 ZONE

The 1-3-1 zone has several advantages: a point guard that directs the placement of the ball, a well-defended middle of the lane, players that are well positioned to take away the three-point shot, and players that are in good positions to set traps. However, in most 1-3-1 situations there's only one player underneath the basket. When the zone rotates to one side, the opposite wing (sometimes a guard) is responsible for both weak-side defense and rebounding. This can create a mismatch: a smaller player might have to rebound or defend against a much taller player near the basket. A diagonal skip pass from one wing to the opposite block can be an effective way of exploiting this mismatch. (An offensive strategy against the 1-3-1 is to start the offense by passing the ball to the wing on the same side as the taller wing defender, leaving the smaller guard alone near the basket.)

This zone defense puts more ball pressure on the wings; unlike the 2-3, it doesn't pack the basket area with defenders. The 1-3-1 can be an effective way to stop outside shots, to prevent drives into the lane, and to trap. But it may not work so well against an opponent that has a dominant post scorer or inside game. She'll have too many one-on-one opportunities against a smaller player.

1-3-1 HALF-COURT TRAPS

1-3-1 zone sets are very conducive to traps. There are four places that traps are most effective in the frontcourt: immediately across the half-court line, in either the right or left corners, and along the baseline, in the right or left corners.

Traps near half-court: As the opposing point guard dribbles the ball over half-court, the defensive point guard should force her toward a sideline. The strong-side player should come up immediately and trap. (If the trap occurs immediately after the point guard crosses half-court, the sideline and half-court lines act as two extra defensive players—once the ball-handler comes over, she can't go back.) The two trappers shouldn't slap at the ball; instead they should try to force a lob pass out of the trap, which one of their teammates should intercept. The weak-side player and power forward should rotate and front the offensive players closest to the ball. The center should be denying the high post.

Traps near the baseline: Traps can be set in the baseline corners, as well. In this case, the trap should involve the low defender (power forward) and the strong-side wing defender. The center should deny the low post, and the weak-side defender should defend the basket. The point guard should intercept any pass out of the trap to the top of the key or away from the basket.

Any kind of 1-3-1 trapping defense can be highly effective, because trapping applies a maximum amount of pressure on the ball. In theory, the only players that are left open are on the weak-side of the court. Trapped players will have a hard time locating their

> *"If you want to know the turning point, it was our layup drill."*
>
> —Darrel Hendric, after losing

teammates; even if they do, they won't have the strength to make that kind of pass accurately out of the trap.

The following are illustrations of half-court traps.

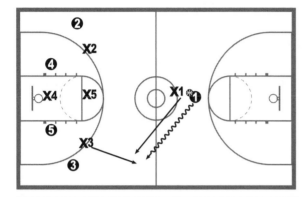

Figure 12.5
1-3-1 Half-Court Trap Setup

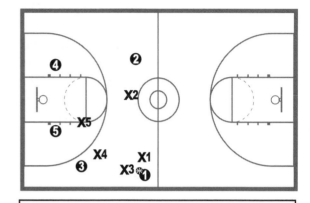

Figure 12.6
1-3-1 Half-Court Trap Left Wing

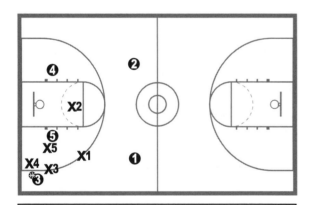

Figure 12.7
1-3-1 Half-Court Trap Left Corner

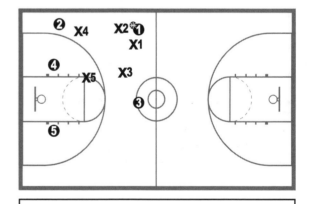

Figure 12.8
1-3-1 Half-Court Trap Right Wing

2-1-2 ZONE DEFENSE

The 2-1-2 zone defense is similar to the 2-3 in the sense that it has an even guard front. However, there are some important differences: in a 2-1-2, the center extends higher up the lane toward the foul line and the two low defenders stay closer in to the basket directly over the right and left blocks.

> *"Give me a smart idiot over a stupid genius any day."*
>
> —Samuel Goldwyn

1-2-2 ZONE DEFENSE

Some coaches consider the 1-2-2 zone the most effective zone defensive set. The point guard picks up high, as she does in a 1-3-1. The first row of defenders (usually the shooting guard and small forward) play just outside the elbows, on either side of the lane. The other two players line up outside the right and left blocks.

The advantage of the 1-2-2 defense lies in its coverage of both wings (from the top of the key to both sides of the baseline) and its excellent coverage of the blocks. Its weakness is in the high post area just below the foul line. If a player can get into the middle of the lane, she may have an open look to the rim.

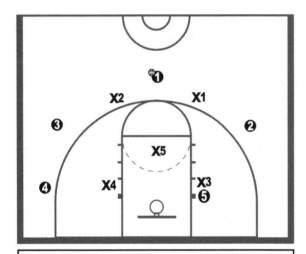

Figure 12.9
2-1-2 Zone Defense

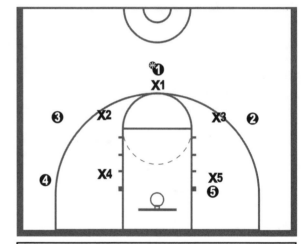

Figure 12.10
1-2-2 Zone Defense

PART FOUR
Special Situations

CHAPTER 13
The Press

A press is a defensive strategy that applies pressure on the offensive team in the backcourt, usually as soon as they inbound the ball. It can take the form of a zone or a man-to-man defense. Typically, presses begin the moment that the ball is in play. However, 3/4-court presses—presses that start at around the three-point line of the backcourt—and presses beginning just past the half-court line can also be effective.

FULL COURT DEFENSE

Press defenses have several objectives. The primary goal is to force the opposing team into a bad or hurried decision: for example, an errant pass, a wild dribble or traveling violation. Bad offensive decisions lead to turnovers and fast break points for the defense. (In that sense, the press is an offensive weapon in itself, as it can lead to high-percentage shots off of steals.) The secondary, and more indirect, goal is to force the offense to alter the pace or tempo of the game in the defense's favor. Pressing eats up time on the clock.

To succeed against a strong press, an offensive team must have execution, teamwork, and timing. But even under the best of circumstances, a pressed offensive team will be forced to entrust the ball to less skilled ball-handlers. For that reason, the press is especially effective against teams that have only one or two truly proficient dribblers. If a team can establish a good press, it can have a major advantage against many opponents!

Because it takes defenders a moment to get into their positions, the best time to set a press is after a made basket (when the opponent has to take the ball out of bounds).

ZONE PRESSES

In my experience, zone full-court presses are more effective than man presses. A ball-handler with momentum can usually beat a single defender. A zone press, however, routinely double-teams the ball, forcing ball-handlers to pass—thus, the zone press better achieves the goal of getting the ball out of the control of the best ball-handler.

Zone full-court presses work the same way that half-court zone defenses do except that full court presses usually involve more traps. Defenders are responsible for guarding players in specific areas of the court, rather than specific matchups.

Almost all zone presses share the following fundamental principles: force the ball to the sideline or corner, trap, and deny the passing lanes. To accomplish these goals, zone presses usually set up with two players trying to trap the ball, two players assigned to steal passes, and one player back to defend the basket. The same trapping principles described in Chapter 10 should be used in the press trap.

Zone presses attempt to force the ball-handler to pick up her dribble and pass the ball away, usually by double-teaming the ball. Furthermore, zone defenders try to dictate what kind of passes the ball-handler can make. Lob or bounce passes are ideal for the defense—they can be easily picked off by lurking teammates. If a dribbler wants to make a forward pass, she must do so at the risk of a turnover. The only open pass she should have is a backward pass (typically, to the player that inbounded the ball).

When playing a press defense, regular defensive slides aren't sufficient. Often press defenders will have to cover a significant distance in order to trap a dribbler or pick off a pass. Press rotation involves sprinting to spots on the floor, not sliding.

THE 1-2-1-1 FULL COURT ZONE PRESS

In my opinion, the full court press that is most effective is the 1-2-1-1 zone press. The positions and responsibilities are described below. (In order to clarify, I've identified press positions by number. These numbers do not necessarily correlate with offensive positions! However, in many cases, they are similar.)

Number 4 plays in the front of the press—immediately in front of the player taking the ball out of bounds. She should be tall and quick with good hands and feet (often, it's the power forward or center). The 4 player puts primary pressure on the inbound pass; her responsibility is to force the ball to be inbounded to the right or left corners, and then follow the pass to trap with one of her teammates. If the ball gets reversed through the inbounder, the 4 player should run to the other side of the court and trap again.

> "There is no comparison between that which is lost by not succeeding and that which is lost by not trying."
>
> —Francis Bacon

> "My only feeling about superstition is that it's unlucky to be behind at the end of the game."
>
> —Duffy Daugherty

If (somehow) the ball makes it over the first line of the press, she should sprint up the court to recover on defense.

Numbers 2 and 3 play the two wings. These defenders line up on opposite ends of the foul line extended, a few feet outside of the lane. Their actions depend on what side of the court the ball is inbounded. The strong-side wing is responsible for trapping on the sideline with the 4 player. She should use her man-to-man fundamentals to keep the dribbler in front of her until the 4 player can get there for the double-team. The weak-side wing player should rotate laterally to the same side of the court as the ball; she is responsible for covering any offensive player in the middle (one that is looking for a pass from the ball-handler). If there's a lateral pass out of the trap, she should intercept it.

Number 1, also known as the "stealer," "thief," or "center-fielder," lines up on the same side as the inbounder level with the top of the key in the backcourt. This player should be quick and decisive and is responsible for any forward pass that comes out of the trap. She should study the opponent's alignment and position herself at the best possible angle for an interception. The number 1 player must also be aware of cutters through the middle of the court.

Number 5 represents the last line of defense. This player plays in the back of the press and protects the basket. She shouldn't go for steals unless she is sure that she can get the ball—if she misses, the basket will be left wide open! The 5 player usually lines up at the half-court line, but shifts back as the ball moves up the court.

The following are diagrams of the 1-2-1-1 zone press showing traps in the corners of the backcourt and rotation by the defenders, the 1-3-1 three-quarters court press (the assignments and rotations are similar to the half-court 1-3-1 zone press defense with traps), and the 1-2-2 three-quarters court press (its primary focus is to force the dribbler to a sideline and into a trap).

An important part of teaching press defense is getting players to anticipate passes and to get back quickly once they have been beaten. To learn how to recover out of a press defense, practice moving the ball past the press; have your players work on turning, sprinting to the lane at the opposite end of

> *"It doesn't matter when you lose. It's like putting earrings on a pig—it don't make a whole deal of difference."*
>
> —Ken Stabler, after a loss in which his quarterback statistics were good

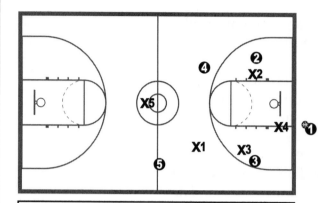

Figure 13.1
1-2-1-1 Matchup Zone Press: Setup

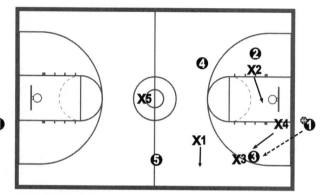

Figure 13.2
1-2-1-1 Matchup Zone Press: Trap
in Right Corner

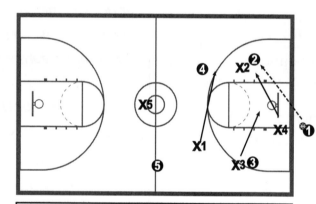

Figure 13.3
1-2-1-1 Matchup Zone Press: Trap
in Left Corner

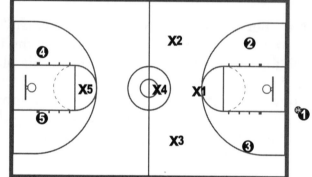

Figure 13.4
1-3-1 Three-Quarters Court Zone Press

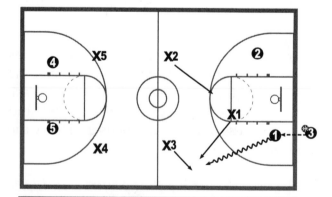

Figure 13.5
1-2-2 Zone Press Rotation

the court, and opening up (to find the offensive players). Emphasize that, even after their press has been broken, they still have to play defense in the half-court.

MAN-TO-MAN PRESSES

Man-to-man full-court presses are based on the same principles as half-court man defense. In fact, a man-to-man press is really nothing more than man-to-man defense extending down the length of the court. Double-teaming and trapping aren't always part of man presses—as I said before, sometimes the object is simply to wear out the offense's primary ball-handler. Ideally, the pressure from the man-to-man press will force the primary dribbler to pass the ball to a weaker teammate that is more susceptible to turnovers.

A defense can step up its man-to-man press by denying all the nearby outlet passes. For example, once a secondary ball-handler has possession of the ball, the defense can ensure that she keeps it by eliminating all of her passing options.

Playing a man-to-man press can be a physically exhausting task. If a defender gets beaten, she must sprint back to the other end of the court and recover her matchup (and then play more defense). For that reason, man-to-man presses are most effective in spurts, at strategic points in the game. They also work well for teams with deep benches. Using the man-to-man press sparingly will ensure that the defenders don't get too tired.

"Our consistency has been up and down all season."

—Robert Parish, discussing an inconsistent Boston Celtics season

DEFENSE BEFORE THE DRIBBLE

If the player with the ball has not yet put it on the floor, the press defender should be the one to initiate the dribble by angling her stance, thus forcing the offensive player to one side (ideally, to her weak hand). She should be in good defensive position, but she should play a little bit off her opponent, to start. There's a lot of court behind the defender—if she gets beaten early, she may not have a chance of catching up.

GUARDING THE DRIBBLER

A defender playing full court man-to-man defense against an active dribbler wants to make her opponent turn as many time as possible before she crosses half-court. Whatever way the offensive player starts to dribble, the defender should quickly cut her

off using the head-on-ball principle, and force her to turn back in the opposite direction. (Ideally, the dribbler's path down the court will look like a series of diagonal lines, each at 45 degree angles to the baseline.) The defender must be careful not to open up too much or overplay the dribble—if she does, the offensive player will have a lane directly down the middle of the court. She should try to stay within one arm's length of the dribbler the whole way down the floor.

Often, defensive slides aren't fast enough to keep up with a ball-handler that has a full head of steam. Sometimes a press defender will have to run alongside her opponent before she can break down into a defensive stance. (In this sense, press defense is different than half-court man-to-man defense.) The goal of the press defender should be to beat her opponent to a spot on the court, plant her feet, and force the dribbler to turn in a different direction. (Once the ball-handler gets within shooting distance of the basket, however, the defender should be back in her low defensive stance.)

DEFENSE ON A DEAD DRIBBLE

When the ball-handler picks up her dribble, her defender should start playing as aggressively as she possibly can. She should "belly up" to her opponent, keeping her arms and hands in constant motion at the level of the ball in order to block the ball-handler's passing lanes and lines of sight. She should also yell "Dead, dead!" or "Ball, ball" to alert her teammates to the dead ball, so that they can deny all the passing lanes.

RUN AND JUMP

Many teams will respond to full court man-to-man press by sending four offensive players down the other end of the court to give space to the primary ball-handler in a one-on-one situation. The so-called "run-and-jump" defense is a counter to this move.

Run-and-jump defense is essentially designed to confuse the ball-handler: it looks like a trap but is really a switching defense. As the defender forces the ball-handler to a sideline, one of her teammates should leave her matchup, sprint over, tightly guard the ball-handler, and yell "Ball!" Meanwhile, the original ball defender should "jump off" to take away the pass to the unguarded player. The jump is most effective if it comes from the strong-side of the court; as the jump unfolds, defenders on the weak-side should shift over to guard any open players.

The run-and-jump works best when the dribbler is traveling at full speed—in that case, it's likely that her head will be down, which will prevent her from seeing the impending jump (before she's in it). The run-and-jump can be modified to work in the half-court, as well as the full.

BEATING THE PRESS

OFFENSE AGAINST A ZONE PRESS

Beating a press begins with the inbounds pass. If the offensive team can put the ball into play before the defenders have a chance to set up, they'll avoid much of the pressure of the press.

After the inbounds pass, the most important thing to do is get the ball into the middle of the court. The sidelines and baselines are danger zones—the defense won't be able to trap effectively without them. Furthermore, offenses should try to defeat zone presses by passing rather than dribbling. The less a player puts the ball on the floor, the less danger she faces from traps. (That said, the dribble can be used to create passing angles.)

Pressing defenses try to stop forward passes; by extension, forward passing is exactly what the offense should try to achieve. Offensive players shouldn't be content with passing the ball from side-to-side all the way down the court. That eats up too much time on the clock.

There are several simple plays that take advantage of these offensive press principles:

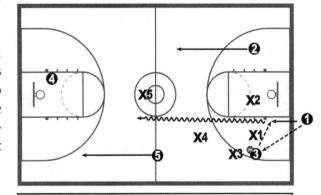

Figure 13.6
Beating the Press with the Give-and-Go

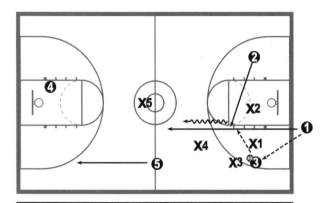

Figure 13.7
Beating the Press with a Second Cutter

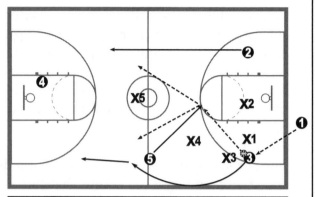

Figure 13.8
Beating the Press with a Post Up

- To break the zone press, one option is to have the point guard take the ball out of bounds, and receive a return pass in the form of a give-and-go down the middle of the court.

- If the point guard is not open, the guard on the opposite side of the ball should cut down the middle after the point guard has cleared out.

- Another play is to have a forward or center post up at the top of the key, and after receiving the pass, turn and pass to players filling the lanes on the sidelines.

- Another strategy is to place the primary ball-handler near half-court since, in many cases, the defense will put their best defenders near the baseline. When she cuts to receive a pass, she might find herself in a mismatch against a slower post player.

The key to beating a zone press is getting the ball over the initial line of defenders—the trappers and the two stealers. If it can do so, an offensive team has a good chance of creating a mismatch on the basket, and scoring an easy layup.

If an offensive player does get trapped, however, her teammates can't stand by and watch. Teammates should find or create passing lanes by making hard cuts to the ball and calling out loudly (to help their teammate find them). They should come as close to the trap as they need in order to rescue the ball (even into a handoff position).

OFFENSE AGAINST A MAN-TO-MAN PRESS

A good ball-handler can beat most defenders one-on-one. Often a good offensive strategy against a man-to-man press is simply to clear out of a guard's way as she dribbles up the court (assuming that the guard is a good ball-handler. This strategy can also be used to exploit a defensive mismatch: for example, a power forward guarding a quicker small forward.) It's possible that the defense will deny or double-team the point guard on the inbounds as she attempts to receive the pass; if that happens, the next time down the court, the point guard should take the ball out of bounds. She can make a pass in, step onto the court, and quickly get the ball back in the middle of the floor.

On her way down the court, the ball-handler will have to use some of the dribbling moves that I discussed in Chapter 4: for example, her crossover and spin dribbles. She should be ready to explode by the defense at any moment (whenever she sees an opening to the rim). Her head should be up and her eyes should be looking for an open teammate.

In some ways, a press can be as much of an advantage for the offense as it is for the defense. A trapping team, with all of its double-teaming and overplaying, leaves itself vulnerable to a numbers mismatch. Confident, poised players running a savvy offense can quickly force a defensive team out of its press, if they attack the defense's weaknesses (and make a few layups).

> *"Pretty similar...I lost all three!"*
>
> —Arnold Palmer, on being asked if his 1966 U.S. playoff loss was similar to two previous playoff losses

CHAPTER 14
Out-of-Bounds Situations

Out-of-bounds situations, in which an offense inbounds (puts into play) a dead ball underneath its own basket, are very common. Proximity alone makes these plays great scoring opportunities. A good screen or cut can put an offensive player in a position to catch the inbounds pass and score immediately (and possibly draw a foul!). In a given game, a team might inbound the ball as many as five to ten times; in a close game, the execution of these out-of-bounds plays can make the difference between a win and a loss. A team should run its out-of-bounds plays to perfection.

OPPORTUNITY TO SCORE

The player that takes the ball out of bounds should be an excellent passer, with good court vision, and a good decision-maker. Her position on the baseline is important: she should be about one foot away from the line, and at least three feet to the side of the basket. (Be careful not to let the ball bounce off the back of the backboard!) Once the ball is in her possession, the inbounder can move as far back from the court as she wants, but is limited to a confined lateral space.

Most passers signal the beginning of the inbounds play by slapping the ball once, loud enough for every teammate to hear, and by yelling "Break!"

The primary goal of an out-of-bounds play is to create an open layup or two-foot shot. As such, these plays typically involve a series of screens and/or cuts to the rim. An inbounder might be tempted to throw the ball to an open player on the wing or at the top of the key—but that kind of pass should be her last option. Her first look should always be inside near the basket.

DEFENSE

Many teams guard out-of-bounds plays with zone defenses. Playing man-to-man defense in such close quarters is risky: good cuts or screens might create mismatches near the basket (or simply, an open shot). Against this sort of quick-hit offensive situation, playing zone defense is, in most circumstances, a safer strategy. The defense I like to use to congest the area near the basket and defend the wing on the side of the ball is shown on the next page.

I also like to place a defender in front of the inbounder attempting to discourage a pass near the basket.

"We can't win at home and we can't win on the road. My problem as general manager is I can't think of another place to play."

—Pat Williams, on losing streak

"I'm not smart enough to talk to my players that many times. After the fourth time out of the first half, I told 'em to stay out there. I didn't have anything to say."

—Jerry Pimm

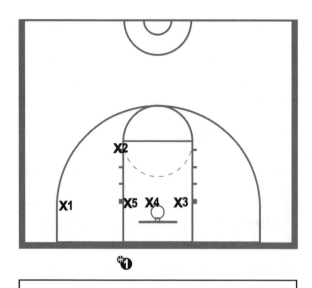

Figure 14.1
Out-of-Bounds Defense

Below are nine out-of-bounds plays that can help win some games for your team.

OUT-OF-BOUNDS PLAYS

PLAY 1: USES A LINE FORMATION

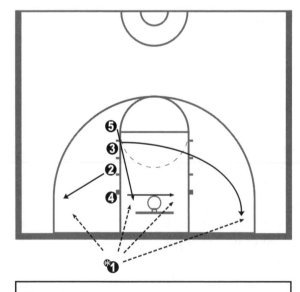

Figure 14.2
Play 1

The 1 takes the ball out of bounds. The rest of the offensive players line up along the strong-side lane line: the 4 first, then the 2, the 3, and lastly, the 5. On the slap, the 4 cuts to the weak-side of the lane and posts up on that block. The 2 cuts to the strong-side corner (and beyond the three-point line if she can shoot the three), the 3 to the weak-side corner (and beyond the three-point line if she can shoot the three). The lane should now be clear for the 5 player to make her move. She should cut down the lane directly to the rim, looking for a bounce pass from the inbounder. After she catches the ball, she shouldn't bring the ball down! She should put it right up to the basket.

PLAY 2: CREATES AN OPEN OUTSIDE SHOT

The team's best shooter (usually the 2 guard) takes the ball out of bounds. The (5) center sets up on the strong-side block, the (4) power forward on the opposite block. The (1) point guard lines up at the strong-side elbow, the (3) small forward on the weak-side elbow. The 2 slaps the ball: the 5 cuts directly to the strong-side corner, the 1 cuts to the strong-side wing, and the 3 floats out to the top of the key. The pass comes into the 5; she passes the ball to the 1, who swings it to the 3. Meanwhile, the 4 moves in a step and sets a screen for the inbounder. The 2 makes a sharp diagonal cut to the weak-side wing (running her defender into the 4's pick). The 3 passes her the ball as she curls out to the wing, and she takes an open shot. If, for some reason,

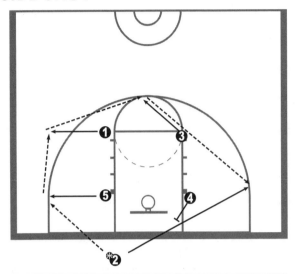

Figure 14.3
Play 2

she doesn't have a shot, she should look into her 4 player, who should be posting up strong after the screen.

Variation on the play: After passing the ball into the 5, the 2 guard fakes a cut to the weak-side. The 5 (having passed the ball to the 1), moves into the block and sets a diagonal screen. The 2 runs her defender off the screen, cuts out to the strong-side corner, and looks for her shot off of a pass from the 1. After the pick, the 5 posts up strong

PLAY 3: CREATES A BACKDOOR LAYUP

This play starts off like Play 2: the 1, 3, 4, and 5 start in the same positions. But instead of passing the ball into the 5, the 2 holds it. The 4 makes a hard cut across the lane to the strong-side box (filling the area the 5 had once been). If the 4 is open, she should get the ball, pivot, and score. Meanwhile, the 3 makes a backdoor cut to the weak-side of the basket, looking for a quick pass for a layup. A safety pass to the 1 is the last option.

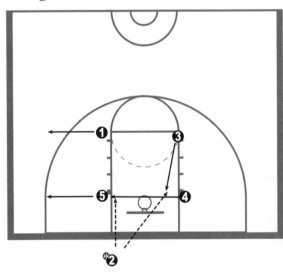

Figure 14.4
Play 3

PLAY 4: USES A SERIES OF POST SCREENS

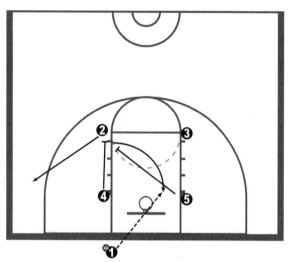

Figure 14.5
Play 4

The 1 takes the ball out of bounds. The 4 sets up on the strong-side block, the 5 on the weak-side block; the 2 goes to the strong-side elbow, and 3 to the weak-side elbow. On the slap, the 4 pivots to the outside, cuts up the lane and sets a backscreen for the 2. The 2 cuts out to the corner, looking for her shot. The 2 is a decoy, luring the defense away from the real action of the play. As the 2 runs to the corner, the 5 cuts to the strong-side elbow and sets a diagonal screen for the 4, who cuts to the weak-side of the basket. If she's open, she should catch the ball and shoot a power layup.

Variation on the play: After setting her pick, the 5 spins and cuts to the basket. As the tallest offensive player, she might be open for a lob pass or a quick two-foot shot.

PLAY 5: USES A CURL CUT

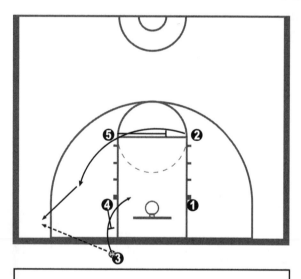

Figure 14.6
Play 5

This time, the small forward (3) takes the ball out of bounds. The 4 lines up on the strong-side box, the 5 at the strong-side elbow, the 1 on the weak-side box and 2 at the weak-side elbow. On the slap, the 5 pivots, cuts across the lane and sets a cross screen for the 2. The 2 runs out to the strong-side wing. Both the 5 and the 1 step back behind the three-point line. On the pass into the 2, the 4 turns and sets a strong-side screen for the 3, who curls around her teammate into the lane. The 2 looks to make an entry pass into the 3.

PLAY 6: THE CHATTANOOGA (FOR A SHOT NEAR THE BASKET)

The 1 takes the ball out of bounds. The 2 lines up at the strong-side block, the 4 at the strong-side elbow, the 5 at the weak-side block, and the 3 at the weak-side elbow. On the slap, the 2 turns, cuts across the lane and sets a cross screen for the 5. The 5 then cuts directly to the strong-side box. At the same time, 4 turns, cuts across the lane, and sets a high cross screen for the 3, who runs out to the strong-side corner. Finally, the 2 turns, cuts up the lane on the weak-side, and sets a backscreen for the 4, who cuts to the rim.

Variation on the play: If the 4 isn't open, the 1 can pass to the 3 in the corner. The 5 then runs out to set a cross screen for 3 on the strong-side wing. The 3 runs her defender off the pick, dribbles to the foul line and shoots.

PLAY 7: THE QUICK SHOT OUT-OF-BOUNDS PLAY

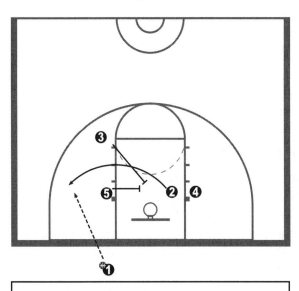

Figure 14.7
Play 6

The point guard takes the ball out of bounds; the 2 lines up in the lane to the left of the basket; the 3 lines up on the strong-side elbow; the 4 lines up on the weak-side block; the 5 lines up on the strong-side block. Players 3 and 5 set a double-screen for player 2 in the lane. Player 2 cuts off the screen to the right corner; shoots immediately off the pass.

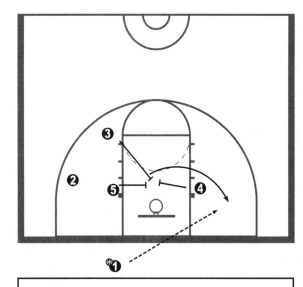

Figure 14.8a
Play 7, Part 1

Figure 14.8b
Play 7, Part 2

Variation on the play: If the 2 isn't open, the 4 and 5 players can turn and set a double-screen for the 3 cutting to the weak-side corner.

"Finish last in your league and they call you an idiot. Finish last in medical school and they call you doctor."

—Abe Lemons

"As a runner Daley Thompson is excellent, as a jumper he is excellent, and as a thrower he is an excellent runner and jumper."

—Cliff Temple

PLAY 8: THE SIMPLE OUT-OF-BOUNDS PLAY (FOR AN INSIDE OR AN OUTSIDE SHOT)

The point guard takes the ball out of bounds, the 2 lines up on the strong-side block, the 3 on the opposite elbow, the 4 on the opposite block, the 5 on the strong-side elbow. Player 2 cuts to the strong-side corner; player 4 posts up on the opposite block; player 3 cuts to the opposite corner; player 5 cuts straight to the basket, looking for a bounce pass or lob pass from player 1.

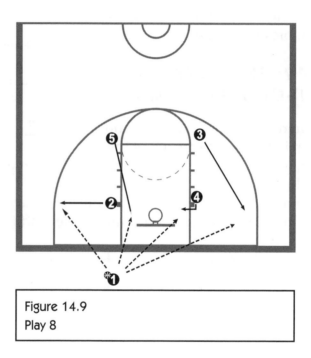

Figure 14.9
Play 8

PLAY 9: MARYMOUNT OUT-OF-BOUNDS PLAY

The point guard takes the ball out of bounds, the 2 lines up on the strong-side block, the 3 on the opposite elbow, the 4 on the opposite block, the 5 on the strong-side elbow. The 2 and 4 cut out to the weak and strong-side corners, respectively, in an attempt to draw defenders out of the lane. The 3 makes a diagonal cut to the strong-side block, looking for the ball. The 5 makes a diagonal cut to the opposite block, looking for the ball. The 3 is the first option, 5 the second, the 2 and 4 the third option.

These plays can be run against a man-to-man or a zone defense. The differences lie in the location of the screens and cuts. When players cut to the basket against a zone, they should look to slip between the defenders, rather than muscling their opponents out of the way.

There are two keys to running successful out-of-bounds plays: the first is to make sure that players know their assignments. The second is to execute, and to execute quickly. Don't let your players stand around looking confused; remember, a game can be won or lost on the basis of one out-of-bounds play. Every player has an important job. Even if she's a decoy, she has to run her assignment to perfection. It's also very important that the passer stay patient and wait for a teammate to cut to the basket, or get open for a two-foot shot. Don't let the passer get into the habit of making the easy pass to a player 20 feet from the basket—that pass will always be open. The bet-

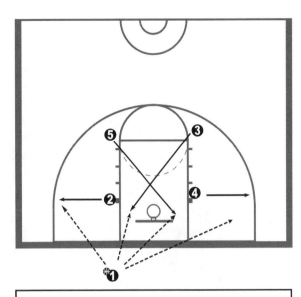

Figure 14.10
Play 9

ter option will be the second or third look that takes a little more time to develop. Those are the looks that will turn into easy baskets.

CHAPTER 15
What Is a Foul?

Referees make bad calls in almost every basketball game; there's simply nothing that a coach, player, or parent can do about. it. So, where do we go from there?

Probably the most misunderstood area in basketball is what constitutes a foul. Most people learn the definition of a foul on the playground or in some other informal setting. I recommend that coaches read the rules that govern their situation (high school, AAU, college, etc.) and clarify any questions with referees before games.

Many players continue to commit the same type of foul over and over again even after different referees call it. Coaches and players need to adapt, and coaches (and parents) need to make sure players are not encouraged to make up their own rules as they see fit.

Usually players who concentrate on the inadequacies of a referee's vision and judgment instead of what they did to commit the foul are only hurting themselves and the team. For example, it is my opinion that many fouls would be avoided if players would learn how to move their feet properly; blaming referees certinly doesn't solve that problem. Constant player criticism of referees should be a concern for a coach (and parent) if it results in the player losing focus on how to play great defense.

> *"The trouble with officials is they just don't care who wins."*
>
> —Tom Canterbury

EDUCATION IS THE KEY

Learning how to play within the rules of the game and learning to adjust to particular referees are two of the most important lessons that players can learn. There's no room for denial on a good basketball team. By extension, players should be coached to accept their mistakes and to learn from them, rather than to complain about fouls on the court. That's the only way that a team, as a whole, will improve.

A savvy team avoids fouling a player taking a wild or off-balance shot. They avoid contact in prime fouling situations—for example, when defending a fast-break layup. Smart teams are also able to gauge the character of particular games. Often, referees will allow more contact in fast-paced pressing games than in half-court

> *"They called fouls like they were getting a commission."*
>
> —Peter Salzberg

contests. Some referees will allow some contact; others will blow the whistle at the first sign of contact. In the first few minutes of the game, coaches and players should pay attention to figure out what kind of fouls the referees are likely to call.

Below, I've included excerpts from high school and NCAA points of emphasis on what constitutes fouls. If players (and coaches) can learn the precise definitions of common fouls and infractions, they have a better chance of playing a smarter game of basketball—one that's faster and more enjoyable for both the athletes involved and the spectators.

(Appendix 1 includes excerpts from NCAA rules which, in my opinion, should be studied by any serious coach or player.)

HIGH SCHOOL AND NCAA POINTS OF EMPHASIS

NATIONAL FEDERATION OF STATE HIGH SCHOOL ASSOCIATIONS (NFHS)

2003-04 POINTS OF EMPHASIS

A. Handchecking:
 1. Any tactic using the hands, arms or body that allows a player, on offense or defense, to "control" (hold, impede, push, divert, slow or prevent) the movement of an opposing player is a foul.
 2. When an offensive player uses his or her hands or body to push-off for position, for spacing, for getting open to receive a pass or to move the ball via pass or dribble, it is a foul.
 3. "Hooking" by the offensive players should be presumed a definite advantage. This is not a judgment call or tactic worthy of a warning. It is a foul and should be called without hesitation.
 4. Any act or tactic of illegal use of hands, arms or body (offense or defense) that intentionally slows, prevents, impedes the progress or displaces an opposing player due to the contact, is a foul and must be called.

"Technical fouls are like traffic tickets. Sometimes you might deserve one and don't get it, but when you do, you don't think you deserve it."

—John Wooden

5. Regardless of where it takes place on the floor, when a player continuously places a hand on the opposing player, it is a foul.
6. When a player places both hands on an opposing player, it is a foul.
7. When a player jabs a hand or forearm on an opponent, it is a foul.

> *"Officiating is the only occupation in the world where the highest accolade is silence."*
>
> —Earl Strom

B. Screening:
1. A legal screener must be stationary prior to contact, with hands and arms close to the body. When these two requirements are not met, and when there is sufficient contact delivered by the screener to bump, slow or displace, it is a foul on the screener.
2. When a screen is blind, or a rear screen, it is only legal when the screened player is allowed a normal step backward. The screened player must then make a legitimate attempt to get around a legal screen without forcing rough or "displacing" contact. This type of contact must result in a foul on the screened player.
3. When a screen is set in view of an opposing player, the screener can get as close as he or she wishes in a legal stationary position. The burden is on the screened player to avoid contact that may result in a foul.

C. Post Play:
1. The offense can "shape up" to receive a pass or to force the defense to deploy or assume a legal guarding position at the side, in front or behind the offensive post player. When the offensive player then uses the "swim stroke," pushes, pins, elbows, forearms, holds, clears with the body, or just generally demonstrates rough physical movements or tactics, this is a foul on the offensive player and must be called without warning.
2. The defense can assume a legal, vertical stance or position on the side, front or behind the offensive post player. When the defense undercuts (initiates lower-body non-vertical contact), slaps, pushes, holds, elbows, forearms or just generally demonstrates rough, physical movements or tactics, this is a foul on the defense and must be called without warning.

3. When a player pushes a leg or knee into the rear of an opponent, it is a foul.
4. When a player dislodges an opponent from an established position by pushing or "backing in," it is a foul.
5. When a player uses hands, forearms or elbows to prevent an opponent from maintaining a legal position, it is a foul.

D. **Rebounding:** A player has a right to any spot on the floor he or she may get to legally. To obtain or maintain a legal rebounding position a player **may not:**
1. Displace, charge or push an opponent.
2. Extend shoulders, hips or knees, or extend the arms or elbows fully or partially in a position other than vertical, so that the opponent's freedom of movement is hindered when contact with the arms or elbows occurs.
3. Bend his or her body in an abnormal position to hold or displace an opponent.
4. Violate the principle of verticality.
5. Better his or her position by other than legal means.

E. **Block/Charge:** A real concern is when players get knocked to the floor and no call is made.
1. Two factors used to determine the responsibility of contact are:
   a. Who was at the spot first?
   b. Was the guard facing the player with the ball with two feet on the playing court?
2. The guard may then move his/her feet and stay within the dribbler's path. The guard should be rewarded for good defense.
3. Contact in front, upper torso, initiated by the offensive player should be a "charge."
4. Contact initiated by the defense (on or off the ball) that involves lower body, non-vertical contact and defending a perimeter player or an airborne player, should be a "block."
5. When a block or charge occurs anywhere on the court, it is a foul and should be called.

F. **Officiating Points:**
1. Was the defensive player placed at a disadvantaged by being displaced or knocked to the floor?

2. Was the defensive player displaced so that he/she could not take the ball out of bounds for a quick throw-in after a score, or within the normal time permitted for any throw-in?

End of Game Situations/Intentional Fouls

Officials must be aware of game situations in the closing moments of a contest. Communication between officials on last-second shots must take place. Game-ending procedures must be reviewed and discussed in pre-game conferences. When a player fouls and the opponent is clearly not playing the ball, an intentional foul must be called.

Reprinted with permission by the NHSF. Rules subject to change annually.

2004 NCAA MEN'S AND WOMEN'S BASKETBALL RULES AND INTERPRETATIONS

POINTS OF EMPHASIS FOR WOMEN

Displacement

Eliminating displacement of an opponent, regardless of where she is on the court, will bring basketball back to a more skillful game that allows freedom of movement. If a player is displaced and cannot continue to cut, screen, post-up, dribble or rebound, a foul shall be called.

1. Displacement as it relates to hand-checking:
   a. The dribbler may not be moved off her path by the use of the forearm by the defender.
   b. The dribbler may not be held, pushed or bumped by the body of the defender.
   c. The defender may not be pushed away by the use of the body or forearm of the dribbler.
   d. Displacement by either the offensive or defense player is a foul.
2. Displacement as it relates to post play:
   a. The defensive post player may not hold or push the offensive post player from her established position with the forearm, body or leg.

> *"I do not participate in any sport with ambulances at the bottom of the hill."*
>
> —Erma Brombeck, on skiing

"We all need to join hands and sing 'Kumbaya.'"

—Brian Williams, on rumors of dissension

    b. The offensive post player may not hold or push the defensive post player from her established position with the forearm, body or leg.

    c. Displacement by either the offensive or defensive player is a foul.

3. Displacement as it relates to screening:

    a. The screener may not use arms, legs or body to hold or push the defensive player off of her intended path around the screen.

    b. The defensive player may not hold or push through the screen with her arms, legs or body to gain an advantage.

    c. Displacement by either the offensive or defensive player is a foul.

4. Displacement as it relates to cutting:

    a. Cutters must be allowed the freedom to move if they get to the path before the defender. Defensive players may not hold or push cutters off of their intended path by using their arms, legs or body.

    b. Cutters may not displace a defensive player in any way by using their arms, legs or body.

    c. Displacement by either the offensive or defensive player is a foul.

5. Displacement as it relates to rebounding:

    a. The use of the arms or body to hold or push by either the offensive or defensive player to get a good position to rebound is a foul.

    b. Backing a player away from the basket with the body and displacing her is a foul.

Reprinted with permission by the NCAA. Rules subject to change annually.

CHAPTER 16
Strategies and Practice Plans

This chapter provides game, practice and coaching strategies that serve as a sort of reminder checklist to be used in conjunction with the rest of the book. Also included are detailed sample practice plans, and ideas for strength and conditioning programs.

COACHING STRATEGIES

Below is a summary compilation of coaching strategies, many of which have been explained throughout this book. This summary is designed to help put coaching strategies at the fingertips of coaches, parents, and players.

OFFENSE

> *"If stupidity got us into this mess, then why can't it get us out?"*
> —Will Rogers

- Encourage players to drive to the basket as much as possible in order to put pressure on the defense.
- Emphasize the importance of the fast break (to get high percentage shots).
- Drill the team in the basic plays of basketball, including screening the ball, passing and screening away, the give-and-go, and clearing out.
- Emphasize spacing and balance. Ideal offensive spacing varies with the age and skill level of the team. There are no firm rules, but usually for younger players, the proper spacing is around 8 to 12-feet apart; and for high school players, from 12 to 15 feet.
- Use out-of-bounds plays underneath the basket as scoring opportunities. Execution is key!
- Make sure that the point guard is the best ball-handler and smartest player on the team. Having a good point guard is like having a coach on the court.
- The way a team executes a play is just as important as the quality of the play itself.
- Move the ball quickly on offense.
- Young teams and teams without a primary ball-handler should consider using a two-guard alignment with a high post player, and two wings. This 2-1-2 alignments gives the ball-handler the option of passing to the opposite guard, the high post player, or a forward cutting out to the wing. Out of this alignment, teams can run the give-and-go or the pass and screen away (and the opposite guard is always around for help!) The high post can act as an additional outlet.
- Always emphasize the fundamentals.

- A player with the ball should make an effort to know where all of her teammates are on the court.
- Players, in general, tend to dribble too high. Practice dribbling low.
- Players should move crisply with and without the ball when playing against a zone defense. When in doubt, dribble penetrate and make a kick-out pass to the wing. Swing the ball from one side of the court to the other: moving the ball fast makes the defense work.

DEFENSE

- Change defenses by switching, for example, from man-to-man to zone or from a half-court trap to a full-court press. I like to mix it up and change defenses continuously throughout the game; players seem to get a kick out of that. (It has the added bonus of confusing the opposing offense!) A good time to change defenses is during a substitution or a timeout, or when players are dropping back from the offensive end of the court.
- Traps are effective tools in basketball. My favorite places to trap are the baseline corners on both ends of the court and just after the ball-handler crosses half-court. Be careful, in general, when you trap. The more advanced the players on offense, the less effective a trapping defense becomes.
- Emphasize the importance of overplaying the ball-handler's strong hand.
- Insist that guards collapse to the ball when it's passed below the foul line.
- Take away the baseline and sideline dribble!
- Consider new defensive strategies, like switching up the defensive matchups, (for example, by putting the point guard in full deny on the wing so that the other team cannot begin its offense).
- Always apply pressure on the ball in the front court.
- The general rule for a defender is to be within one arm's length of the ball-handler. Another way to teach it (to get her even closer) is to tell the defender to be as close to the ball-handler as possible without making any physical contact.
- Good defense is about applying pressure, forcing the other team to make mistakes, and forcing them to take low percentage shots.
- Challenge every shot on defense—don't allow any free baskets!

"The President doesn't want any yes-men and yes-women around him. When he says no, we all say no."

—Elizabeth Dole

- Don't commit foolish fouls (like reaching in to steal the ball).
- Trapping a defensive rebounder can be an effective way of delaying the fast break. But there is a downside: in this situation, many players are prone to fouling. Also, they typically don't get back on defense as fast. If you encourage that kind of trapping, you'll find that players (both forwards and guards) start to hang around to see what the rebounder's doing with the ball, putting themselves at a defensive disadvantage. For that reason, I like to teach players to get back as soon as the opposing team gets a defensive board.
- On defense, take away the dribbler's strong hand, the baseline and the sidelines. (As a defender, think about actually planting your foot on the line to stop the dribbler's progress—she'll only have one direction to go, and that's backward, which will make your job a lot easier.)
- Players commit a disproportionate number of fouls when they reach in an attempt to steal the ball. My guess is that some players that were able to steal the ball when they were in grade school don't realize that older players know how to protect it better. Try to avoid foolish reach-in fouls.
- A simple technique to determine if your team is making a reasonable effort to rebound is to count the number of jerseys near the basket when the ball hits the rim. That's a good way to quickly tell how many of your players are crashing the boards.

OTHER STRATEGIES AND HELPFUL HINTS

- Coaching younger players is different than coaching older, more experienced players. The youth game tends to be more of an inside game, so coaches should design an offensive strategy geared toward getting the ball down low near the basket.
- Coaches can consider assigning players to the same side of the court on both offense and defense (if the team's playing a zone). This can reduce confusion and eliminate missed defensive assignments.
- Use your timeouts wisely: for example, to avoid turnovers (by anticipating when a player might lose control of the ball in a trap). This can be an effective strategy for helping a team win in a close game.
- Play against better teams in order to expose your squad to a higher level of speed and ability.
- Use your substitutions as opportunities to change the offense or defense without burning time-outs.

"They do one-armed push-ups so they can count with the other hand."

—Al McGuire, on football players

- If you keep statistics, keep track of turnovers, steals, and rebounds, and fast-break points scored and given up.
- Force taller players to learn how to handle the ball and play on the outside; similarly, make the guards play under the basket every now and then.
- Tape each game; analyze the strengths and weaknesses of individual players and the team. Consider taping practices as well. (Review the tapes with the team. This is well worth the time, but be sure to make the criticism constructive!)
- Prior to games, meet with your team to get the players focused on what needs to be accomplished. (A sample of what to cover prior to a game is discussed in Chapter 2.) The team should also meet after the game in order to review, for example, what went right and what went wrong. These meetings should be instructive rather than critical!
- Remember to coach the players and not the referees.
- Remind your team to take good shots.
- Emphasize the importance of teamwork, hustle, and staying focused.
- Coaching is all about what you emphasize. Many coaches teach the same things—what really separates coaches is what they drive home to their players.
- Remind the team that discipline is not something that is done *to* players, but rather something done *for* the benefit of them and the team.
- Many games are decided by four points or less; the team that can execute out-of-bounds plays and make free throws has a much greater chance of winning.
- Teach and emphasize footwork at practice. (Many players travel because they get into the habit of moving their pivot foot just before they put the ball on the floor.)
- Everything else being equal, the team that wants it more usually wins. Keep your team focused on the goals at hand.
- Focus your defense on stopping the top scorer (or two). Don't defend each player on the opposing team equally.
- Encourage players to get personal trainers and basketball tutors, if they can afford them. There simply isn't enough time at practice to work every skill to perfection; more importantly, players need to stay in shape all year round. At the very least, encourage players to shoot outside of practice.

"When we started, we used to make very little money and have a lot of fun. Now we make a lot of money and have no fun at all. I like it better this way."

—Abe Lemons

Some coaches like to use an easy-to-remember numbering system for defensive alignments. A popular method is a double-digit system: the first number indicates if the defense is a man, zone or a pressing defense; the second number indicates where on the court the pressure should be applied. For the first digit, a number 2 means a man-to-man defense, a number 3 means a straight-zone defense and a number 4 means a press defense. To understand the second digit, you first must break the court down into four areas. The number 4 signifies the area closest to your team's basket, extending from the baseline to the top of the key; the number 3 signifies the area from the top of the key to the half-court line; the number 2 area extends from the half-court line to the top of the key; and the number 1 area extends from the top of the key to the baseline. Under this numbering system, a "24" would be a fullcourt man-to-man defense and a "31" would be a straight zone defense starting near the top of the key in the back-court. (Coaches or point guards can either call these numbers out vocally, or use their hands to signal them. If they're using hand signals, the left hand should show the first number, the right hand the second.)

Also, don't forget to let players know what you, as a coach, are looking for—what is expected of them as players. Let them know that they need to, for example, show enthusiasm in games, hustle between drills, and show up early to practices. Make it clear that, when corrected or given instructions, they should never respond with "I know." (If they really knew they wouldn't have done it to begin with!) Players need to agree to let coaches train them. To that end, tell players not to give an explanation or a rebuttal in response to constructive criticism from coaches; instead, simply ask that they try to do it better the next time. Tell them to maintain eye contact when coaches are speaking, and most importantly, to never talk while he's talking! (I think players forget how much body language on and off the court can influence a coach's opinion of them). Finally, tell your players never to argue with referees.

REWARDS AND CONSEQUENCES

It's important that a coach develop team rules that are reasonable and easy to understand. He should apply these rules consistently, but also should leave some room for flexibility. A consistent system of rewards and consequences creates a unified team with a high morale, in addition to making disciplinary questions easier.

> *"When I want your opinion, I will give it to you."*
>
> —Samuel Goldwyn

> *"It's about 90 percent strength and 40 percent technique."*
>
> —Johnny Walker, world middleweight wrist-wrestling champion

"Motivational" consequences can include doing push-ups, running sprints, running suicides, or doing defensive slides. Also, a player can be required to explain to a coach or assistant coach what mistake she made, and why, when the situation arises. The most obvious consequence, of course, is to reduce the player's court time.

Not all "motivational" consequences involve conditioning; some are simply rewards designed to make practices more fun and competitive. A coach might, for example, award a player a soft drink for making a left-handed layup or a T-shirt for stealing the ball twice in a game. In scrimmages, a coach might reward the winning team with soft drinks after practice while making the losers run one sprint.

"The kid is slower than erosion."

—Gordon Chiesa

PRACTICE TIPS

I've organized the drills in the next part of this book (Part 5: Drills) so that coaches can prepare an almost unlimited number of practice plans tailored to their needs. A coach can choose to use a few drills from every section, or to use several drills from only one or two sections, in order to focus on particular skills and principles.

Section 1 Individual Skills
- Basic Ballhandling Drills (Drills 1)
- Dribbling Drills (Drills 2)
- Footwork, Jumping, and Conditioning Drills (Drills 3)
- Passing and Catching Drills (Drills 4)
- Shooting Drills (Drills 5)
- Rebounding Drills (Drills 6)

"I look at the NBA as a football game without the helmet."

—Tom Tolbert

Section 2 Breakdown of Team Offense
- Fast-Break Drills (Drills 7)
- Breakdown of Team Offense Drills (Drills 8)

Section 3 Defense Skills
- Individual Defense Drills (Drills 9)
- Screening Drills (Drills 10)
- Breakdown of Team Defense (Drills 11)

Section 4 Team Offense and Defense
- Drills for Guards (Drills 12)
- Drills for Forwards (Drills 13)
- Team Offense and Defense (Drills 14)
- Special Situation Drills (Drills 15)

Section 5 Concluding Practice
- Fun Drills (Drills 16)

Below are sample practice plans to get you started.

SAMPLE TWO-HOUR PRACTICE PLANS

SAMPLE PRACTICE 1: EMPHASIZES SHOOTING, BALLHANDLING, AND CONDITIONING

"I'm in favor of drug tests, just so long as they are multiple choice."

—Kurt Rambus

"When Irish eyes are smiling, watch your step."

—Gerald Kersh

Time (in min)	Drill	Activity
3		Personal shooting (shooting by yourself)
2	Drill 5.2	Perfect Shooting Form Drill
2	Drill 5.6	2-4-6-8 Drill
5		50 shots in a group (three shooters, three rebounders, three balls at each basket)
1		Full court jog (around the court two times, dribbling a basketball)
4		Stretch
3	Drill 4.5	Meet the Pass Drill
2	Drill 16.8	Single-Line Rebounding Drill
8	Drill 5.9	Half-Court Layup Drill (from right and left sides, also shoot jump shots)
5	Drill 5.23	Half-Court Olympic Drill
3		Meeting at center circle
2		Water break
2	Drill 5.11	Full Court Two-Minute Layup Drill
5	Drill 4.12	Full Court Weave Drill
5	Drill 4.11	Full Court Side-Center-Side Drill
6	Drill 7.2	Three-on-Two, Two-on-One Drill
5		Shoot free throws
5	Drill 5.5	Mikan Drill
5	Drill 5.8	Elbow Layup Drill

6	Drill 5.13	Two Player Elbow-to-Elbow Drill
6	Drill 5.14	Three-Player Elbow-to-Elbow Drill
5	Drill 5.24	Continuous Pressure Shooting Drill
8	Drill 5.26	Low Post Footwork and Shooting Drill
4		Water break
15	Drill 14.2	Scrimmage
3		Closing meeting at center circle

SAMPLE PRACTICE 2: EMPHASIZES DEFENSE, REBOUNDING AND CONDITIONING

Time (in min)	Drill	Activity
3		Personal shooting (shooting by yourself)
5		50 shots in a group (three shooters, three rebounders, three balls at each basket)
1		Full court jog (around the court two times, dribbling a basketball)
4		Stretch
3		Meeting at center circle
3	Drill 4.5	Meet the Pass Drill
2	Drill 16.8	Single Line Rebounding Drill
7	Drill 5.9	Half-Court Layup Drill (from the right and left sides)
5	Drill 5.23	Half-Court Olympic Drill
2		Water break
5	Drill 9.1	Zig-Zag Drill
4	Drill 6.1	Bread-and-Butter Rebounding Drill
7	Drill 6.9	Two-on-Two Rebounding Drill
7	Drill 6.8	Weak-Side Box Out Rebounding Drill
7	Drill 11.21	Ball-Line, Mid-Line Drill
4	Drill 11.1	Deny the Wing Drill
5	Drill 11.7	Wing Closeout Drill
5	Drill 11.9	Take Away the Baseline Drill
5		Shoot free throws
6	Drill 11.27	Herding Drill
4		Water break
5	Drill 11.17	Give-and-Go Defense Drill
6	Drill 11.18	Jump to the Ball Drill
12	Drill 14.2	Scrimmage
3		Closing meeting at center circle

"You bring the smoke, I'll bring the mirrors."

—Business executives

"I think the world is run by C students."

—Al McGuire

SAMPLE PRACTICE 3: EMPHASIZES THE FAST BREAK (OFFENSE AND DEFENSE)

Time (in min)	Drill	Activity
3		Personal shooting (shooting by yourself)
5		50 shots in a group (three shooters, three rebounders, three balls at each basket)
3		Meeting at center circle
1		Full court jog (around the court two times, dribbling a basketball)
4		Stretch
4	Drill 4.5	Meet the Pass Drill
4	Drill 16.8	Single Line Rebounding Drill
5	Drill 5.9	Half-Court Layup Drill (from right and left sides)
5	Drill 5.23	Half-Court Olympic Drill
4		Water break
2	Drill 5.11	Full Court Two-Minute Layup Drill
5	Drill 4.12	Full Court Weave Drill
5	Drill 4.11	Side-Center-Side Drill
6	Drill 7.2	Three-on-Two, Two-on-One Drill
5		Shoot free throws
7	Drill 6.14	Rebound/Outlet Drill
8	Drill 8.36	Fast-Break Rebounding Drill
6	Drill 11.28	Press Recovery Drill
6	Drill 7.5	Five-Man Break Drill
4		Water break
20	Drill 14.2	Scrimmage
5	Drill 16.4	Knockout Drill
3		Closing meeting at center circle

SAMPLE PRACTICE 4: EMPHASIZES TEAM OFFENSE AND DEFENSE

Time (in min)	Drill	Activity
2		Personal shooting (shooting by yourself)
5		50 shots in a group (three shooters, three rebounders, three balls at each basket)
3		Meeting at center circle

"In basketball, the first person to touch the ball shoots it. Either that or the coach carefully diagrams a set play and then the first player to touch it shoots it."

—Gene Klein

"The best cure for insomnia is to get a lot of sleep."

—Senator S. I. Hayakawa

1		Full court jog (around the court two times, dribbling a basketball)
4		Stretch
4	Drill 4.5	Meet the Pass Drill
5	Drill 5.9	Half-Court Layup Drill (from the right and left sides)
4		Water break
6	Drill 6.10	Location Drill
5	Drill 12.3	Full Court One-on-One Drill
5	Drill 14.5	Recognition Drill
5	Drill 11.24	Wing Trap Drill
4		Water break
8	Drill 7.5	Five-Man Break Drill
6	Drill 11.28	Press Recovery Drill
5	Drill 10.3	Back Screen Drill
8		Out-of-Bounds Plays
8	Drill 8.8	Ten Ways to Beat a Zone Drill
12	Drill 14.1	Shell Drills
12	Drill 14.2	Scrimmage
5	Drill 16.4	Knockout Drill
3		Closing meeting at center circle

INDIVIDUAL WARM-UP AND SKILLS ROUTINE

The individual routine that I provide below is ideal for players that want to improve on their own time, or for players that arrive early to practice and want to warm up, separate from the team. I have found that the 2-4-6-8 drill (See Drill 5.6), in particular, is useful to young players, not only as an individual basketball warmup, but also as a form of mental preparation that takes place before practice begins.

- Stretch
- Right-hand dribble (30 seconds)
- Left-hand dribble (30 seconds)
- Crossover dribble (30 seconds)
- Spin dribble (30 seconds)
- 2-4-6-8 Drill, directly in front of the rim (at least eight shots)
- Jump shots 5 feet from basket (five shots from same spot, jump high)
- Jump shots 10 feet from basket (five shots from same spot, jump high)

"When we came out on the floor, I saw Looie and the three refs deciding where they were gonna eat right after the game."

—Tom Green, asked when he knew he was in for long night

"Nobody goes there anymore. It's too crowded."

—Yogi Berra

- Jump shots 15 feet from basket (five shots from same spot, jump high)
- Jump shots 20 feet from basket (five shots from same spot, jump high)
- Post moves from the right block (power dribble, baby hook, up-and-under, etc.)
- Post moves from the left block
- Individual rebounding: toss the ball off the backboard and practice perfect rebounding form (five times)

STRENGTH AND CONDITIONING

Why is conditioning so important? Basketball is a physically demanding sport. It is a game of quickness, acceleration and deceleration, jumping, fast starts, sharp turns, cuts and running. It has been estimated that a high school basketball player can run several miles in a 32-minute game. It is, therefore, important that players are in top physical condition. For this reason, both in-season and off-season training programs are necessary in order to develop speed, strength, coordination, agility, and endurance.

"Pay attention to the details!"

—Most good coaches

There is some controversy surrounding strength training for young athletes. Some coaches believe that strength training should not start until high school, since young players lack the hormone levels needed to achieve significant strength gains. Furthermore, intense weight training might injure growth plates and/or young bones. However, there's no denying that physical strength is an asset for players at all levels, because it makes basketball movements more efficient and effective. Resistance training is a good alternative to weightlifting for ambitious young players. Grade and middle school girls can get stronger by utilizing their own body weight: by doing push-ups, sit-ups, chin-ups, leg raises, and dips. Once they reach high school, though, girls that aspire to be varsity players should hit the weight room under close supervision.

It's true that most basketball players have neither the time nor the motivation to engage in a comprehensive conditioning and strengthening program outside of practice. But kids that are involved in alternative activities that build endurance and coordination, like soccer or volleyball, will reap some of the same benefits.

As a practical matter, players that don't have time to complete a full resistance program should focus on strengthening their fingers, hands, wrists, and forearms. This will achieve maximum results relative to the amount of time spent. In fact, players should be able to see a noticeable improvement in their shooting and dribbling abilities in a period of only a few weeks. Players can improve hand and arm strength by using dumbbells and thera-bands. This type of low-impact exercise strengthens while minimizing the chance of injury.

When players do begin to lift weights, they must be properly supervised, both by coaches and other players that act as "spotters" for individual exercises: bad technique can quickly lead to injuries. Players should never lift weights over their heads without close supervision. In most cases, basketball lifters should focus on legs, back, and shoulders, in addition to arms and hands.

"Very simple. Nothing will work unless you do."

—John Wooden, on the secret of winning

PART FIVE
Drills

DRILLS
Introduction

Properly executing drills in practice will produce positive results in games. Players cannot simply be told or shown how to develop a skill necessary for competitive success; instead, they need to practice that skill to perfection, day after day. By consistently incorporating the proper drills into practices, coaches will make skills like cutting, pivoting, dribbling, passing, screening, shooting, defending, and rebounding part of their players' muscle (as well as visual) memories.

THE ULTIMATE TEACHING TOOL

Coaches should have a plan for every practice. That plan should be based on tried-and-true methods of teaching the game of basketball—and those methods include effective drills. A coach that is not armed with an intimate knowledge of top-notch drills will have a very difficult time coaching effectively, because drills are the tools needed to develop basketball success.

In the following chapters, I make a point of incorporating drills that address all aspects of the game, from the most basic basketball fundamentals to the most unusual situations. The drills can be adapted for any age or skill level, from beginner to collegiate. (I like to say that a complete study of the drills in this book will provide the reader with the equivalent of a Ph.D. in drillology. In coaching circles, this is a distinguished honor!)

Below are some suggestions on how to run drills.

POINTS TO REMEMBER

MAKE DRILLS INTERESTING (AND THEY WILL BEG FOR MORE)

No player is going to like running suicides up and down the court. Effective drills can accomplish the same level of conditioning, be competitive, and leave a player in a positive state of mind.

START WITH THE BASICS

Teach and run each drill properly before moving on to a more advanced version. Don't be afraid to start slowly—the important thing is to instill good technique into the players. Once the players have the drills down, though, run them at game speed. Early in the

> *"We only have one person to blame, and that's each other."*
>
> —Barry Beck, New York Ranger, on who started a brawl

season, drills should stress conditioning and fundamentals. Later, a coach should shift his drills to more team-oriented concepts.

SHELL DRILLS

A great way to introduce drills, as well as team offenses and defenses, is to "shell" through them (run them with only an offense or a defense on the court). Break the drills down into one-on-one, two-on-two, and three-on-three components.

PLAN AHEAD

Certain types of drills work best at the beginning of practices—typically, these drills help players warm up. By contrast, other drills are effective at the end of practices, when players are tired (it's always good to force players to execute when they are feeling exhausted). Conditioning drills should be paired with less demanding shooting drills. The moment a drill starts to become boring, it's time to move on: when players lose interest in what they are doing, their technique invariably slips.

FUNDAMENTALS ARE KEY

The fundamentals of basketball form the foundation of competitive success. By extension, the best drills focus on developing fundamental skills. Drilling skills improperly, allowing poor form or relaxed concentration, will encourage bad basketball habits. Once those habits take hold, they are very difficult to break. (On the other hand, early development of proper fundamental skills will stick with a player for her entire career.)

IT'S WHAT YOU EMPHASIZE THAT MATTERS

State an emphasis for each practice. Setting forth goals at the beginning of practice helps players remember fundamental concepts. Coaches can organize the day's drills around those goals so that they can really drive the point home to their players.

Remember, it's what you emphasize that really makes a difference. Practice time is limited, so it is particularly important that coaches emphasize (through drilling) the fundamental concepts that are most pertinent. Drills can help focus a players in the right direction.

> *"The Orlando Magic were so bad last season, the cheerleaders stayed home and phoned in their cheers."*
>
> —Pat Williams

Every drill has a purpose, and that purpose should be made known to players before the drill begins. If need be, break the drill down into its component parts and explain them one by one, to make each teaching point crystal clear.

Drills don't always have to be focused on an isolated skill. One way for a coach to enhance the effectiveness of his practices is to break down the team's offensive and defensive schemes into drill components. That way he can tackle multiple fundamental skills and team concepts at the same time.

SET THE TONE AND ESTABLISH RULES

Drills are an ideal place to instill a sense of teamwork and discipline, and to emphasize the importance of hard work. Coaches should communicate up front that drills are neither the time nor place for talking or socializing. (But don't forget to have a sense of humor at the appropriate times.)

BE ENTHUSIASTIC

Often players have a hard time believing that drills are as important as, for example, scrimmaging. Coaches should be enthusiastic about every drill—your attitude will rub off on the players.

ADD COMPETITION, REWARDS AND PENALTIES

Competitive drills naturally elicit more effort out of players. A coach might consider developing a system of penalty and reward that measures an individual's or a team's performance during drills (just for a little added incentive).

NAME THE DRILLS

Drill names should be short and descriptive. After a few weeks of practice, players should know exactly what to do when a drill name is called. It's helpful to hand out written descriptions of drills, too.

DEVELOP YOUR OWN DRILLS

Devise your own drills that incorporate your team's particular schemes and that take into account your unique personality.

> *"I love exercise. I could watch it all day."*
>
> —Bill Russell

> *"He's a quick learner, but he forgets quick too."*
>
> —Mychal Thompson, on an NBA player

"Make the easy pass."

—John Wooden

"You get guys taking part from MIT and guys who can't spell MIT."

—Sylvester Stallone, on arm wrestling

KEEP DRILLS SHORT AND HUSTLE!

As a general rule, each drill should last around 4 to 8 minutes. Don't allow for too much time between drills. Players should have the chance to recover their breath, but then they should be back running the next drill. Hustling between drills is almost as important as hustling in the drills themselves.

OVERVIEW OF DRILLS

Some of the drills that follow focus on single skills; others incorporate more than one fundamental principle. I've also included drill variations; typically these variations describe a more advanced or more competitive alternative to the original drill.

As you will see, some drills are most effective when run by a small group of players, but others require the entire team. (No matter what, good drills don't let groups of players stay inactive for long.) As an additional teaching tool, I've included diagrams to assist coaches and players.

Let's get drilling!

Some drills may target more than one skill and be equally valuable when learning offense and defense, passing and shooting, etc. As a result, some drills have been included in more than one chapter with slight modifications.

KEY TO DIAGRAMS

Path of player	→
Path of ball	----→
Dribble	ᴡᴡᴡᴡ→
Screen	——⊢
Ball	✳
Offensive player	➊ ➋ ➌ ➍ ➎ ⬤
Player with ball	✳➊ ✳➋ ✳➌ ✳➍ ✳➎ ⬤
Defensive player	**X1 X2 X3 X4 X5 X5**
Coach	ℂ
Assistant Coach	𝔸ℂ

Solid black circles represent additional offensive players
X with no numbers are additional defensive players

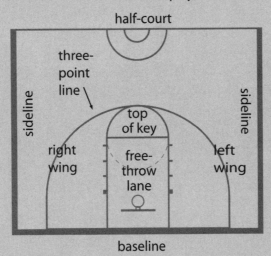

The right and left sides are determined when facing the basket. This may confuse you at first: for instance, the right wing is on the right side of the court but on the left side of the page.

The "elbow" refers to the point where the free-throw line intersects with the line coming from the baseline, also known as the lane line. The right elbow is where the lines meet on the right side of the court (facing the basket) and the left elbow is where they meet on the left side.

Court dimensions:
The court is 50 feet wide and 94 feet long (47 feet to half-court).
The free-throw line is 15 feet from the point directly under the backboard.
The outside of the three-point line is 19 feet 9 inches from the point directly under the rim.

DRILLS SECTION 1
Individual Skills

DRILLS I
Basic Ballhandling Drills

STATIONARY BALLHANDLING

These next drills help players develop a comfortable feel for the ball. They can be used by players waiting their turn while other teammates are shooting or scrimmaging, or included at the beginning of practice as a fun warm-up.

DRILL 1.1 FIGURE 8 DRILL

1. Spread your feet to shoulder-width; bend your knees, and angle slightly forward at the waist
2. Start with the ball in your right hand; position your left hand in back of your body at knee-height, at the midpoint of the distance between your feet
3. Swing the ball through your legs with your right hand; transfer it to your left hand
4. Bring the ball around in front of your left knee; swing it through your legs with your left hand, transfer it to your right hand (positioned in back of your body at knee height)
5. Bring the ball around in front of your right knee; swing it through your legs with your right hand, transfer it to your left hand

- Repeat 10 times
- Repeat again in the reverse direction
- Every ballhandling drill should be executed with your head facing forward, and your eyes up

DRILL 1.2 FIGURE 8 DRILL WITH A DROP IN THE MIDDLE

- This drill is identical to the Figure 8 Drill, except that the player drops or bounces the ball each time she brings it between her legs
- Repeat 10 times as quickly as possible; change directions and repeat
- Keep your eyes up

DRILL 1.3 FIGURE 8 RUN

1. Start in a crouched position with the ball in your right hand
2. Make a long stride with your left leg; drop your left hand down
3. Transfer the ball between your legs into your left hand
4. Make a long stride with your right leg; bring the ball around in front of your left knee
5. Transfer it between your legs to your right hand
6. Make another long stride with your left leg; bring the ball around in front of your right knee
7. Transfer it between your legs to your left hand

• Perform continuously for the length of the court, as quickly as possible

DRILL 1.4 AROUND THE KNEES DRILL

1. Spread your feet several inches apart; bend your knees and angle slightly forward at the waist
2. Start with the ball in your right hand; position your left hand in back of your knees
3. Swing the ball clockwise behind your knees; transfer it to your left hand
4. Bring the ball around in front of your knees; transfer it to your right hand
5. Increase the speed of the ball as much as possible

• Repeat 10 times going clockwise
• Repeat again going counterclockwise

DRILL 1.5 AROUND THE WAIST DRILL

1. Spread your feet to shoulder-width; loosen your knees
2. Start with the ball at waist level, in your right hand
3. Swing the ball clockwise behind your body
4. Bring your left hand in back of your body to meet the ball; transfer the ball from your right hand to your left hand
5. Swing the ball around in front of your body; bring your right hand around to meet it
6. Transfer the ball from your left hand to your right hand
7. Increase the speed of the ball as much as possible

• Repeat 10 times going clockwise
• Repeat again going counterclockwise

DRILL 1.6 BOUNCE AND CATCH DRILL

1. Spread your feet to slightly further than shoulder-width apart
2. Start by holding the ball over your head with both hands
3. Swing the ball down in front of your waist; release it so that it bounces between your legs
4. Quickly bring your arms around in back of your body
5. Catch the ball at waist level as it bounces up behind you

• Repeat 10 times

DRILL 1.7 DROP AND CLAP DRILL

1. Start with your feet together
2. Bend your knees, angle forward at the waist
3. Hold the ball behind your waist with both hands; drop it
4. Bring your hands around in front of your knees; clap once
5. Quickly swing your hands behind your knees in time to catch the ball after one bounce

• Repeat 10 times

DRILL 1.8 FINGERTIP DRILL

1. Spread your feet a few inches apart
2. Start by holding the ball in front of your face with only the fingertips of both hands
3. Tap the ball lightly back and forth between your hands (using only your fingertips)
4. Raise the ball over your head; bring it down to waist level; bring it down to ankle level
5. Continuously tap the ball back and forth as you move it up and down your body

• Repeat the up-and-down motion 10 times

DRILLS 2
Dribbling Drills

STATIONARY DRIBBLING DRILLS

These drills teach players to dribble without looking at the ball (with their heads and eyes up); they also improve players' feel for the ball.

DRILL 2.1 SIT DRIBBLING DRILL

1. Sit on the floor
2. Start by dribbling the ball low, with your right hand
3. Dribble the ball clockwise behind your back, as far over to your left hip as possible
4. Transfer the ball to your left hand; dribble it low, around to the front of your body
5. Transfer the ball to your right hand

• Repeat 10 times going clockwise
• Repeat again going counterclockwise

Variation of the Sit Dribbling drill:
• Start by dribbling the ball low, with your right hand
• Dribble 3 times with each finger on your right hand
• Repeat with your left hand

DRILL 2.2 WALL DRIBBLING DRILL

1. Stand facing the wall about one arm's length away
2. Dribble the ball off the wall with your right hand, just above head level
3. Use only your finger pads, not your palm, to control the ball
4. Keep your elbow at a 90-degree angle
5. After 10 dribbles, extend your elbow slowly up and out. Finish by dribbling off the wall with a completely straight arm
6. Repeat with your left hand

Variation of the Wall Dribbling Drill:
• Use only the index finger and thumb of your hand, then the middle finger, the ring finger, and the little finger

DRILL 2.3 CONTINUOUS CROSSOVER DRIBBLING DRILL

1. Spread your legs to shoulder-width; bend your knees
2. Without watching the ball, perform continuous crossover dribbles in front of your body (staying in the same place)
3. Repeat the dribble behind your body (but don't look back at the ball!)

- Keep the ball below knee level
- Execute 10 repetitions, front and back

Variation of the Continuous Crossover Dribbling Drill:
- Walk down the court performing continuous front-crossover dribbles

CHANGE OF DIRECTION DRIBBLING DRILL

DRILL 2.4 DRIBBLE AROUND THE COACH DRILL

1. Line up in a row at the half-court line, facing one basket; each player has a ball
2. The coach stands at the foul line, facing the players
3. Dribble at the coach; when you reach him, execute the dribbling move that he calls out; for example, crossover, spin, behind-the-back, retreat, or between-the-legs
4. Score a layup

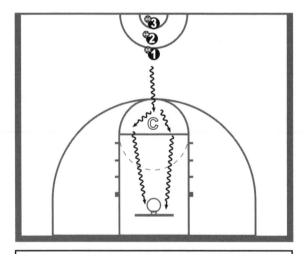

Dribble Around the Coach Drill

FULL COURT DRIBBLING DRILLS

These next drills develop players' ability to dribble on the run and to change directions quickly, their conditioning, and their footwork. Players should not look at the ball while they are dribbling, but instead should see the entire court!

DRILL 2.5 CONE DRIBBLING DRILL

1. Position cones or chairs 10 to 15 feet apart, extending lengthwise down the court
2. Keeping your dribble alive, weave around the cones—the first time down, crossover dribble at each change of direction in order to work both dribbling hands

• Repeat the drill using spin and behind-the-back dribbles to change directions

DRILL 2.6 FULL COURT SPEED DRIBBLING DRILL

1. Dribble with your right hand down the court at a full sprint (using a speed dribble)
2. Make a layup at the far end of the court
3. Speed dribble with your right hand to the other end of the court; make a layup

• Repeat 2 times
• Repeat the drill using the left hand

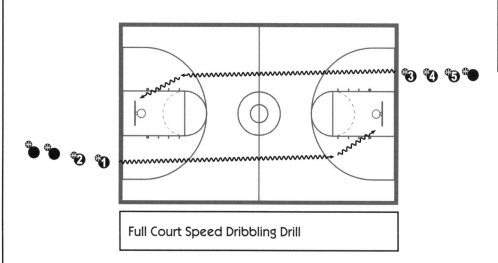

Full Court Speed Dribbling Drill

Variation of the Full Court Speed Dribbling Drill:
- Have each dribbler match up to a defender of comparable speed. Give the dribbler a two step (or more) head start, and have the defender try to catch her and deflect the ball from behind (see Full Court Chase Drill in Drills 11)

DRILL 2.7 FULL COURT CONTROL DRIBBLING DRILL

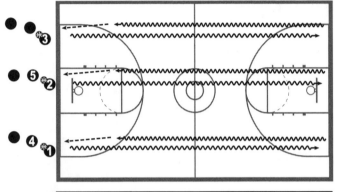

1. Line up along the baseline (2 or 3 players in each line)
2. [Players 1–3] Control dribble the length of court with your right hand, keeping the ball low
3. At the far end of the court, jump stop and pivot 180 degrees; control dribble back down the court with your left hand
4. Jump stop 15 feet from next teammate in line and make a bounce pass to her
5. Return to the end of the line as the drill continues

Full Court Control Dribbling Drill

Variation of the Full Court Control Dribbling Drill:
- Zig-zag down the court, changing dribbling hands with each change of direction

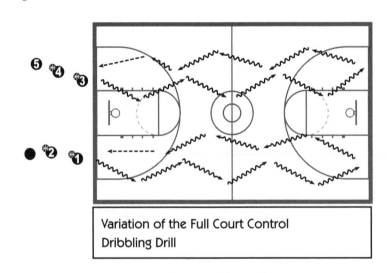

Variation of the Full Court Control Dribbling Drill

DRILL 2.8 FULL COURT VARIETY DRIBBLING DRILL

1. Line up in three or four lines across the baseline
2. [Players 1–3] Control dribble out to the free-throw line with your right hand
3. At the free-throw line, the first "change" point, listen to the coach as he calls out a dribbling move. The move could be a crossover dribble, spin dribble, in-and-out dribble, behind-the-back dribble, or retreat dribble
4. Repeat the dribbling change (as per the coach's instructions) at the half-court line and the far free-throw line
5. At the far end of the court, jump stop and pivot
6. Speed dribble back down the court and pass the ball to the next teammate in line

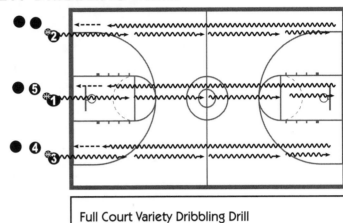

Full Court Variety Dribbling Drill

TWO-BALL DRIBBLING DRILL

This drill helps develop a feel for the ball. (Don't forget to dribble with your head and eyes up!)

DRILL 2.9 TWO-BALL DRIBBLING DRILL

1. Line up as if executing the Full Court Control Dribbling Drill
2. Dribble down the court with two basketballs (one in each hand), bouncing each ball at the same time
3. At the far end of the court, jump stop and pivot
4. Dribble both balls back down the court; pass the balls to the next teammate in line

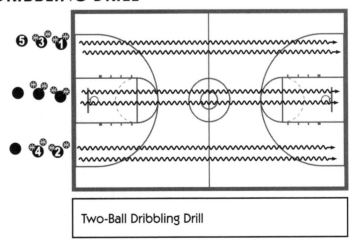

Two-Ball Dribbling Drill

Variation of the Two-Ball Dribbling Drill:

• Use an alternating dribble down the court
• Dribble from sideline to sideline instead of the length of court

TEAM/PARTNER DRIBBLING DRILLS

These drills practice changing directions quickly using different types of dribbles. (Did I remember to mention that it's important to dribble with your head and eyes up?)

DRILL 2.10 PARTNER DRIBBLING DRILL

1. Pair up and spread out down the length of the court; start facing each other about 20 feet apart
2. On the coach's whistle, start dribbling toward one another with the right hand
3. Listen as the coach calls out a dribbling move, like the spin, crossover, between-the-legs, and in-and-out dribbles
4. Execute the move to the left, go past your partner, and continue dribbling to the other side of the court
5. Dribble back toward your partner and execute the move called out by the coach

- Repeat 5 times
- Repeat again starting with the left hand

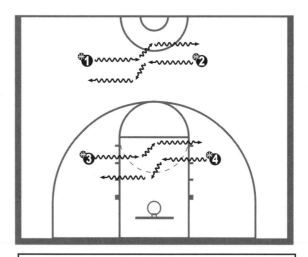

Partner Dribbling Drill

DRILL 2.11 FOUR CORNER DRIBBLING DRILL

1. Line up in the four corners of the half-court
2. [Players 1–4] On the coach's whistle, dribble to the center of half-court
3. Listen as the coach calls out a dribbling move like the spin, crossover, between-the-legs, and in-and-out dribbles
4. After making a dribble, move to the corner diagonal to the starting point

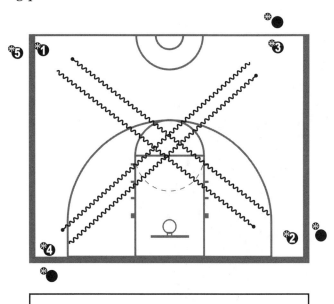

Four Corner Dribbling Drill

Variation of the Four Corner Dribbling Drill

- After a spin dribble, move to the corner to the right or left of the starting point (depending on the direction of the dribble)
- Repeat until each player has executed each move in both directions

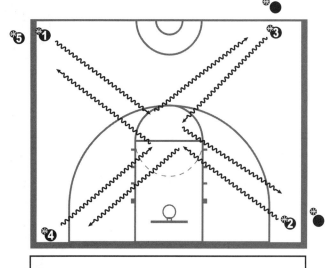

Four Corner Dribbling Drill

DRILLS 3
Footwork, Jumping, and Conditioning Drills

INDIVIDUAL OFFENSIVE MOVES

In these drills players perform stationary fundamental basketball moves with the ball.

DRILL 3.1 TRIPLE-THREAT DRILL

1. Form one line on the right wing (with the coach at the top of the key)
2. [Player 1] Execute a V-cut down to the block and out again
3. Catch the pass from the coach and reverse pivot into triple-threat position
4. After 2 seconds, pass the ball back to the coach and go to the end of the line

Variation of the Triple-Threat Drill:
- After pivoting into triple-threat position, execute a jab-step or rocker step
- Drive to the basket for layup or a pull-up jump shot

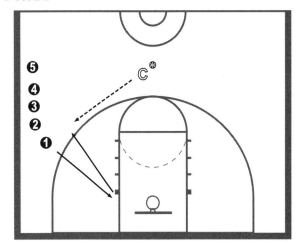

Triple-Threat Drill

DRILL 3.2 JAB STEP DRILL

1. Form one line at the top of the key; the first player out is defense, the second player offense with a ball
2. [Player 1] Execute a jab step into the defender
3. Read the defense, and drive to the basket for a layup or pull-up for a short jump shot
4. The second time through the line, execute a jab step/pullback or a jab step/crossover; drive to the basket

Variation of the Jab Step Drill:
- Instead of driving to the basket, pull back and shoot a long jump shoot after the jab step

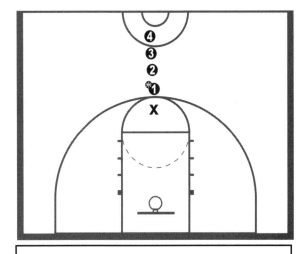

Jab Step Drill

PIVOTING

These drills develop proper pivoting mechanics. Pivoting is one of the most important fundamentals to learn; time teaching it is time well spent!

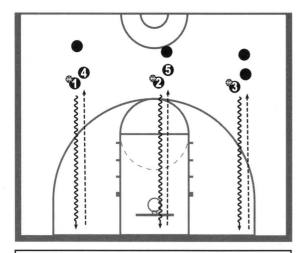

Pivoting Drill

DRILL 3.3 PIVOTING DRILL

1. Form three or four lines across the court, even with the top of the key and facing the basket; the first player in each line has a ball
2. [Players 1–3] Control dribble to the baseline; stop
3. Front pivot, and pass to the next players in line

Variation of the Pivoting Drill:
- Use a reverse pivot instead of a front pivot

DRILL 3.4 DOUBLE-TEAM AND PIVOT DRILL

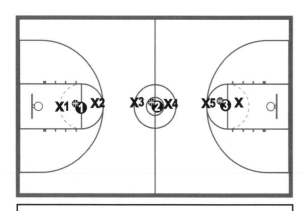

Double Team and Pivot Drill

1. Divide up into teams of three, one offensive player and two defenders
2. Spread out around the entire court
3. [Offensive players with basketballs] Use pivots to keep the ball away from the two attacking defenders; try to keep your body between the defenders and the ball
4. [Two defenders] Try to tip the ball away from the offensive player

- After 15 seconds, rotate positions: one defender goes to offense, and the offensive player goes to defense
- After 15 seconds, rotate again and repeat

JUMP STOPPING

This drill develops the ability to come to a balanced and controlled stop, without traveling, and to establish a pivot foot. Many post players use the jump stop to great effect.

DRILL 3.5 JUMP STOP DRILL

1. Form several lines along the baseline, 2–3 players in each line
2. On the coach's whistle, sprint down the court
3. When the coach calls "stop," jump stop immediately
4. When the coach calls "go," resume the sprint

Variation of the Jump Stop Drill:
• Give each player a ball; jump stop off the dribble

FOOTWORK DRILLS

DRILL 3.6 PERIMETER RUNNING DRILL

1. Line up in single file on the sideline
2. On the coach's whistle, start an easy jog around the perimeter of the court
3. Listen as the coach calls out agility/footwork moves, which can include:
   a. jump stop
   b. stride stop
   c. front pivot (after a jump stop)
   d. reverse pivot (after a jump stop)
   e. jab step (after a jump stop)
   f. crossover step
   g. spin move

4. After executing each move, continue jogging until the next call

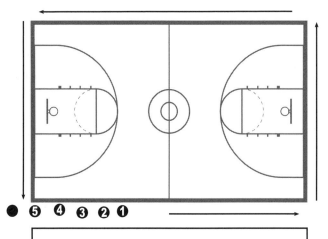

Perimeter Running Drill

LOW POST FOOTWORK

DRILL 3.7 LOW POST FOOTWORK DRILL

1. Form two lines, one behind the right block and one behind the left
2. One offensive post player from each line steps out; each player has a ball facing away from the basket
3. [Right post] Execute an up-and-under (crossover) to the baseline by pivoting on your right foot: face the basket, step through with your left foot to the basket, and shoot a right-handed layup (without a dribble)
4. [Left post] Pivot on your left foot: face the basket, step through with your right foot to the basket, and shoot a left-handed layup (without a dribble)
5. [Right post] Execute up-and-under (crossover) to the middle by pivoting on your left foot: face the basket, step through with your right foot into the lane and shoot a left-handed baby hook shot (without a dribble)
6. [Left post] Pivot on your right foot: face the basket, step through with your left foot into the lane and shoot a right-handed baby hook shot (without a dribble)

- Execute the following low post moves with drop step, face-up with a pump fake and shot, crossover step without a dribble (described above), crossover step with a dribble to the middle of the lane, power dribble to the basket and layup. Repeat until each player has executed each move from the right and left blocks.

Variation of the Low Post Footwork Drill:
- Add a wing player on each side of the court to make a bounce pass into the low post
- Add a defender
- As a warmup, execute all the moves without a ball

SPEED AND CONDITIONING

DRILL 3.8 SUICIDE DRILL

1. Spread out along the baseline
2. On the coach's whistle, sprint to the opposite baseline and back
3. On the second whistle, sprint to the opposite foul line, and back, then to the opposite baseline, and back
4. On the third whistle, sprint to the half-court line and back, opposite foul line and back, then to the opposite baseline and back
5. On the fourth whistle, run a full suicide: foul line and back, half-court line and back, opposite foul line and back, opposite baseline and back

- At every turn, players should plant one foot, pivot, and explode back in the opposite direction
- Players should be timed on the full suicide

Variation of the Suicide Drill:
- Have players dribble a ball as they run
- Run sprints relay-style in miniteams

JUMP ROPE

DRILL 3.9 JUMP ROPE DRILL

1. Line up extending down the court; each player has a jump rope
2. On the coach's whistle, jump rope with both feet
3. On the next whistle, switch to jumping on the right foot
4. On the next whistle, switch to jumping on the left foot
5. On the next whistle, speed jump with both feet

- Coaches can allot anywhere from 30 seconds to 2 minutes between whistles

Variation of the Jump Rope Drill:
- Incorporate double-jumps (on every jump, players swing the rope twice around them)
- Incorporate boxer-jumps (quick changes between the right and left feet)
- Count the number of jumps in 30 seconds

AGILITY EXERCISES

DRILL 3.10 LEG BOUNDS

1. Spread out along the baseline
2. Stand at the end line with your legs together, your arms tucked into your sides, and your knees bent. Jump out, as far and as high as possible, thrusting your arms up and extending your body
3. Land in the same crouched position; take off again immediately
4. Continue jumping until you reach the far baseline
5. Jump back to the opposite baseline

DRILL 3.11 SQUAT JUMPS

1. Stand with your feet shoulder-width apart; put your hands behind your head and lace your fingers together
2. Squat down and quickly explode up; jump as high as possible
3. Land, squat, and jump again

• Count the number of jumps in 30 seconds

DRILL 3.12 STRING JUMPING DRILL

1. Tie a string between the legs of two chairs (or coaches can hold the string), about 4 feet apart (the string should be 12 to 18 inches off the floor)
2. Stand to one side of the string; put your feet together, your arms to your sides
3. Squat down and then explode up and over the string, using your legs and arms for power
4. Land and quickly jump back over to the other side

• Perform continuously for 1 minute

DRILL 3.13 CONE JUMPING DRILL

1. Line up 6-inch cones extending down the court (one for each player)
2. [Players] Stand to the right of your cone
3. On the coach's whistle, jump with both feet together over your cone; immediately back jump over again

- Jump continuously for 30 seconds; rest and repeat again
- Repeat jumping forward and backward over the cone (instead of left and right)

Variation of the Cone Jumping Drill:
- Extend a line of cones down one sideline; have the players jump continuously over each cone until they reach the end of the cone line

DRILL 3.14 SIDELINE JUMPING DRILL

1. Line up along one sideline, standing with both feet together to the right of the line
2. On the coach's whistle, jump quickly over the line; land with your feet together. Immediately jump back over the line.

- Repeat continuously for 30 seconds; rest and repeat again
- Repeat jumping forward and backward over the line (instead of right and left)

Variation of the Sideline Jumping Drill:
- Jump side-to-side traveling down the sideline; jump continuously from one end of the court to the other

DRILL 3.15 WALL TAPS DRILL

1. Stand in front of a wall
2. Jump up as high as you can; tap the wall with both hands

- Repeat continuously for 30 seconds

Variation of the Wall Taps Drill:
- Stand below the basket; jump up and tap the backboard (or net)

DRILLS 4
Passing and Catching Drills

BASIC PASSING DRILLS

These drills develop good passing and catching fundamentals.

DRILL 4.1 WALL PASSING DRILL

1. Stand about six feet from the wall
2. Make 20 chest passes to a spot level with your chest; concentrate on snapping your wrists and holding your follow-through
3. Step back two feet and make 20 more chest passes

• Repeat using bounce passes

Variation of the Wall Passing Drill:
• See how many chest or bounce passes players can make in 30 seconds

DRILL 4.2 MAN IN THE MIDDLE DRILL

1. Split up into groups of three, each group with a ball; spread out around the court
2. Two players start facing each other, no more than 15 feet apart; one player starts in the middle facing the ball
3. [Outside players] Pass the ball back and forth; pivot; use chest passes and bounce passes; use fakes to draw the defender away from the direction that you intend to pass. Try not to lob pass over the head of the inside player!
4. [Inside player, or "man"] Try to deflect the ball; when you do, take that passer's place on the outside

• The "man" must play the ball tightly on defense. If she sits back, the offensive player could hold the ball forever! The object is to force the outside players to fake and pivot.

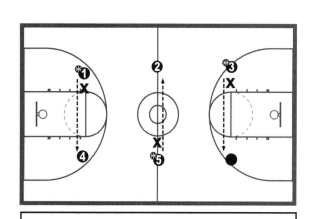

Man in the Middle Drill

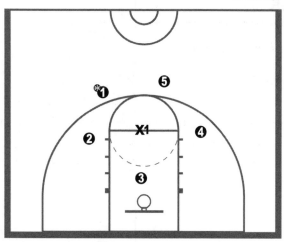

Bull in the Ring Drill

DRILL 4.3 BULL IN THE RING DRILL

1. Form a circle of five or six players, several feet apart
2. Put one defensive player in the middle of the circle
3. [Players 1–5] Pass the ball to your teammates without allowing the defender to get a touch; you may not pass to a teammate standing directly on either side of you
4. The passer whose ball is deflected becomes the defender

- Passers should fake and pivot, but not dribble or pass over the head of the defender.

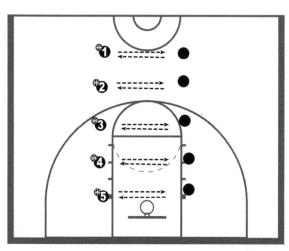

Partner Passing Drill

DRILL 4.4 PARTNER PASSING DRILL

1. Pair up; line up along either side of the lane, extending out toward the half-court
2. Practice passing back and forth: use chest passes, bounce passes, overhead passes, and one-handed passes
3. [Passers] Keep both eyes on the target; call out the name of your partner; step in the direction of every pass
4. [Players receiving pass] Provide a target with both palms facing the ball; point your fingers to the ceiling; call for the ball
5. [Passers] Hold your follow-through until the ball reaches the target

- Practice both left-handed and right-handed passes.
- Emphasize talking! Call out the receiver's name on every pass.

Variation of the Partner Passing Drill
- See Drill 4.10 for Full Court Partner Passing Drill

HALF-COURT PASSING DRILLS

These drills develop good passing and catching form for players in motion.

DRILL 4.5 MEET THE PASS DRILL

1. Form two lines approximately 25 feet apart, facing each other
2. [Player 1] Pass to player 2
3. [Player 2] Pass to player 3
4. [Player 3] Pass to player 4, etc.
5. After making a pass, run to the left and go to the end of the opposite line

- Don't slow down or flinch when catching a pass
- Passers call out the receivers' names; receivers run forward to meet each pass
- Receivers should provide targets with their fingers pointing to ceiling and their palms facing the ball
- Each player should make a chest pass, then bounce pass, then flip pass handoff

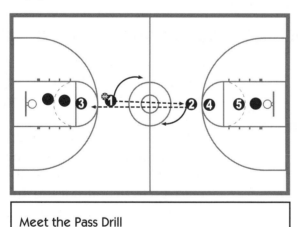

Meet the Pass Drill

- You can also run this drill diagonally in the half-court—it can be good warmup for practice or a game
- Emphasize talking!

DRILL 4.6 SPEED PASSING DRILL

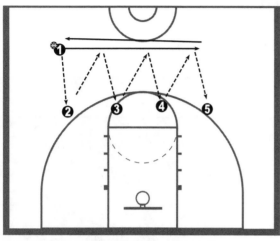

Speed Passing Drill

1. Spread out into lines extending across the court; the first player in each line has a ball
2. [Player 1] Step out and face your teammates; pass the ball to player 2 in line; defensive slide toward the end of the line
3. [Player 2] Quickly pass the ball back to player 1
4. [Player 1] Pass the ball to player 3; defensive slide down the line
5. [Player 3] Quickly pass back to player 1, etc.
6. Once the first player reaches the end of the line, she should slide-and-pass back up the line to her original position

- Use chest passes, bounce passes, and overhead passes
- Call out the name of the player on every pass to emphasize talking

Variation of the Speed Passing Drill:
- Use two basketballs

DRILL 4.7 FOUR CORNER PASSING DRILL

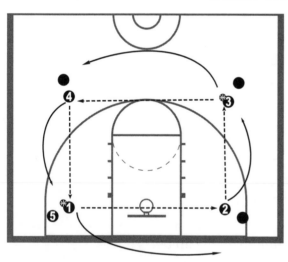

Four Corner Passing Drill

1. Form four lines in a square formation around the key; both the right baseline corner line and the left wing corner line have a ball
2. [Player 1] Pass to player 2; follow your pass, go to the end of the line
3. [Player 3] Pass to player 4; follow your pass, go to the end of the line
4. [Player 2] Pass to the next player in the next line; follow your pass, go to the end of the line
5. [Player 4] Pass to the next player in the next line; follow your pass, go to the end of the line, etc.

- After one minute of continuous passing, switch directions

DRILL 4.8 FLASH PASSING DRILL

1. Form one line to the right of the basket on the block; position one player at the left block
2. One coach stands at the top of the key; another stands on the left wing
3. The coach at the top of the key passes to the coach at the wing
4. [Player 2] Make a flash cut to the high post
5. [Player 1] Cut out to the short corner
6. The coach can pass to either the high post or the corner
7. [Player 2] If the ball comes to you, catch the pass, square, and immediately make a bounce pass to player 1 cutting to the basket for a layup
8. [Player 1] If the ball comes to you, catch the pass, square, and immediately make a bounce pass to player 2 cutting down the lane to the basket

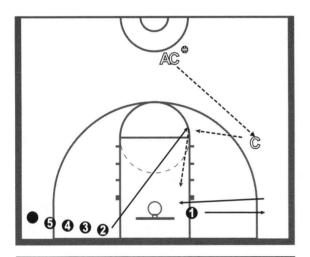

Flash Passing Drill, Part 1

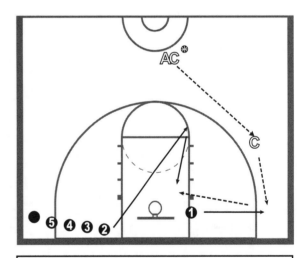

Flash Passing Drill, Part 2

DRILL 4.9 KENTUCKY PASSING DRILL

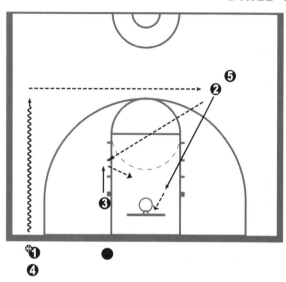

Kentucky Passing Drill

1. Form three lines: one at the right baseline corner, one to the left of the top of the key, and one at the right block
2. [Player 1] Dribble hard up the sideline; jump stop, pivot, and pass to player 2
3. [Player 2] Step forward to meet the ball; pass to player 3; make a hard cut down the lane to the basket
4. [Player 3] Step up to catch the pass; pivot, square, and throw a lead bounce pass to player 2 for a layup
5. [Player 3] Rebound the shot; dribble over to the baseline; go to the end of the line
6. Repeat

- Every player should be square to her target before passing the ball
- After one series, switch sides of the court

FULL COURT PASSING DRILLS

These drills improve passing skills on the sprint, as well as overall conditioning.

DRILL 4.10 FULL COURT PARTNER PASSING DRILL

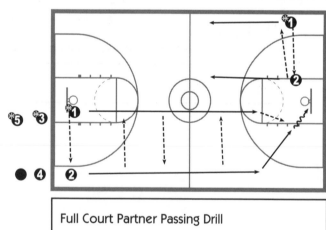

Full Court Partner Passing Drill

1. Form two lines on the right side of the baseline; the first players in each line are partners
2. Sprint down the court, passing the ball back and forth; call out the name of your partner on each pass
3. [Inside player] Keep the ball as you near the opposite foul line (use a dribble, if you have to); jump stop at the foul line
4. [Outside player] At the foul line extended, make a hard diagonal cut to the basket; catch the bounce pass from your partner and shoot a layup
5. Return down the other side of the court (the player that was on the inside now runs the outside lane)

6. Repeat starting on left side of the court (shooting left-hand layups)

- Call your partner's name on every pass.

Variation of the Full Court Partner Passing Drill:
- Use heavy or extra large basketballs to work on arm strength (without a bounce pass or a shot)
- Instead of sprinting down the court, defensive slide

DRILL 4.11 SIDE-CENTER-SIDE DRILL

1. Form three lines on the baseline; players in the right line stay in the right lane of the court; the center line stays in the center lane; the left line stays in the left lane
2. The ball starts in the center lane
3. [Players 1, 2, and 3] Sprint down the court
4. [Player 1] Pass to one wing (in this diagram, player 3)
5. [Player 3] Pass back to player 1
6. [Player 1] Pass to player 2
7. [Player 2] Pass back to player 1
8. Repeat the length of the court

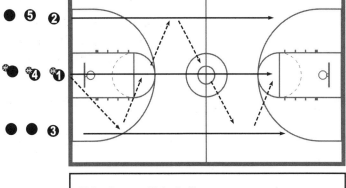

Side-Center-Side Drill

- The entire drill should be run at sprint speed; every pass should be a lead pass
- The first time through, use chest passes. Run the drill back down the court using bounce passes

DRILL 4.12 FULL COURT WEAVE DRILL

1. Form three lines on the baseline; the players in the center line have basektballs
2. [Player 1] Pass to player 3; run behind her and fill the outside lane
3. [Player 3] Pass to player 2; run behind her and fill the outside lane
4. [Player 2] Pass to player 1; run behind her and fill the outside lane
5. [Player 1] Throw a lead pass to player 3
6. [Player 3] Catch the ball and score a layup

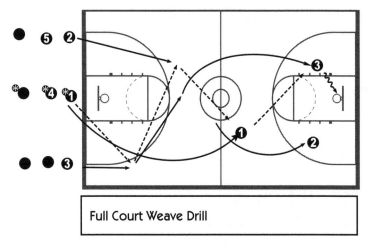

Full Court Weave Drill

- As soon as the first three players are past the half-court, the next three players start

Variation of the Full Court Weave Drill:
- Specify the maximum number of passes allowed before the layup (between four and six)
- Run weave with four or five players instead of three

DRILL 4.13 FULL COURT OLYMPIC DRILL

1. Form three lines on one baseline: only one player in the middle line, 2 players in the left and right lines; the middle player, and the second player in each of the wing lines have basketballs

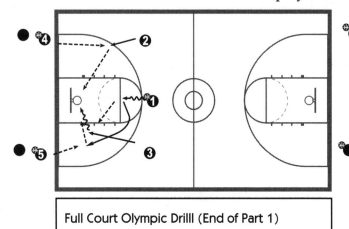

Full Court Olympic Drilll (End of Part 1)

2. Form two lines on the opposite baseline (2 players each); first two players have basketballs
3. [Players 1–3] Weave down the court; shoot a layup
4. [Two nonshooters, in this diagram, players 1 and 2] Pull up within your range; catch passes from players 4 and 5 and shoot jump shots; rebound the balls and dribble to the baseline; join the two baseline lines
5. [Players 4 and 5] After passing, run out onto court and call for the ball as outlets; weave back down the court with the layup shooter (in this diagram, player 3)

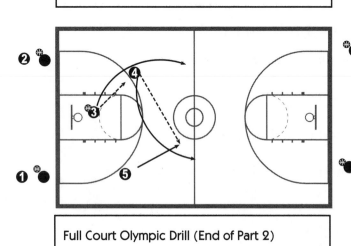

Full Court Olympic Drill (End of Part 2)

- After weaving down the court, either player 3, 4, or 5 will shoot a layup. The three nonshooters pull up for jump shots (receiving passes from the two baseline players, who then become outlets). The layup shooter rebounds her own shot and weaves back down the court with the two outlets.

- Run the drill continuously for 3 to 6 minutes
- Call for the ball before catching a pass
- See the Half-Court Olympic Drill 5.23

FAST-BREAK PASSING

DRILL 4.14 TRAILER WEAVE DRILL

1. Form four lines on the baseline; designate one of the outside lines as the "trailer" line (in this diagram, player 4's line); the ball starts two lines away from the trailer
2. [Player 4] Sprint down the court; when you reach the top of the key in the front court, make a diagonal cut toward the basket
3. [Players 1–3] Weave down the court; after a maximum of three passes, throw a lead pass to the trailer for a layup; rebound the basketball
4. [Player 4] After you shoot, sprint down the opposite side of the court; cut to the basket at the far top of the key
5. [Players 1–3] Weave back down the court; after a maximum of three passes, make a lead pass to the trailer for a layup

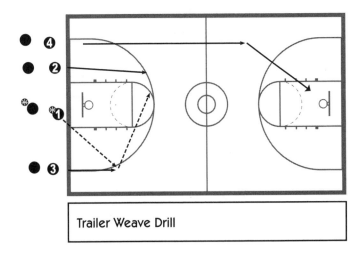

Trailer Weave Drill

- The ball may not touch the floor at any point

GETTING OPEN

The next drills emphasize the importance of getting open, calling for the ball and stepping to the pass. They help break the habit of excessive dribbling, and are also useful for learning how to beat a zone press.

DRILL 4.15 DEAD BALL DRILL

1. Play game of two-on-two, three-on-three or four-on-four with no dribbling allowed

DRILL 4.16 PRESSURE PASSING DRILL

1. Form three lines along the baseline (the first three players in each line constitute one team)
2. The first team out is defense, the second team offense
3. Each offensive player must stay in her lane (right, center, or left) and is allowed a maximum of two dribbles
4. [Player 1] Take two hard dribbles up the court; use pivots to keep the ball away from defender 1 once you pick up your dribble
5. [Players 2 and 3] Sprint up the court; when player 1 picks up her dribble, V-cut back hard to the ball with your hands up (but stay in your lane)
6. [Defenders 2 and 3] Play hard deny defense; try to prevent your player from catching the ball
7. [Player 1] Pass to the open player

• Continue until the offense makes it to the other end of the court

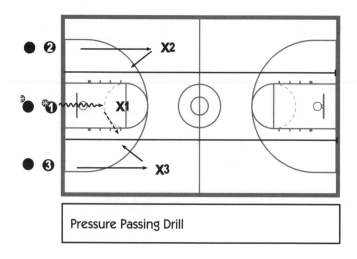

Pressure Passing Drill

DRILLS 5
Shooting Drills

STATIONARY SHOOTING DRILLS

These shooting drills force players to concentrate on proper shooting form, the key building block of a consistent shot. They are ideal warmup drills.

DRILL 5.1 WRIST SNAP DRILL

1. Start with both arms by your side
2. On the coach's whistle, lift your arms into a mock shooting position
3. On the second whistle, quickly extend your shooting arm so that your elbow is completely locked; keep your wrist flexed and cocked
4. On the third whistle, snap your wrist forward, keeping your fingers loose (at the end of your motion, your fingers should be pointed to the floor)

DRILL 5.2 PERFECT SHOOTING FORM DRILL

1. Hold the ball in your strong hand with your nonshooting hand resting on the side of the ball; support it with your finger pads, not your palms
2. Bend your elbows and cock your shooting wrist; bring the ball into proper shooting position (below chin level, just to the side of your face)
3. Snap your shooting arm and your wrist so the ball goes straight up into the air
4. Hold your follow-through while the ball is in the air
5. Catch the ball with only your shooting hand; bring it down into shooting position

- Grip the ball properly (the fingers of the shooting hand should be across the seams; nonshooting hand should rest on the side of the ball)
- Watch the seams to ensure that the ball has proper backspin; make sure that the path of the ball is straight up and down
- Keep your shooting elbow in
- Release the ball with with the "shooting fork"

Variation of the Perfect Shooting Form Drill:
- Use perfect shooting form to "shoot" to a teammate approximately 10 feet away

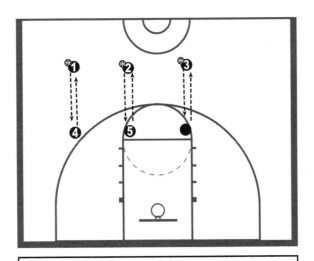

Variation of the Perfect Shooting Form Drill

DRILL 5.3 LIE DOWN AND SHOOT DRILL

1. Lie down on the floor with a ball
2. Repeat the Perfect Shooting Form Drill while lying on the floor (make sure that the ball goes straight up!)

• Focus on snapping your wrist, releasing with the "shooting fork," and creating proper backspin

DRILL 5.4 MARYMOUNT CHAIR SHOOTING DRILL

1. Set up rows of folding chairs—one chair for each player
2. Sit on the edge of the chair, keeping your back straight and your feet on the floor (toes directly below your knees), pointed forward
3. Position the ball in your shooting hand: your fingers should be perpendicular to the seams, and your wrist cocked so that your fingers are pointed toward the ceiling
4. Rest your shooting forearm lightly on your thigh so that the ball is directly over your knee
5. Stand up from the chair by pushing off the ground with your feet and legs; keep your head in the middle of your stance and be sure not to lean too far forward
6. As you stand up, raise your arms and the ball; when you are halfway out of your squat, your upper arm should be parallel to the floor (forearm perpendicular) and your wrist should be completely cocked; as you straighten your legs, your elbow and wrist should snap forward in an "up and out" shooting motion

7. Snap your wrist and fingers through the seams using the "shooting fork," and the ball will travel straight up in the air
8. When you release the ball, your shooting elbow should be level with your forehead; your nonshooting hand should be frozen in front and to the side of the head with your fingers pointing to the ceiling
9. Hold your follow-through as the ball is in the air; catch the ball and bring it immediately back into the shooting position
10. Slowly sit back down on the edge of the chair, reversing the shooting motion; when you make contact with the chair, your shooting forearm should be resting lightly on your thigh

- Repeat 20 times; switch hands and repeat
- If chairs are not available, then squat into low position

FUNDAMENTAL SHOOTING DRILLS

These next drills involve shooting at the basket from close range. They should be included at the beginning of every practice.

DRILL 5.5 MIKAN DRILL

1. Start by standing just to the right of the basket, with a ball
2. Make a layup (or baby-hook shot) with your right hand; rebound the ball before it hits the floor
3. Step across the basket; plant your right foot and drive your left knee up

4. Shoot a layup (or baby-hook shot) with your left hand; rebound the ball before it hits the floor
5. Step across the basket; plant your left foot and drive your right knee up
6. Shoot a layup (or baby-hook shot) with your right hand; rebound the ball before it hits the floor

- Repeat continuously for 30 seconds
- Players waiting to shoot should execute individual dribbling and ballhandling drills

Mikan Drill

DRILL 5.6 2-4-6-8 DRILL

1. Start by standing directly in front of the basket, two feet away
2. Hold the ball in your shooting hand; bring it into proper shooting position
3. Shoot the ball one-handed, using perfect form (the nonshooting hand should be at your side or behind your back)
4. After two shots from two feet, step back to four feet and shoot, then to six feet, and finally to eight feet; shoot every shot one-handed
5. Try to make every shot a "swish"

- Grip the ball properly and release with the shooting fork
- Hold your follow-through
- Make sure the ball has proper backspin

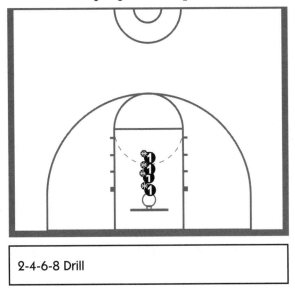

2-4-6-8 Drill

DRILL 5.7 SWISH DRILL

1. Split up into pairs, each pair at a basket; one player is the shooter, the other player the rebounder
2. [Shooter] Start at the right baseline, three feet from the basket; shoot the ball until it goes through the hoop without touching the rim
3. Step back one step; repeat
4. Step back another step; repeat
5. After making three "swishes," move outside of the right block; repeat the three-step process
6. Repeat from inside the foul line, outside the left block, and the left baseline
7. [Rebounder] Make crisp passes to the shooter

LAYUP DRILLS

These next drills develop proper layup form by teaching players to take big steps, jump high and to not shoot too far underneath the basket).

DRILL 5.8 ELBOW LAYUP DRILL

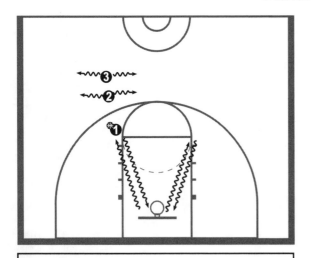

1. Start at the right elbow
2. Dribble toward the basket with your right hand; make a right-handed layup
3. Rebound ball before its hits the floor; dribble with your right hand to the left elbow
4. Pivot; dribble toward the basket with your left hand; make a left-handed layup
5. Rebound the ball before it hits the floor; dribble to the right elbow with your left hand

• Repeat the drill continuously for 30 seconds (each player counts the number of baskets that she makes)
• Players waiting to shoot should execute individual dribbling and ballhandling drills

Elbow Layup Drill

DRILL 5.9 HALF-COURT LAYUP DRILLS

1. Form two lines above the top of the key, one on the right side and one on the left side; two players are on the right wing; first player on right side and first player on wing have basketballs
2. [Player 1] Dribble hard to the basket; shoot a right-handed layup; jog to the end of the left line
3. [First player in left line] Sprint to the basket; rebound the ball
4. Dribble out along the baseline; make a crisp pass to wing, player 4; jog to the end of that line
5. [Player 2] As soon as the first player shoots, drive hard to the basket, receive a bounce pass from wing, player 5, and shoot a right-handed layup
6. [Player 5] Make bounce pass to player 2 and go to end of right line

7. [Player 4] Receive pass from rebounder; pass to player 3 cutting to basket
8. [Player 3] As soon as player 2 shoots, drive hard to the basket, receive a bounce pass from player 4, and shoot a right-handed layup

- Repeat continuously for 2 minutes
- Next time, have cutters in the right line stop at the elbow and shoot jump shots
- This can be a great warmup drill at the beginning of practices or before games

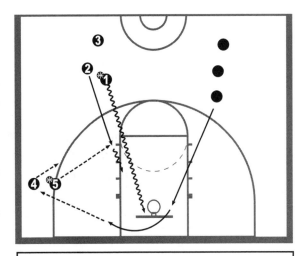

Half-Court Layup Drill

Variation 1: Half-Court Layup Drill:
- Form two lines at half-court, one to the right and one to the left of the top of the key; two balls start on the right side
- [Player 1] Dribble hard to the basket; shoot a right-handed layup; jog to the end of the left line
- [Player 4] Sprint to the basket; rebound the ball
- Dribble out along the baseline; make a crisp pass to the next player in the right line; jog to the end of that line
- [Player 2] As soon as the first player shoots, dribble hard to the basket and shoot a right-handed layup
- [Player 5] Rebound the ball

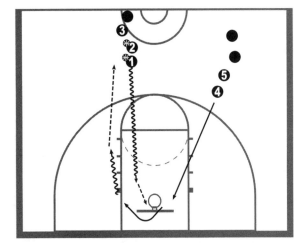

Half-Court Layup Drill Variation 1

- Repeat until every player has shot; switch sides of the court (shoot left-handed layups)
- Practice some layups starting from the center of the court (since many fast break layups in a game don't come from a side angle)

Variation 2: Half-Court Layup Drill:
- Player 1 passes to player 4 and cuts to the basket; player 4 makes a lead pass back to her for a layup and then rebounds the shot

Variation 3: Baseline Layup Drill
- Form two lines at the baseline, one in the right corner and one in the left corner; two balls start on the left side
- [Player 1] Dribble hard to the basket; shoot a right-handed layup; jog to the end of the other line
- [Player 4] Rebound and pass to player 2
- Repeat continuously; switch sides of the court

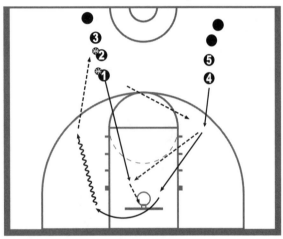

Half-Court Layup Drill Variation 2

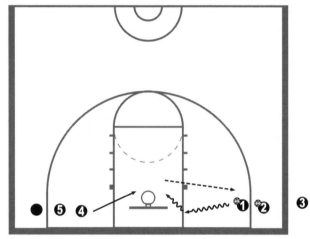

Baseline Layup Drill Variation 3

DRILL 5.10 FOUR-BALL LAYUP DRILL

1. Form two lines above the top of the key, one on the left side and one on the right side, both facing one basket
2. The first two players in each line have basketballs
3. [First players in right line] Drive to the basket; shoot a right-handed layup; grab your own rebound; pass to the third player in the opposite line
4. [First player in left line] Drive to the basket; shoot a left-handed layup; grab your own rebound; pass to the next player in the opposite line
5. [Second player in right line] Drive to the basket, etc.

- Run continuously
- A player should not begin her drive until the player on the other side is shooting her layup

FULL COURT LAYUPS

DRILL 5.11 FULL COURT TWO-MINUTE LAYUP DRILL

1. Form two even lines at either end of the court, to the right of the basket
2. Two coaches line up just above the top of each key; each coach faces a baseline
3. Pass the ball to the coach on your side of the court; sprint by him and catch a flip pass
4. Speed dribble down the court and score a layup

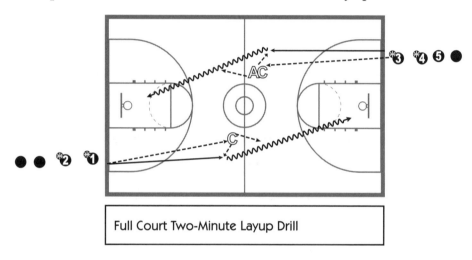

Full Court Two-Minute Layup Drill

- Make as many layups as possible in a 2-minute interval
- After 2 minutes, repeat starting on the left side of the court

Variation of the Full Court Two-Minute Layup Drill:
- Make the two lines into teams and have them compete to see who makes the most layups

DRILL 5.12 HALF-COURT/FULL COURT LAYUP DRILL

1. Form two lines near the top of the key, one on the left side and one on the right; the coach with a basketball should be near half-court
2. Two balls start in the right wing line
3. [Player 1] Pass to player 2; make a hard diagonal cut to the basket

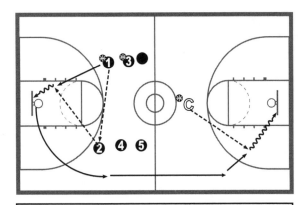

Half-Court/Full Court Layup Drill

4. [Player 2] Make a lead bounce pass to player 1 for a layup; follow the shot and rebound the basketball; make an outlet pass to player 3
5. [Player 1] After the layup, sprint out to the opposite sideline and down to the far end of the court; catch a lead pass from the coach and score another layup
6. After making the second layup, pass the ball to the coach

• Repeat continuously for 3 minutes

TEAM SHOOTING DRILLS

In these drills, players take longer range shots at game speed.

DRILL 5.13 TWO PLAYER ELBOW-TO-ELBOW DRILL

1. One offensive player lines up on one elbow, as a shooter with a ball; another player stands in front of the basket, as a rebounder
2. [Shooter] Shoot the ball; hold your follow-through and then cut to the opposite elbow
3. [Rebounder] Rebound the ball before it hits the floor; pass it quickly back to the shooter
4. [Shooter] Shoot again; cut to the opposite elbow

• Shoot a total of ten shots
• Switch shooter and rebounder
• The rebounder should work on rebounding stance, timing, and catching ball at the top of her jump

Variation of the Two Player Elbow-to-Elbow Drill:
• Move out to three-point range
• Change shooting locations (move away from the elbow)

DRILL 5.14 THREE PLAYER ELBOW-TO-ELBOW DRILL

1. Divide into groups of three, each group at a basket
2. Form a triangle: right elbow, left elbow, and in front of the basket
3. Two players have basketballs (one of the shooters and the rebounder)
4. [Player 1] Shoot from the right elbow; follow your shot
5. [Player 3] Pass to player 2 at the left elbow (and move to right elbow)
6. [Player 2] Shoot, follow your shot
7. [Player 1] After you get the rebound, pass the ball to the player 3, now relocated at the right elbow; spot up at the left elbow
8. [Player 2] After you get the rebound, pass the ball to player 1 at left elbow
9. [Player 3] After your shot, rebound and pass to player 2, etc.

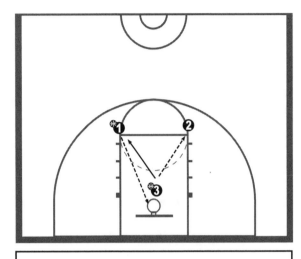

Three-Player Elbow-to-Elbow Drill

- Repeat continuously

Variation of the Three-Player Elbow-to-Elbow Drill:
- Move out to three-point range
- Shoot bank shots from right and left wings
- Have teams of three keep track of the number of shots they make

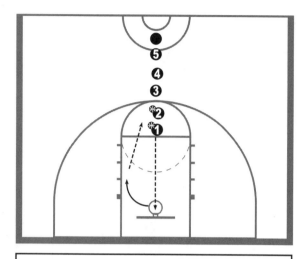

One-Line Rapid Fire Shooting Drill

DRILL 5.15 ONE-LINE RAPID FIRE SHOOTING DRILL

1. Form one line starting at the foul line, facing the basket (first 2 players in line have basketballs); put 2 minutes on the clock
2. [Player 1] Shoot the ball; rebound your own shot
3. [Player 1] Pass the ball to player 3; go to the end of the line
4. [Player 2] Shoot the ball; rebound your own shot
5. [Player 2] Pass the ball to player 4; go to the end of the line
6. [Player 3] Shoot the ball, etc.

- Count the number of made shots in 1 minute
- This drill works on a range of shots: it can be run at the foul line or beyond the three-point line; a team can also shoot bank shots from the right and left wings

DRILL 5.16 TWO-LINE RAPID FIRE SHOOTING DRILL

1. Form two lines, one at each elbow (or any two analogous points on the court); have two teams compete to see how many shots they can make in 1 minute, or to see which team can make 20 shots first

DRILL 5.17 AROUND THE WORLD DRILL

1. Pair up; spread out to every available basket (one player is the shooter, one the rebounder)
2. [Shooter] Shoot five shots from the right baseline, right wing, top of the key, left wing, and left baseline (25 total)
3. [Rebounder] Rebound the shots quickly; make crisp passes back to the shooter
4. [Shooter] Keep your feet moving; step into every pass; jump high on every shot; release the ball as quickly as possible

- Players should shoot some shots off the dribble
- The rebounder should work on rebounding stance, anticipation, timing, catching the ball at the top of her jump, and making a quick pass after the rebound

DRILL 5.18 HOT SHOTS DRILL

1. Start at the foul line (after the first shot, you can move anywhere on the court)
2. Shoot continuously for 60 seconds; get your own rebound after each shot and dribble to any spot on the floor

- Players are awarded ten points for made shots from the top of the key, five points for shots made from the foul line, two points for shots outside the lane and one point for layups
- Make it a contest to see which player can score the most points in a minute

DRILL 5.19 ONE-MAN SHOOT AND FOLLOW DRILL

1. Spread out around the baskets (each player with a ball)
2. Bounce the ball to yourself (using backspin), as if mimicking a pass; catch the ball and pivot toward the basket
3. Shoot or drive to the hoop; get your own rebound
4. Make three shots from any three spots on the floor and then relocate

- Repeat for 3 minutes
- Work on making quick pivots; use pump fakes
- Shoot bank shots from the right and left wings

DRILL 5.20 ONE-SPOT DRILL

1. Divide into groups of three, two basketballs per group; one player is the shooter, one player the rebounder, and one player the passer
2. [Player 1] Shoot continuously from one spot for 1 minute; step into every shot
3. [Player 3] Make crisp passes to player 1, the shooter; pass to her outside hand (away from imaginary defender)
4. [Player 2] Try to rebound every ball before it hits the ground; make accurate passes to player 3, the passer

- After 1 minute, switch positions: shooter goes to rebounder, rebounder goes to passer, passer goes to shooter
- Move out to three-point range and repeat
- The shooter can dribble one or two times before shooting to practice under game conditions

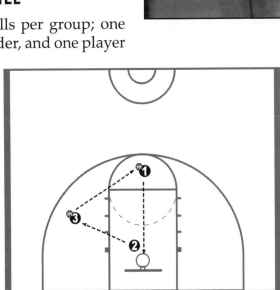

One-Spot Shooting Drill

DRILL 5.21 RACE THE CLOCK DRILL

1. Divide the team equally; send the groups to opposite ends of the court
2. Each half of the team has to make ten shots from the right baseline, right wing, top of the key, left wing and left baseline (50 total) in 5 minutes

Variation of the Race the Clock Drill:
- Have the two teams compete against each other to see which group can make ten shots from each spot the fastest

DRILL 5.22 NBA SHOOTING DRILL

1. Split the team in half; send each group to opposite ends of the court; first player out has a ball
2. Start outside the three-point line; shoot a three-point shot (a made shot counts as three points)
3. Rebound your shot, dribble the ball outside the three point line
4. Take two dribbles and shoot a pull-up jumper (a made shot counts as two points)
5. Rebound your shot, dribble the ball outside the three-point line
6. Take three dribbles and shoot a layup (a made shot counts as one point)
7. Shoot a foul shot (a made shot counts as one point)

- One possession is a complete cycle of four shots (one three-pointer, one pull-up jumper, one layup and a foul shot)
- A perfect round of five possessions will score 35 points
- Keep score and make it a contest

DRILL 5.23 HALF-COURT OLYMPIC DRILL

1. Form three lines at half-court, one on the right side, one in the center, one on the left side; send two players to the baseline (players 4 and 5 to the right and left of the basket)
2. Two balls start in the center line; players 4 and 5 both have a ball
3. [Player 1] Throw the ball to one wing (in this diagram, player 3)
4. [Player 2] Make a hard cut to the basket
5. [Player 3] Throw a lead pass to the cutter, player 2
6. [Player 1] After your pass, loop behind player 3 and spot up for a shot at the right wing or corner

7. [Player 3] After your pass, loop behind the cutter, player 2, and spot up for a shot at the left wing or corner
8. [Players 4 and 5] Pass to the player spotting up on your side of the court; go to the end of one of the half-court lines
9. [Player 2] Rebound your shot, dribble outside the sideline and pass the ball back to the center line; get in back of one of the three lines at half-court
10. [Players 1 and 3] Rebound your shot; take ball to the baseline and pass to the next set of shooters

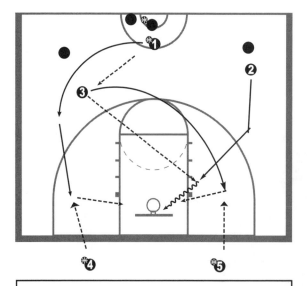

Half-Court Olympic Drill

• Run continuously for 3 minutes
• This is a great warmup drill at the beginning of practice or before games
• See the Full Court Olympic Drill 4.13

DRILL 5.24 CONTINUOUS PRESSURE SHOOTING DRILL

1. [Player 1] Start at the right elbow
2. [Player 2] Start under the basket, with the ball; pass to player 1
3. Run at player 1 with your hands up; try to block her shot
4. [Player 1] Shoot the ball under pressure
5. Follow your shot; rebound and pass to player 2 (who should be spotting up for a shot at the right elbow)
6. Run at player 2 with your hands up

• Repeat continuously
• Change shooting locations to different spots on the court

LOW POST SHOOTING

DRILL 5.25 LOW POST SHOOTING DRILL

1. Form one line at the top of the key; one player stands outside the right block (player 2), another on the left wing (player 3)
2. [Player 2] Make a hard flash cut into the lane
3. [Player 1] Pass into the post; go to the right block
4. [Player 2] Catch the ball, square up, shoot a six foot shot (don't forget to pump fake!); rebound the ball and pass it to player 3
5. [Player 3] Pass back to the top of the key, go the end of that line

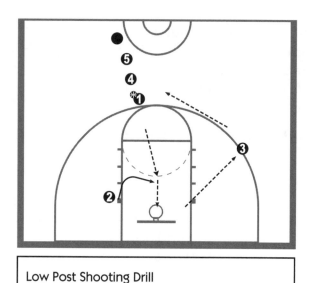

Low Post Shooting Drill

- Repeat continuously for 2 minutes
- Switch sides of the court

Variation of the Low Post Shooting Drill:
- After receiving the pass, execute drop step, face-up with pump fake and shot, crossover step without a dribble, crossover step with a dribble or power dribble to the basket

LOW POST FOOTWORK AND SHOOTING

DRILL 5.26 LOW POST FOOTWORK AND SHOOTING DRILL

1. Form two lines, one behind the right block and one behind the left
2. One offensive post player from each line steps out; each player has a ball
3. Execute the following low post moves: drop step, face-up with pump fake and shot, crossover step without a dribble, crossover step with a dribble to the middle of the lane, power dribble to the basket, and layup
4. Go to the end of the opposite line
5. Repeat until every player has executed two moves to the right and the left

Execute the crossover as follows:
1. Execute up-and-under (crossover) moves to the middle
2. [Right post] Pivot on your right foot; face the basket
3. Step through with your left foot to the basket, and shoot a right-handed layup
4. [Left post] Pivot on your left foot; face the basket
5. Step through with your right foot to the basket, and shoot a left-handed layup
6. Execute up-and-under (crossover) moves to the baseline
7. [Right post] Pivot on your left foot; face the side of the basket
8. Step through with your right foot into the lane; shoot a left-handed baby hook shot
9. [Left post] Pivot on your right foot; face the side of the basket
10. Step through with your left foot into the lane; shoot a right-handed baby-hook shot

DRILLS 6
Rebounding Drills

BASIC REBOUNDING DRILLS

These drills teach proper rebounding positioning and form.

DRILL 6.1 BREAD-AND-BUTTER REBOUNDING DRILL

1. Line up on the right side of the rim, with a ball
2. Toss the ball off the backboard
3. Jump up and catch the ball with both hands at the peak of your jump with the elbows locked; land with your feet spread more than shoulder-width apart, your hips low, knees bent, and elbows out
4. Chin the ball

- Repeat at least ten times
- Practice timing your jump so that you reach the ball at the peak of your leap

Variation of the Bread-and-Butter Rebounding Drill:
- After the rebound, pump fake and make a shot
- After the rebound, pivot to the outside pretending to outlet into a fast break

Another Variation:
1. Throw the ball off the backboard; explode to the ball and catch it with both hands at the peak of your jump
2. Pivot 180 degrees on your left foot; stay low in triple-threat position
3. Pivot another 180 degrees your left foot (this should bring you back into your original position)
4. Throw the ball off the backboard again
5. Pivot 180 degrees on your right foot; stay low in triple-threat position
6. Pivot another 180 degrees on our right foot to face the basket

DRILL 6.2 TIP DRILL

1. Line up near the basket, one player on the right side and two players on the left side of the rim
2. [First player on the left] Throw the ball over the rim to the opposite side of the backboard; quickly run behind player on right
3. [Player on the right] Jump up, catch the ball, and tip (pass) the ball before you land off the backboard and back over to the other side of the rim; quickly run behind the player on the left
4. [Second player on left] Jump up, catch the ball and tip (pass) the ball (before landing) off the backboard, etc.

- Run continuously for 30 seconds

DRILL 6.3 BACK TO THE BASKET DRILL

1. Form one line in front of the basket
2. [First player in line] Start six feet in front of the basket in the middle of the lane, facing away from the hoop
3. The coach throws the ball up so that it bounces off the backboard
4. [Player] Pivot, spot the ball, and go after the rebound; grab the ball and land in a balanced stance
5. Keep the ball high; finish the basket

- After the basket, go to the end of the line
- Don't forget to pump fake!

BOXING OUT

DRILL 6.4 CIRCLE BOX OUT DRILL

1. Pair up; one pair lines up in the middle of the lane, the other at the top of the key; the offensive players should be outside (away from the ball)
2. The coach stands at the foul line, with a ball
3. [Defenders 1 and 2] When the coach puts the ball on the floor, box out the offensive player
4. [Players 1 and 2] Try to touch the ball as it rests on the floor

- One repetition ends when the defense successfully keeps the offense away from the ball for 5 seconds (or when the offense touches the ball)
- Switch offense and defense between repetitions

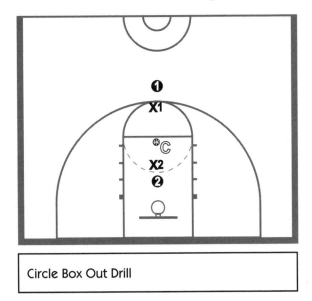

Circle Box Out Drill

DRILL 6.5 TRIANGLE BOX OUT DRILL

1. Split up into teams of three, the first team out is offense, the second team defense; the coach has a ball on the left wing
2. Defender 1 is at the high post, defender 2 is near the right block, defender 3 on the left block; players 1–3 line up just outside of their defenders
3. [Players 1–3] On the coach's whistle, run clockwise around the defender's triangle; when the coach's shot goes up, crash the boards hard
4. [Defenders 1–3] Stay stationary until the shot goes up; when it does, find the nearest offensive player, step toward her, and box her out (the player that you box will not necessarily be the player you were originally matched against!)

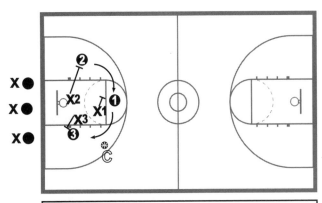

Triangle Box Out Drill

5. Keep sliding your feet after you make contact with your opponent; don't allow the offensive player to escape your box out

6. After three repetitions, send the offensive players in the other direction (counterclockwise)

- The defenders' goal is to allow the ball to bounce on the floor before releasing to pick it up; their main focus is the box out, not the ball!
- The offensive players' goal is to rebound the ball off the rim
- The coach may require each stationary player to call out the name of the player she plans to box out
- This is a useful drill for practicing rebounding against a zone offense
- Make it competitive; keep track of the rebounds grabbed by each team

Variation of the Triangle Box Out Drill:
- Send the defenders in motion and keep the offensive players still until the shot goes up
- Have both the defenders and the offensive players stand still until the shot goes up

DRILL 6.6 CLOSE OUT/BOX OUT DRILL

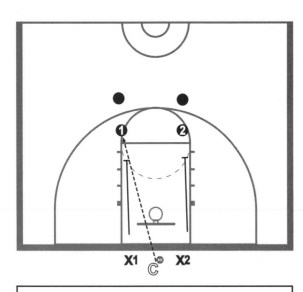

Close Out/Box Out Drill

1. Form four lines: two facing the basket at the elbows and two on the baseline; the coach stands with a rack of balls on the baseline with a basketball

2. Coach passes to player 1

3. [Player 1] Shoot the ball

4. [Players 1 and 2] Crash the offensive boards

5. [Defenders 1 and 2] On the pass, close out to your players

6. As the shot goes up, turn and box out

- If the offensive team gets the rebound, the offense stays for another round; defense goes to the back of the opposite line
- The defense gets one point for every defensive rebound; the offense gets two points for every offensive rebound
- Each team keeps track of their score

DRILL 6.7 KILLER INSTINCT DRILL

1. Split up into groups of three; each player is a rebounder
2. Line up around the basket
3. On the coach's shot from the wing, go hard after the ball
4. [Player that rebounds the ball] Put the ball back up; play it live until it goes in the basket
5. [Two nonrebounders] Play double-team defense; try to prevent the rebounder from scoring
6. After a made shot, the coach shoots again

- After one player makes three baskets, the other two players run one sprint; the next group of three steps onto the court

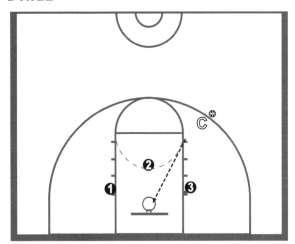

Killer Instinct Drill

Variation of the Killer Instinct Drill:
- Have the three rebounders start outside the key (from the right and left wing, and above the foul line)

DRILL 6.8 WEAK-SIDE BOX OUT REBOUNDING DRILL

1. Pair off; the first two players out are offense, the second two defense; the coach has the ball on one wing
2. [Players 1 and 2] Line up on the opposite side of the court as the coach, well outside the lane (in this diagram, on the right side of the court)
3. [Defenders 1 and 2] Match up to the offensive players in help defensive position (both feet inside the lane)
4. When the coach's shot goes up, find your players and box out
5. [Players 1 and 2] Crash the weak-side boards hard

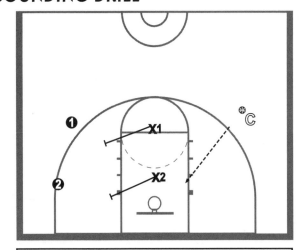

Weak-Side Box Out Rebounding Drill

- If the defense rebounds the ball, they rotate to offense and the next defensive pair steps in
- If the offense rebounds the ball, the defense runs one sprint and plays defense again

DRILL 6.9 TWO-ON-TWO REBOUNDING DRILL

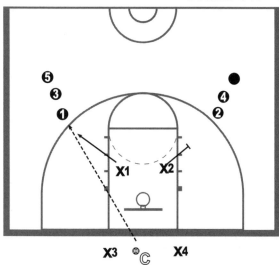

Two-onTwo Rebounding Drill

1. Form four lines: two facing the basket on the right and left wings, two on the right and left blocks; the coach has a ball on the baseline
2. The coach passes to one of the wing players (in this diagram, player 1)
3. [Player 1] Catch the ball; shoot immediately
4. [Player 2] Read the shot; crash the offensive boards
5. [Defender 1] Close out on the shooter; turn and box out on the perimeter
6. [Defender 2] Find the crashing player 2; box out on the weak-side

• After the rebound, defenders 1 and 2 go to the end of the wing lines, players 1 and 2 to the end of the baseline lines

DRILL 6.10 LOCATION DRILL

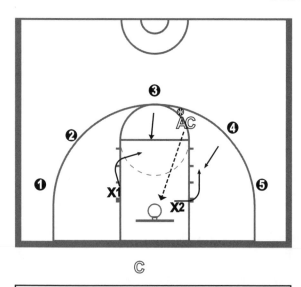

Location Drill

1. Line five offensive players up around the perimeter; two defenders start in the lane facing away from the basket
2. One coach stands on the baseline, another near the foul line
3. The baseline coach points to two offensive players so that the defenders cannot tell which players were selected (in this diagram, players 3 and 4); the assistant coach shoots
4. [Players 3 and 4] Crash the boards hard; use fakes or a roll move to spin off defenders 1 and 2, if you can
5. [Defenders 1 and 2] Identify the two offensive rebounders chosen; move your feet, turn and box out away from the basket
6. Try to let the ball bounce once on the floor before picking it up

• If defenders rebound, the two offensive rebounders go to defense, and the defenders take their places around the perimeter; if not, they defend again

DRILL 6.11 STOP, DROP, AND REBOUND DRILL

1. Form two lines near the top of the key
2. [Defenders 1 and 2] Step out into the lane
3. On the coach's whistle (and then shot), drop and do one push-up
4. [Players 3 and 4] When the coach shoots (after the whistle), crash the offensive boards
5. [Defenders 1 and 2] Stand up quickly and move your feet; find the offensive players and box out

• Switch lines, repeat

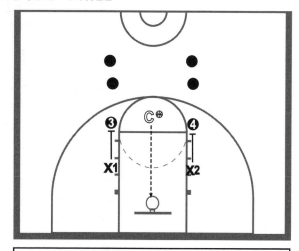

Stop, Drop, and Rebound Drill

OFFENSIVE REBOUNDING

DRILL 6.12 REBOUNDING ROLL DRILL

1. Form one line at the top of the key; one defender stands in the middle of the lane
2. The coach stands with a ball just outside the lane
3. [Player 1] Step out to below the foul line, facing the basket
4. [Defender 1] Stand facing player 1
5. On the coach's shot, turn and box out in stationary position
6. [Player 1] Step into the defender; pivot and roll either to the right or the left side so that you end with the defender on your back
7. Go after the rebound hard
8. Score a basket after the rebound

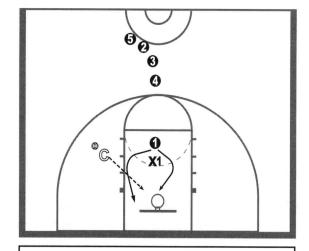

Rebounding Roll Drill

Variation of the Rebounding Roll Drill:
• Player 1 can fake in one direction and go around the other side without rolling

FREE THROW REBOUNDING

DRILL 6.13 FREE THROW REBOUNDING DRILL

1. Line up defensive and offensive players along the lane, mimicking a free throw scenario; coach shoots the ball
2. [Defenders 3 and 4] On the shot, step into the lane and box out players 3 and 4
3. [Defenders 1 and 2] Step into the high post area, blocking out the shooter; look for a long rebound
4. [Players 3 and 4] Step quickly into the lane and fight for the rebound.

- In high school players are allowed in the lane as soon as the ball hits the rim or backboard; under NCAA rules, players can enter the lane upon the shooter's release

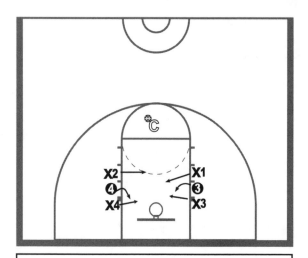

Free Throw Rebounding Drill: High School

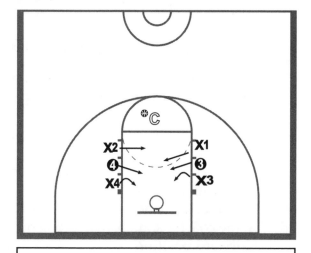

Free Throw Rebounding Drill: NCAA

FAST-BREAK REBOUNDING

This drill shows how to quickly initiate a fast break off a rebound.

DRILL 6.14 REBOUND/OUTLET DRILL

1. Form four lines: one line of guards on each wing, and one line of forwards on each block with basketballs
2. [Forwards] Toss the ball off the glass; rebound the ball at the top of your jump
3. Pivot to the outside; locate your outlet player
4. [Guards] Call "outlet" to let your forward know where you are
5. [Forwards] Make a lead pass to the outlet player
6. [Guards] Dribble hard past the half-court line (as if beating a defender)

• Each post player should repeat from the right and left sides

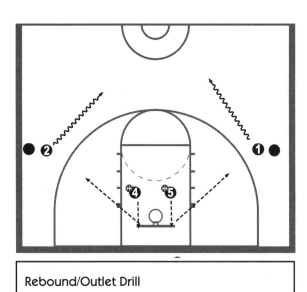

Rebound/Outlet Drill

DRILLS SECTION 2
Team Offense

DRILLS 7
Fast-Break Drills

TEAM FAST BREAK

These drills teach players how to run an effective fast break.

DRILL 7.1 THREE-MAN BREAK DRILL

1. Form three lines on the baseline; first three players out are offense (with one ball)
2. [Player 1] Throw the ball off the backboard; rebound and pivot out to the wing
3. [Players 2 and 3] Make a hard V-cut back to the ball; call "outlet"
4. [Player 1] Pass the ball to a wing player (in this diagram, player 3); fill the lane behind her
5. [Player 3] Speed dribble down the middle of the court
6. [Player 2] Sprint down the court; at the opposite top of the key, make a hard diagonal cut to the basket; catch a bounce pass from player 3 and score a layup; run to the opposite wing
7. [Player 1] Rebound the ball; throw the ball off the backboard; outlet it to player 3 (who should be on the wing)
8. [Players 1-3] Break back down the court in the same manner with player 1 making a layup

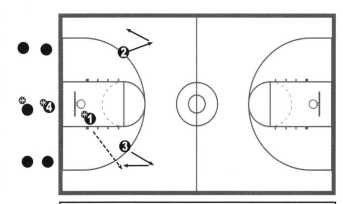

Three-Man Break Drill, Part 1

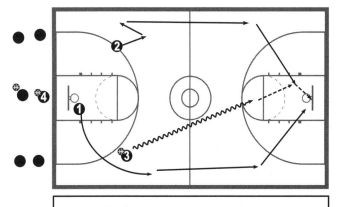

Three-Man Break Drill, Part 2

- After the first group of three finishes, another group steps onto the court
- The rebounder can take a power dribble before passing the ball to the wing

DRILL 7.2 THREE-ON-TWO, TWO-ON-ONE DRILL

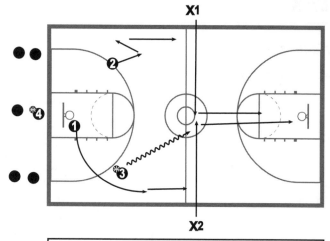

Three-on-Two, Two-on-One Drill, Part 1

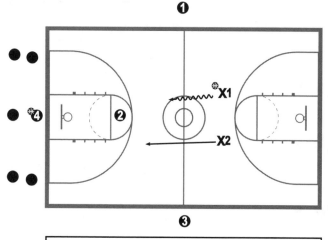

Three-on-Two, Two-on-One Drill, Part 2

1. Form three lines on the baseline; two players line up on either side of the half-court line
2. [Players 1–3] Toss a ball off the backboard; outlet it and break down the court (just as in the Three-Man Break Drill)
3. [Defenders 1 and 2] On the toss, step onto the court, back-peddle and defend in tandem the opposite basket
4. After a shot, rebound the ball and run a two-man break down the court
5. [Shooter, in this diagram, player 2] Sprint down the court and get back on defense
6. [Two nonshooters, in the diagram, players 2 and 3] Go to either side of the half-court line; play defense against the next three offensive players

- The top defensive tandem player should stop the ball; the lower defender should play the first pass
- If the shot is made, the rebounder should step out of bounds before passing to her teammate
- The rebounder can take a power dribble before outletting to the wing

Variations of the Three-on-Two, Two-on-One Drill:
- Continue the drill by having the two-on-one defender play one-on-one against the shooter if there is a rebound
- Begin the drill with four players breaking down the court against three defenders; after the rebound run three-on-two break against the last two players that touched the ball

DRILL 7.3 THREE-ON-TWO PLUS ONE BREAK DRILL

1. Three offensive players line up across the baseline, three defenders across the foul line; coach is near the foul line with a basketball
2. The coach passes the ball to one offensive player (in this diagram, player 2
3. [Defender opposite the ball, in this diagram Defender 2] Sprint and touch the baseline
4. [Players 1–3] Fast break down the court; try to score a basket three-on-two
5. [Defenders 1 and 3] Play tandem defense
6. [Defender 2] Sprint down the court and rejoin your defensive team as quickly as you can after touching the baseline
7. [Shooter] After the rebound or basket, sprint back down the court and play defense
8. [Defender 1 and 3] Rebound the ball and break down the court; try to score a basket two-on-one

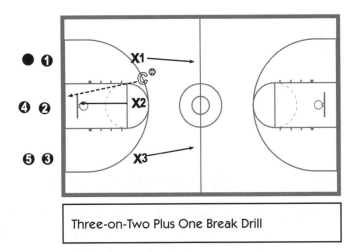

Three-on-Two Plus One Break Drill

Variation of the Three-on-Two Plus One Break Drill:
• Begin the drill with five or four players on each team instead of three

DRILL 7.4 CELTICS FAST-BREAK DRILL

1. Form two lines, one on the baseline and one at the wing; first player in the baseline line steps out (in this diagram, player 2)
2. [Player 2] Throw the ball off the backboard; pivot and outlet to player 1
3. [Player 1] Speed dribble down the court and make a layup
4. [Player 2] Sprint down the court; rebound the made shot (and put back any missed shots)

5. Inbound the ball to player 1 (now on the opposite side of the court)
6. [Player 1] Speed dribble down the court and make a layup; go to the end of the baseline line
7. [Player 2] Go to the back of the wing line

- The next rebounder waits to take the ball out of the net and outlets to the next player at the wing
- Rebounders can take a power dribble before outletting to the wing

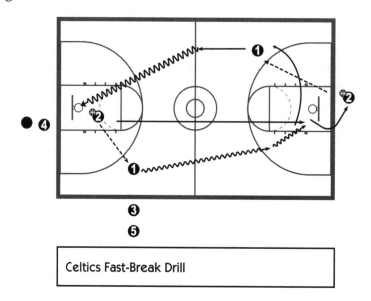

Celtics Fast-Break Drill

DRILL 7.5 FIVE-MAN BREAK DRILL

1. Five offensive players (positions 1–5) start around the basket; the 3, 4, and 5 players are in a rebounding triangle, the 2 is just inside the foul line (looking for a long rebound), the 1 (point guard) is at a wing
2. The coach tosses the ball off the backboard
3. [2, 3, 4, or 5 player] Rebound the ball; outlet to the point guard
4. Run the fast break down the court: fill all the lanes and run wide
5. [Point guard] Dribble toward top of key at other end; make bounce pass to one of your teammates for a layup or shot
6. [Nonshooter] Inbound the ball to player 1; break back down the court with the other players
7. Continue breaking until you score four baskets

DRILL 7.6 POST FAST-BREAK DRILL

1. Post players line up on the baseline; guards line up at a wing (one guard at a wing at the other end of the court)
2. [Player 5] Throw the ball off the backboard; pivot and outlet to player 1
3. Sprint down the court
4. [Player 1] Pass the ball ahead to player 2
5. [Player 2] Take a couple of dribbles to put yourself into good position to make a post entry pass
6. [Player 5] Cut directly to the basket for a layup or stop on the block and post up; catch the pass from player 2 and score a basket
7. [Player 2] After the pass, run to the other side of the court; call outlet
8. [Player 5] After the layup, step out-of-bounds and inbound the ball to player 2
9. Sprint down the court
10. [Player 2] Dribble down the court, wide on the wing; pass ahead to player 5
11. [Player 5] Finish the layup

- Player 1 fills player 2's spot
- Another post player steps out, rebounds, outlets; the drill continues
- The rebounder can take a power dribble before making the outlet pass to the wing

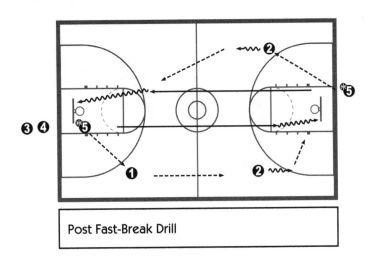

Post Fast-Break Drill

BASIC PLAYS

DRILL 8.1 GIVE-AND-GO DRILL

1. Three players (positions 1–3) line up on the perimeter; two players (4 and 5) start on the blocks
2. [Player 1] Pass to player 2
3. [Player 4] Cut to the opposite side of the lane to clear out for player 1
4. [Player 5] Cut to the short corner to clear out
5. [Player 1] Make a give-and-go cut down the lane to the basket
6. [Player 2] Make a lead bounce pass to player 1 for a layup
7. Repeat on the opposite side of the court; pass to player 3; players 4 and 5 clear out in the opposite direction

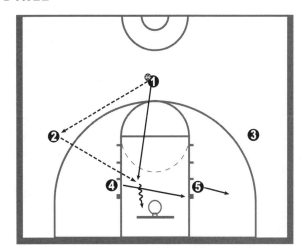

Give-and-Go Drill

• Run the give-and-go from the wing (players 2 and 3 pass to player 1 and cut to the basket for a layup)

DRILL 8.2 BACKDOOR DRILL

1. Three players (positions 1–3) line up on the perimeter; two players (4 and 5) start on the blocks
2. Two defenders match up to players 2 and 4
3. [Player 1] Dribble to the right side of the court
4. [Player 5] Cut to the short corner to clear out
5. [Player 4] Cut to the block on the opposite side of the lane
6. Player 2] Make a hard backdoor cut to the basket
7. [Defender 2] Slide to stay with your opponent

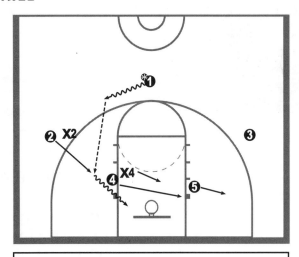

Backdoor Drill

8. [Player 1] Make a lead pass to player 2 for a layup
9. Repeat on the opposite side of the court (player 1 dribbles left, player 4 cuts to the short corner, player 5 cuts to the opposite side of the lane, player 3 cuts backdoor)

DRILL 8.3 CLEAR OUT DRILL

1. Starts the same as the Backdoor Drill, but is continuation of the play
2. [Player 2] If you don't get the pass, continue your cut to the opposite wing
3. [Player 1] Drive to the basket in the "cleared out" space: down the right side of the lane
4. Repeat on the opposite side of the court (player 3 goes to the opposite wing, point guard drives down the left side of the lane)

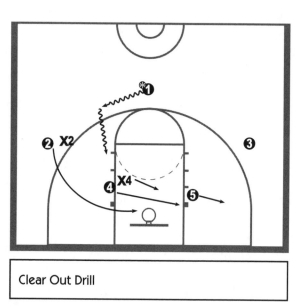

Clear Out Drill

DRILL 8.4 HIGH POST HANDOFF DRILL

1. One player [player 2] starts on the right block, another on the right wing [player 1]
2. [Player 2] Cut to the high post
3. [Player 1] Pass to player 2; make a jab step and then a cut down the middle of the lane looking for a handoff; make a layup if you get the ball

4. [Player 2] Handoff to player 1; if you don't, fake the handoff, pivot and shoot the ball
5. If you hand the ball off, slide down the lane looking for a rebound

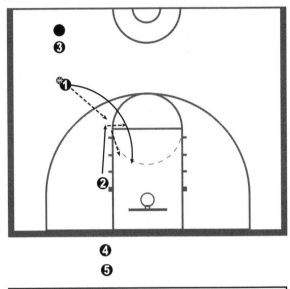

High Post Handoff Drill

DRILL 8.5 HIGH POST GIVE-AND-GO DRILL

1. Three players (positions 1–3) line up on the perimeter; two players (4 and 5) start on the blocks
2. [Player 1] Dribble to the right side of the court
3. [Player 5] Cut up to the elbow
4. [Player 4] Cut to the opposite block side of the lane to clear out
5. [Player 1] Pass to player 5; make a give-and-go cut to the basket
6. [Player 5] Pivot and make a bounce pass to player 1 for a layup
7. Repeat on the opposite side of the court (player 1 dribbles left, player 4 cuts to the elbow, player 5 to the opposite block)

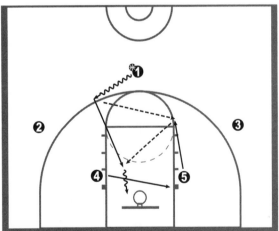

High Post Give-and-Go Drill

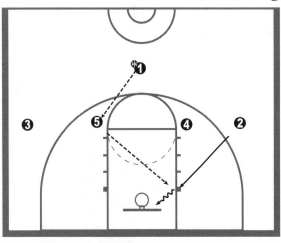

High 1-4 Drill

DRILL 8.6 HIGH 1-4 DRILL

1. Player 1 lines up at the top of the key; the other four players line up across the foul line extended
2. [Player 1] Pass the ball to player 5
3. [Player 2] Make a backdoor cut to the basket
4. [Player 5] Pivot toward the basket and make a bounce pass to player 2
5. [Player 2] Catch the ball and finish the layup

- Repeat with player 3 making the backdoor cut
- Repeat on the opposite side of the court (pass to player 4, players 3 and/or 2 cut backdoor)

Variations of the 1-4 Drill:
- After the pass into the high post, have player 1 make a slash cut down the lane, looking for a handoff or give-and-go from the post
- Pass to player 2 and have player 4 drop to the block and post up
- Pass to player 3 and have player 5 drop to the block and post up

DRILL 8.7 PASS AND SCREEN AWAY DRILL

1. Three offensive players line up on the perimeter; three defenders match up
2. [Player 1] Pass to player 3; screen away for player 2
3. [Defender 1] Hedge the screen by briefly stepping out into the path of player 2
4. [Player 2] Come off the screen toward the top of the key
5. [Defender 2] Fight over top of the screen
6. [Player 1] Pivot and cut to the basket; if you don't get a pass, stop and cut out to the left wing
7. [Player 3] Look to pass to player 1 for a layup; if she's not open, reverse the ball to player 2
8. [Player 2] Pass the ball to player 1; screen away for player 3, and continue the drill

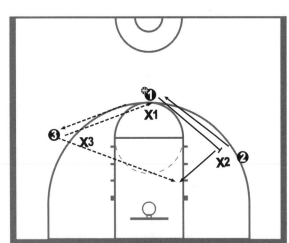

Pass and Screen Away Drill

DRILL 8.8 TEN WAYS TO BEAT A ZONE DRILL

1. Five offensive players line up on the perimeter; five token defenders line up in a 2-3 zone
2. [Offensive players] Attack the defense using the following principles:

- Reverse the ball quickly to the weak side
- Find an open area and fill it
- Penetrate the gaps with the dribble and pass
- Shoot over the zone
- Overload one side of the zone
- Pass the ball to the low post area, or a post player cutting to the foul line area
- Set screens
- Feed the post and pass the ball back out to the perimeter
- Run a fast break before the zone gets set up
- Get offensive rebounds

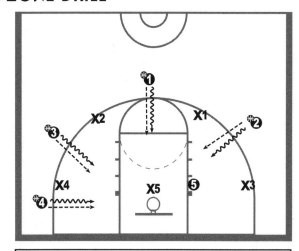

Ten Ways To Beat a Zone Drill

CUTTING DRILLS

In these drills players perform basic cutting moves to get open without the ball.

DRILL 8.9 TWO-PLAYER CUTTING DRILL

1. Form two lines; one at the top of the key, one on the right wing; the first player at the top of the key has ball
2. [Player 1] Dribble two times toward right wing
3. [Player 2] Execute a V-cut down to the block and back to the wing; call for the ball
4. [Player 1] Jump stop, pivot toward player 2, and pass the ball to her outside hand
5. [Player 2] Catch the pass, pivot into triple-threat position
6. [Player 1] V-cut to get open
7. Dribble two times; pass the ball to player 1

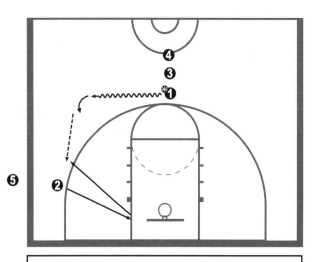

Two-Player Cutting Drill

- Repeat until both players have caught the ball five times

DRILL 8.10 X-CUT DRILL

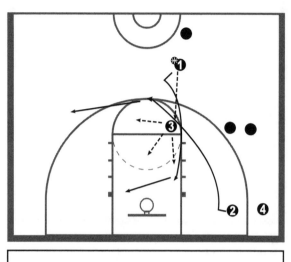

X- Cut Drill

1. Form three lines: one along the baseline, one on the foul line extended, and one near the top of the key with a ball (player 3 steps out to the high post)
2. [Player 1] Pass into the post; make a jab step toward the top of the key
3. [Player 2] Fake a cut along the baseline, then explode into a diagonal cut in front of player 3; finish on the opposite wing
4. [Player 1] After the baseline player makes her cut, make a cut in front of the post player; cut down the lane and across the block; and finish on the opposite baseline
5. [Player 3] Hand the ball off to one of the cutting players, or keep the ball, pivot, and make a jump shot

DRILL 8.11 GETTING OPEN DRILL

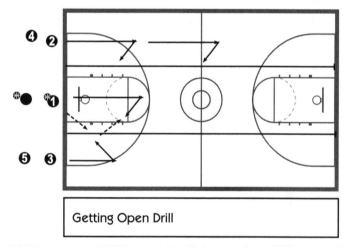

Getting Open Drill

1. Form three lines along the baseline, corresponding to three lanes on the court (right, center, and left); the line in the center has basketballs
2. [Players 2 and 3] Sprint out 10–15 feet, pivot, and V-cut back toward player 1 (the player with the ball)
3. [Player 1] Pass to one of the wings (in this diagram, player 3)
4. [Players 1 and 2] Sprint out past player 3, pivot, and V-cut back toward player 3 (the player with the ball)
5. [Player 3] Pass to player 1 or player 2

• Repeat until all three players are at the other end of the court

DRILL 8.12 CUT OFF OF THE POST DRILL

1. Form four lines: two along the baseline, on either side of the basket, and two to the right and left of the top of the key; the top two lines have basketballs
2. [Players 1 and 2] Step out from the baseline to the mid-post, on either side of the lane
3. [Players 3 and 4] Pass the ball to the post on your side
4. Make a jab step fake toward the corner, and then cut over top of the post player; angle the cut down the center of the lane
5. Receive the ball from the post on a flip pass, or handoff; make a layup

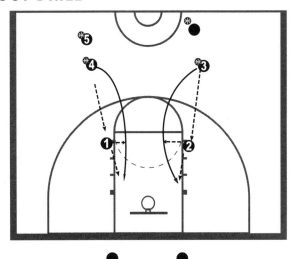

Cut Off of the Post Drill

• Cutters go to the end of the baseline lines; passers go to the end of the top of the key lines

DRILL 8.13 MIDDLE CUT DRILL

1. Form two lines, to the right and left of the top of the key; only one line has a ball (in this diagram, the line on the right side)
2. [Player 1] Pass to player 2; jab step fake to the right corner, and then make a cut down the middle of the lane
3. [Player 2] Throw a lead bounce pass to the cutting player 1
4. [Player 1] Finish the layup, rebound the ball, pass to player 2, and go to the end of the opposite line
6. [Player 2] Pass to player 3; jab step fake to the corner and make a cut down the middle
7. Catch the the pass from player 3, make the layup, rebound the ball, pass it to player 3, and go to the end of the opposite line

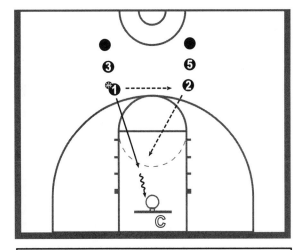

Middle Cut Drill

• Run continuously for 3 minutes

DRILL 8.14 BACKDOOR CUTTING DRILL

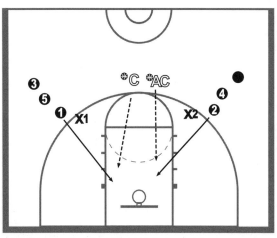

Backdoor Cutting Drill

1. Form two lines, one on each wing; the first player out is defense, the second player offense
2. Two coaches, with basketballs, stand at the top of the key
3. [Defenders] Play token deny defense
4. [Players 1 and 2] Make a series of cuts and pivots until you beat the defender backdoor
5. Catch the ball from the coach and make a layup; return to the same line and play defense on the next teammate in line
6. [Defenders] Go to the end of the opposite line

Variation of the Backdoor Cutting Drill:
• After catching the backdoor pass, make a jump stop; reverse pivot, and kick it out (not literally, of course) to the next player in line for a three-point shot

DRILL 8.15 FLASH CUT DRILL

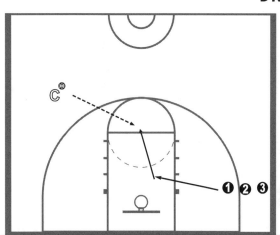

Flash Cut Drill

1. Form one line, extending out to the sideline from the left block
2. The coach stands on the opposite wing, with the ball
3. [Player 1] Take a couple of steps into the lane, plant your inside foot, and make a hard cut to the high post/foul line
4. Extend your outside arm and hand as a target; call for the ball
5. Catch the pass from the coach and pivot into triple-threat position, facing the basket
6. Pass the ball back to the coach and return to the end of the line

• Repeat starting from the right side

Variation of the Flash Cut Drill:
• After the pass from the coach, pivot and shoot the ball; rebound your own shot
• After the pass from the coach, pivot and drive to the basket
• Put a defender in the lane; if she denies the cut to the elbow, pivot and cut backdoor

DRILL 8.16 TWO-PLAYER PASSING AND CUTTING DRILL

1. Pair up; line up in two lines at the half-court line about 15 feet apart, facing the basket
2. First pair out is defense, second pair is offense
3. [Player 1] Dribble toward the top of the key
4. [Player 2] Read the defense and make a cut to get open: this cut can be a V-cut, middle cut, or backdoor cut
5. Cut and pass until one offensive player scores
6. [Defenders] Play on-ball and deny defense

DRILL 8.17 THREE-PLAYER PASSING AND CUTTING DRILL

1. Identical to Two-Player Passing and Cutting Drill, except with three offensive players and three defenders

DRILL 8.18 THREE-PLAYER RESPONSE DRILL

1. Start with three offensive players; one at the top of the key with the ball, and one on each wing
2. [Player 1] Pass to one of the wings (in these diagrams, player 2)
3. Execute a without-the-ball move: a give-and-go, screen away, or fade
4. [Player 3] React to the move, and fill the open position at the top of the key; catch the pass from player 2 if she doesn't pass to player 1
5. Continue passing and cutting until at least 4 passes are made, then shoot a layup or jump shot

- The player at the top of the key can pass to either wing before executing a move

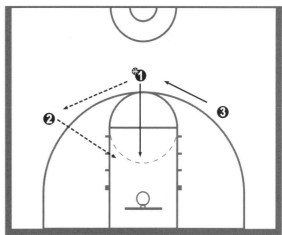

Three-Player Response Drill: Give-and-Go

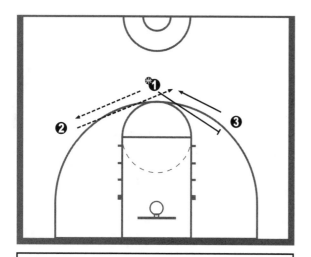

Three-Player Response Drill: Screen Away

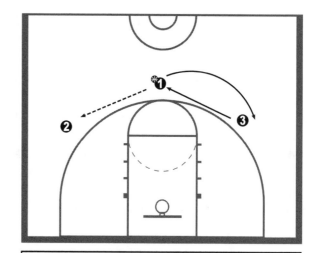

Three-Player Response Drill: Fade

SCREENING DRILLS

These next drills develop a player's ability to recognize screens, set screens and roll to the basket.

DRILL 8.19 PICK AND CURL CUT DRILL

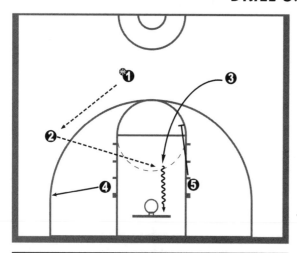

Pick and Curl Cut Drill

1. Five offensive players line up on the perimeter; player 1 has the ball
2. [Player 1] Pass to player 2
3. [Player 5] Cut up to the left elbow; set a screen for player 3
4. [Player 4] Cut out to the short corner
5. [Player 3] Run shoulder-to-shoulder off the screen; make a curl cut into the lane
6. [Player 2] Make a bounce pass to player 3
7. [Player 3] Catch the pass; finish the layup
• Repeat on the opposite side of the court

Variation of the Pick and Curl Cut Drill:
• Have five defenders match up

DRILL 8.20 PICK POSITION DRILL

1. Form three lines on the baseline
2. [First group] On the coach's whistle, sprint to the foul line; jump stop and assume the proper screening stance
3. On the next whistle, sprint to the half-court line, jump stop and "screen" again
4. [Second group] Begin on the second whistle and sprint to the foul line; jump stop and assume the proper screening stance

• Continue the drill until every player has screened at the near foul line, half-court line, far foul line, and far baseline

DRILL 8.21 STAGGER SCREEN DRILL

1. Three offensive players line up on the perimeter; the coach stands on the right wing
2. [Player 1] Pass to the coach
3. [Players 1 and 2] Set a staggered screen for player 3 (player 2 picks below the foul line, player 1 at the foul line)
4. [Player 3] Cut over top of the screens; look to make a cut to the basket
5. [Players 1 and 2] If player 3 catches a pass, pop out to the top of the key and the wing, respectively
6. If she doesn't get the pass, make cuts to the basket

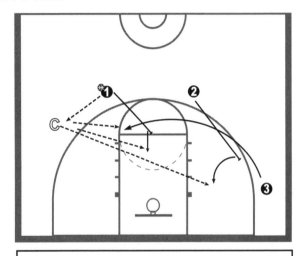

Stagger Screen Drill

Variation of the Stagger Screen Drill:
• Add three defenders to the drill

DRILL 8.22 TWO-PLAYER SCREENING DRILL

1. Form two lines, one at the top of the key with a ball and one on the right wing; the coach stands on the left wing
2. [Player 1] Pass the ball to the coach; screen away for player 2 (there's no defense in this drill, but practice good screening position anyway)
3. [Player 2] Make a hard cut off the screen: either cut to the high post or backdoor to the basket

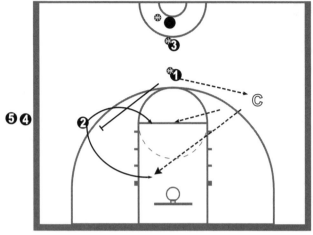

4. Catch the coach's pass and shoot a jump shot or a short bank shot
5. [Player 1] After the screen, roll to the basket and rebound

Variation of the Two-Player Screening Drill:
- [Player 1] If player 2 decides to cut to the basket off your screen, roll to the high post; look for a pass from the coach. If player 2 cuts to the high post, roll to the basket

Two-Player Screening Drill

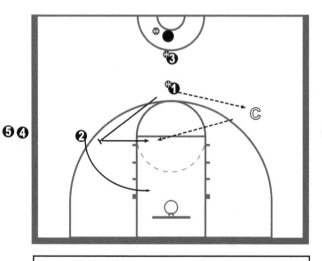

Two-Player Screening Drill:
Screener Cuts High

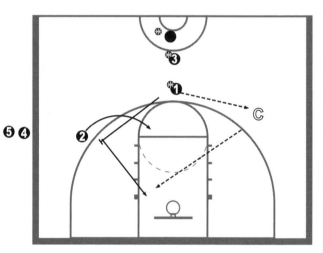

Two-Player Screening Drill:
Screener Cuts Low

DRILL 8.23 TRIANGLE DRILL

1. One offensive player lines up on the right wing, one on the right block, and one on the right side of the foul line in the high post
2. [Player 1] Dribble toward the baseline
3. [Player 2] Set a down screen for player 3 (on an imaginary defender)
4. [Player 3] Cut to the high post; catch the pass from player 1 and pivot into triple-threat position, facing the basket
5. [Player 2] After you screen, pivot and seal your imaginary defender
6. [Player 3] Make a bounce pass into player 2
7. [Player 2] Make a post move and score

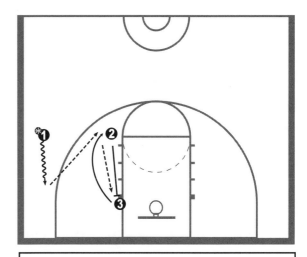

Triangle Drill

- Use post moves from Drill 3.7 (drop step, crossover, etc.)
- Switch sides of the court and repeat

Variation of the Triangle Drill:
- Add three defenders

DRILL 8.24 POST-TO-GUARD PICK-AND-ROLL DRILL

1. Form two lines, one on the left wing (with a ball), and one on the baseline; first two players out are offense
2. [Player 2] Set a back screen for player 1
3. [Player 1] Set up your defender by taking a jab step in the opposite direction that you plan to drive
4. Drive over the top or to the baseline side (in this diagram, over the top)
5. [Player 2] Pivot and roll to the basket
6. [Player 1] Pass the ball to the roller (player 2) cutting to the basket
7. [Player 2] Shoot a layup

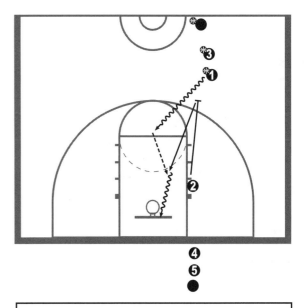

Post-to-Guard Pick-and-Roll Drill

- Switch sides of the court

Variation of the Post-to-Guard Pick-and-Roll Drill:
- Add two defenders

DRILL 8.25 READING THE DEFENSE DRILL

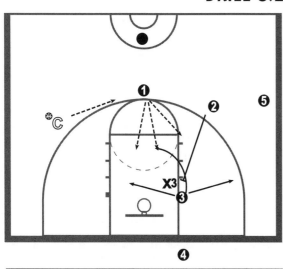

Reading the Defense Drill

1. Form three lines, one at the top of key, one on the left wing and one on the baseline; the ball starts with the coach on the right wing
2. First player out from the baseline line is defense, second player offense
3. [Player 2] On the coach's pass to player 1, set a down screen on defender 3
4. [Player 3] Read your defender as you cut off the screen
5. If defender 3 follows on your heels, make a curl cut into the lane for a short shot
6. If defender 3 goes behind the screen (on the basket side of the pick), make a flare cut out to the left wing and spot up for a jump shot
7. If defender 3 overplays the screen over the top, make a hard backdoor cut
8. [Player 1] Read player 3; make a pass to player 3 to score

• Switch sides of the court and repeat

DRILL 8.26 POST PICK-AND-SEAL DRILL

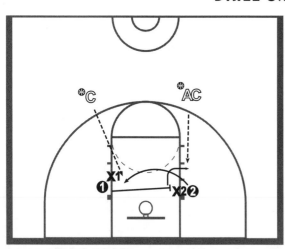

Post Pick-and-Seal Drill

1. Two offensive players line up on the right and left blocks; two defenders match up
2. Two coaches stand on both sides of the top of the key, each with a basketball
3. [Player 1] Set a cross screen on defender 2
4. [Player 2] Run your defender off the screen; cut across the lane
5. [Defenders 1 and 2] Switch on the screen
6. [Player 2] As you come across the lane, catch a pass from the coach and shoot a layup or make a post move
7. [Player 1] After you screen, turn and seal defender 2; use your outside hand as a target; catch a pass from the second coach
8. Make a post move and score

• Repeat until every player has played both offensive and defensive positions

- Defenders should let the offensive players receive the passes and score at the beginning of the drill
- See Drill 3.7 for post moves

DRILL 8.27 PERIMETER PICK-AND-ROLL DRILL

1. Three offensive players line up around the perimeter; the player at the top of the key has a ball
2. Three defenders match up
3. [Player 1] Pass to player 2; screen defender 2
4. [Defender 1] Call out "screen right" and leave room for defender 2 to go over the pick
5. [Player 2] Dribble over top of the screen
6. [Defender 2] Fight over the top of the screen
7. [Player 1] When player 2 passes your shoulder, pivot and roll to the basket
8. [Player 2] If player 1 is open, pass her the ball; if not, pass to player 3 on the left wing and repeat the drill
9. [Player 1] If you catch the ball, score a layup; if not, turn and sprint out to the right wing

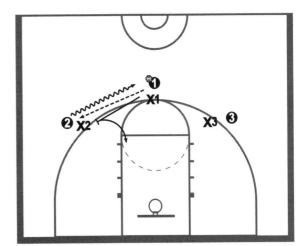

Perimeter Pick-and-Roll Drill, Part 1

- Run the drill continuously until the offense scores or the defense gets a rebound
- Switch offense and defense

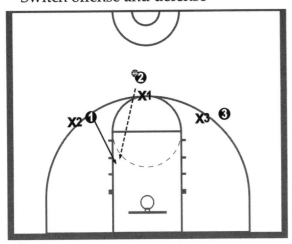

Perimeter Pick-and-Roll Drill, Part 2

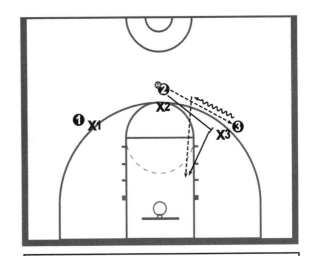

Perimeter Pick-and-Roll Drill, Part 3

DRILL 8.28 HIGH POST PASS-AND-SCREEN DRILL

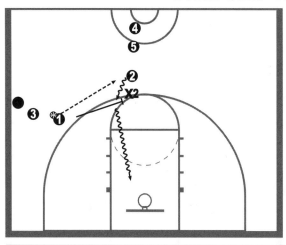

1. Form two lines: one on the right wing, the other near the top of the key
2. One defender matches up to player 2
3. [Player 1] Pass to player 2; jab step toward the baseline
4. Set a screen on defender 2
5. [Player 2] Square to the basket; run your defender off the screen, drive to the basket, and score a layup
6. [Player 1] Roll to the basket after setting the screen

- After one repetition, two new players step in; the player that set the screen goes to defense

High Post Pass-and-Screen Drill

FEEDING THE POST

These drills teach players how to get open in the low post, and how to create open passing lanes.

DRILL 8.29 POST ENTRY PASSING DRILL

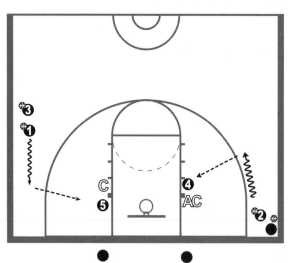

1. Guards form two lines: on the right wing, high, and on the left wing, low
2. Posts form two lines on the baseline
3. [Posts 4 and 5] Step out and in good post up position
4. [Coaches] Play 3/4 high side defense near right block; 3/4 low side defense near left block
5. [Guard 1] Dribble down toward the baseline and make a good entry (bounce) pass into the post
6. [Guard 2] Dribble up the three-point line and make a good entry (bounce) pass into the post
7. [Posts 4 and 5] Make a post move and score

- The post players should work on maintaining good position, sealing, calling for the ball, and catching it with both hands

Post Entry Passing Drill

- Guards and posts should switch sides after catching each pass
- See Drill 3.7 for post moves

DRILL 8.30 HIGH-LOW PASSING DRILL

1. Two offensive players line up on the right and left blocks; two defenders match up; the coach starts on the right wing with a ball
2. [Player 2] Cut to the foul line
3. [Defender 2] Try to deflect the pass
4. [Player 1] As soon as player 2 catches the ball, make a front cut over the top of your defender into the lane
5. Sit down low and wide; keep your arms locked in a strong frame position
6. [Defender 1] Try not to let her seal you
7. [Player 2] Throw player 1 the ball (make a chest or bounce pass, depending on the defense)
8. [Player 1] Make a post move and score

- Switch offense and defense
- See Drill 3.7 for post moves

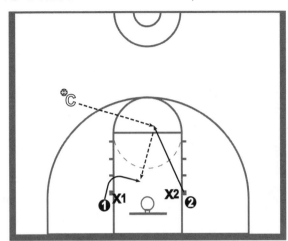

High-Low Passing Drill

POST OFFENSE AND DEFENSE

DRILL 8.31 ONE-ON-ONE IN THE LOW POST DRILL

1. One offensive player lines up on the left block; one defender matches up; the coach stands on the right wing with a ball
2. [Player 1] Make a hard cut to the right block or mid-post
3. [Defender 1] Play 3/4 deny defense (high or low, depending on the location of the ball)
4. [Player 1] When you catch the coach's pass, make a post move and score
5. Play the ball live until you make a basket or until the defender gets the rebound

- Switch sides of the court and repeat
- See Drill 3.7 for post moves

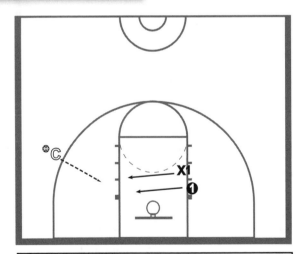

One-on-One in the Low Post Drill

Variation of the One-on-One in the Low Post Drill:
- If the defender fronts the offensive player, the offensive post player should seal and look for a lob pass
- Put four passers on the perimeter; allow the offensive post player to cut anywhere around the lane as the ball gets reversed; the four perimeter players should enter the ball as soon as the post player gets open

DRILL 8.32 TWO-ON-TWO IN THE LOW POST DRILL

1. Three guards line up on the perimeter; two forwards start in the post, one on either block; two post defenders match up
2. [Guards] Pass or dribble the ball around the perimeter; pass the ball into the post as soon as one of the forwards gets open
3. [Offensive post players] Get open using cuts and cross screens; use seal moves and post moves to score
4. [Defensive post players] Play tough post defense

AVOIDING TRAPS OFF OF SCREENS

DRILL 8.33 DOUBLE-TEAM (TRAP) RECOGNITION DRILL

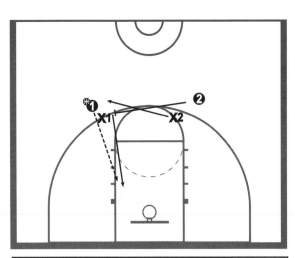

Double-Team (Trap) Recognition Drill

1. Two offensive players line up on the perimeter, one with a ball (in this diagram, player 1); two defenders match up
2. [Player 2] Set a screen for player 1
3. [Defender 2] Jump out and double-team player 1 as she starts to dribble over the screen
4. [Player 2] Recognize the double-team; make a hard cut to the basket
5. [Player 1] Back dribble to give yourself space; pass over top of the defenders to player 2 for a layup

- Switch offense and defense

ONE-ON-ONE DRILLS

DRILL 8.34 ONE-ON-ONE THREE DRIBBLE DRILL

1. One offensive player starts at the top of the key with a ball; one defender matches up
2. [Player 1] Attack the basket; use a maximum of three dribbles to score; stay within a 15-foot lane (see diagram)
3. [Defender 1] Try to cut off the driver's angle to the basket; box out and rebound after the shot

Variation of the One-on-One Three Dribble Drill:

- Put an additional offensive player on a wing; if the attacking guard is forced to pick up her dribble, allow her to pass to her teammate and cut back to the ball to get three more dribbles
- Repeat the drill from the right and left wings, and right and left corners (each with a 15-foot lane)

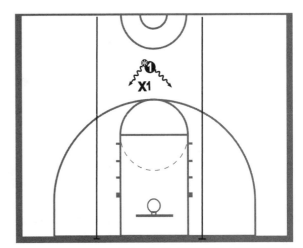

One-on-One Three Dribble Drill

FAST-BREAK DRILLS

DRILL 8.35 SIX-PASS FAST-BREAK DRILL

1. Line up extending down the court (on each side of the court, there should be one passer on the near wing, one at the half-court line, and one at the far wing on the opposite end of the floor)
2. [Players 1–4] Line up on both baselines, to the left of the basket (each line should have two basketballs)
3. [Players 1 and 3] Pass the ball to the first passers (coaches in this example) and sprint up the court
4. [First Passers] Give the cutters lead passes up the middle
5. [Players 1 and 3] Catch the return passes; pass to the passers at half-court
6. [Second Passers] Give the cutters lead passes up the sideline
7. [Players 1 and 3] Catch the return passes; pass the ball to the last passers; make hard diagonal cuts to the basket

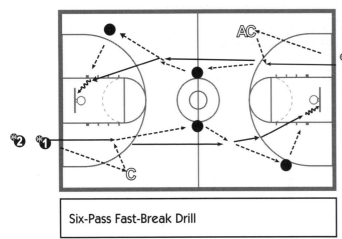

Six-Pass Fast-Break Drill

8. [Third Passers] Give the cutters lead bounce passes to the hoop

9. [Players 1 and 3] Shoot layups; start again from the closest baseline

10. [Players 2 and 4] Begin when players 1 and 3 get to half-court

FAST-BREAK REBOUNDING DRILLS

In this drill players practice making quick outlet passes after rebounds.

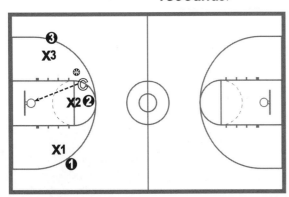

Fast-Break Rebounding Drill, Part 1

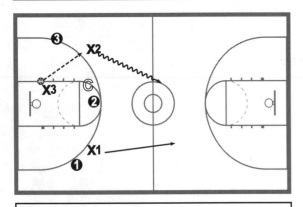

Fast-Break Rebounding Drill, Part 2

DRILL 8.36 FAST-BREAK REBOUNDING

1. Form three lines on the baseline, left, center, and right; the first three players out are offense, second three defense
2. The coach stands at the foul line with a ball
3. [Defenders 1–3] On the coach's shot, turn and box out the offensive players; grab the rebound
4. [Defender 2] As the player closest to the rebounder, call for the ball as an outlet
5. [Defender 3] Pivot to the outside and pass to defender 2; now you're on offense
6. [Defenders 1–3] Run a fast break and make a layup

• The defenders' goal is to grab the rebound and make a quick outlet pass
• As soon as the defense breaks down the court, the three offensive players go to defense, and a new offensive team steps in

DRILLS SECTION 3
Defense

DRILLS 9
Individual Defense Drills

INDIVIDUAL DEFENSE

These drills focus on fundamental defensive footwork and slides.

DRILL 9.1 ZIG-ZAG DRILL

1. Form three lines across the baseline; first three players out are defense, next three are offense with basketballs
2. [Offensive players] Dribble diagonally down the court in a 15-foot lane using the dribble designated by the coach (such as crossover dribble, spin dribble, etc.) to change direction; stay in your lane
3. [Defenders] Slide and completely cut off the dribbler's angle, maintaining your head-on-ball position (but don't go for the steal)
4. Use your feet to overplay the dribble and force the offensive player to turn in another direction; keep a wide stance (your arms should be extended to the side with your palms facing the ball); stay low (keep your head below the chin level of the dribbler)
5. Continue "turning" the dribbler down the length of the court

- The offensive players should dribble at one-half to three-quarters speed to allow the defender to get into position (head-on-ball)
- When one group reaches the top of the key, the next group begins
- Switch offense and defense when reach the end of the court

Variations of the Zig-Zag Drill:
- Pin your hands and arms behind your back as you play defense
- Once the offensive player crosses half-court, force her to stay on one side of the court (as if you wanted to keep the ball in her weak dribbling hand); try to funnel her into a baseline corner
- When she reaches the half-court line, the offensive player can play the ball live
- Run the drill sideline-to-sideline instead of fullcourt

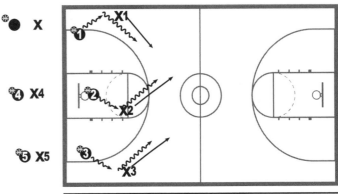

Zig-Zag Drill

DRILL 9.2 KILLER DEFENSE DRILL

1. Form three lines on the baseline
2. The first player out of the left line is defense, the second player out is offense with a ball; the three players at the baseline each have a ball
3. [Player 1] Try to beat your defender to the half-court line; use as many dribbles as you need
4. [Defender 1] Force the offensive player to turn as many times as you can (but don't go for the steal)
5. At the half-court line, turn and sprint back to the basket
6. [Player 2] Call out "layup," "jump shot," or "three-pointer"; make the appropriate pass to the former defender (defender 1) now cutting to the hoop
7. [Defender 1] Shoot the ball as instructed by player 2
8. Play defense again to the half-court line but on the other side of the lane against player 3

Killer Defense Drill

DRILL 9.3 PARTNER MIRROR DRILL

1. Pair off and line up across the court; offensive players have basketballs, defenders match up
2. [Offensive players] On the coach's whistle, make stationary offensive moves: jab steps, pass fakes, pump fakes, etc.
3. [Defenders] React to the offensive players; retreat, slide to the right or left, or step forward
4. Move quickly and stay low the whole time; keep both hands up, with one following the ball
5. Stay within an arm's length of the offensive player

Variation of the Partner Mirror Drill:
• Have the pairs spread out all over the court; on the whistle, offensive players can take two dribbles in any direction (in addition to making stationary moves); defenders must slide and cut off the dribblers' angles

DRILL 9.4 TEAM MIRROR DRILL

1. Form lines across the court facing the coach (who is standing on the foul line)
2. Drop down into good defensive position
3. React to the coach's directions: if he points to your left, slide twice to your left (remember, you are mirroring his actions); if he points to your right, slide twice to your right; if he jab steps, make two retreat steps; if he puts the ball up in the air, advance forward and yell "shot"

DRILL 9.5 LANE SLIDE DRILL

1. Split up, four players to a basket
2. Line up on the right side of the lane line, extending from baseline to foul line; start at least two feet away from the player in front of you, facing half-court with your left foot on the lane line
3. On the coach's whistle, slide to the other side of the foul lane; touch the opposite lane line with your right foot
4. Push off and slide back in the opposite direction; touch the lane line with your left foot

• Repeat continuously for 30 seconds

Variation of the Lane Slide Drill:
• Have pairs of players face each other as they slide; make sure that each player is keeping up with the other

DRILL 9.6 BLOCK DRILL

1. Split up into groups of four or five, each group to a basket
2. Put a block on the right and left sides of the lane and on the foul line
3. [First player out] Line up in the middle of the lane, even with the box
4. On the coach's whistle, slide to the right block; pick it up
5. Slide to the left block; pick it up and replace it with the one you are carrying
6. Sprint to the foul line; pick up the block and replace it with the one you are carrying
7. Sprint to the baseline

DRILL 9.7 ANTICIPATION DRILL

1. Two offensive players line up: one on the right elbow and the other on the left elbow, facing the basket; one defender starts in the middle of the lane; the coach stands underneath the basket with a ball
2. The coach passes to one of the offensive players
3. [Defender] Read the coach's eyes and body language; try to deflect the ball

• The offensive players are stationary

DRILL 9.8 FULL COURT SLIDES DRILL

1. Spread out along the baseline, everyone facing same sideline
2. On the coach's whistle, defensive slide to the foul line; reverse pivot
3. Defensive slide to the half-court line (now leading with the opposite foot); reverse pivot
4. Slide to the far foul line; reverse pivot
5. Slide to the baseline

Variation of the Full Court Slides Drill:

- Form two lines on the left block, on each end of the court
- On the coach's whistle, slide across the lane; pivot and slide diagonally to the right hash mark; sprint to the opposite hash mark
- Pivot and slide diagonally to the left block on the opposite side of the court (facing center court); slide across the lane; pivot and slide diagonally to the hash mark; sprint to the opposite hash
- Pivot and slide to the left block (where you started)
- The next time through, backpedal instead of sprint the sideline legs of the drill
- Always slide facing center court when moving toward the basket and away from center court when you're moving away from the basket

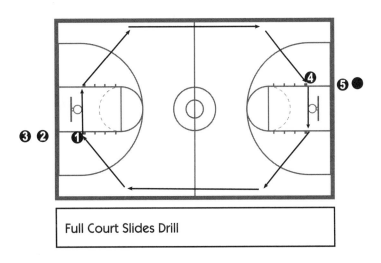

Full Court Slides Drill

DRILL 9.9 BASIC TRAINING DRILL

1. Form four lines on the baseline; first four players step out to form a line even with the foul line
2. [First players out] On the coach's whistle, slap the floor, get into defensive stance and start rapid foot fire (running in place on the balls of your feet, as quickly as you can)
3. If the coach points to the right far corner (at the other end of the court), slide three times on a diagonal to the far right; if the coach points to the left far corner, slide three times on a diagonal to the far left
4. If the coach calls "up," jump up and yell "shot"; if the coach calls down, drop down into a push-up and get back up again
5. On the second whistle, sprint the remaining length of the court

- Once the first group starts to sprint, the second group of four steps on the court; first group jogs around and gets back in line

DRILL 9.10 TAG DRILL

1. Form one line on the baseline, each player with a ball
2. One defensive player lines up on the near top of the key; another lines up on the far top of the key line
3. [First offensive player out] Dribble down the court; try to get past half-court without being tagged by the first defender (whose boundaries are the near top of the key line, extended, and the half-court line)
4. Try to get to the opposite baseline without being tagged by the second defender (whose boundaries are the half-court line to the far top of the key line extended)
5. [Next offensive player] Start dribbling as soon as the first dribbler crosses half-court

- Any player that gets tagged takes the place of the defensive player

Variation of the Tag Drill:
- Make the center circle a "free zone" where players can rest

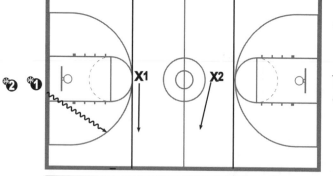

Tag Drill

PERIPHERAL VISION

DRILL 9.11 PERIPHERAL VISION DRILL

1. Five offensive players line up: one at the top of the key, one on each wing and one in each corner—each with a ball
2. One defender starts in the middle of the lane, facing the perimeter; the coach stands on the baseline out of the vision of the defender, also facing the perimeter
3. The coach points to one of the perimeter players
4. [Offensive player] Drive to the basket
5. [Defender] Use your peripheral vision to locate the driving player; position yourself to cut her off before she reaches the basket
6. Try to take a charge

- The dribbler becomes the defender; the defender takes her place on the wing

Variation of the Peripheral Vision Drill:
- Have another perimeter play drive to the basket as soon as the first player shoots; the defender must pick up the new attacker

DRILLS 10
Screening Drills

SCREENS

These drills are equally useful for teaching offensive and defensive screening techniques.

DRILL 10.1 DOWN SCREEN DRILL

1. One offensive player starts near the top of the key with a ball; another starts on the left block
2. Two defenders match up; the coach stands on the right wing
3. [Player 1] Pass to the coach; set a down screen on defender 2
4. [Defender 1] Drop down away from the screen; make room for defender 2 to get through
5. [Player 2] Make a hard cut to the foul line
6. [Defender 2] Run between the screener and your teammate, defender 1; cut off the passing lane between the coach and player 2
7. Intercept the pass, if you can

• Switch sides of the court and repeat

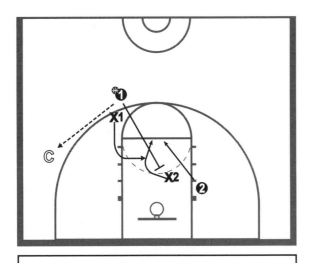

Down Screen Drill

DRILL 10.2 DOWN SCREEN CUT TO THE WINGS DRILL

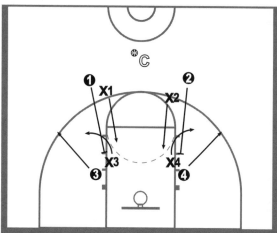

Down Screen Cut to the Wings Drill

1. Two offensive players line up on the right and left of the top of the key, two on the right and left blocks; four defenders match up; the coach stands at the top of the key with a ball
2. [Players 1 and 2] Set down screens for players 3 and 4
3. [Defenders 1 and 2] Move away from your player to allow your teammate to run through the screen
4. [Players 3 and 4] Cut hard to the wing; put up your outside hand as a target
5. [Defenders 3 and 4] Run through the screen; try to get a hand in the passing lane between the coach and your player

• Switch offense and defense and repeat

DRILL 10.3 BACK SCREEN DRILL

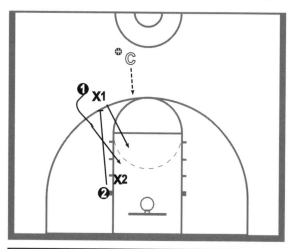

Back Screen Drill

1. One offensive player lines up to the right of the top of the key; another lines up at the right block
2. Two defenders match up; the coach stands at the top of the key with a ball
3. [Player 2] Set a back screen on defender 1 (remember to give her some space, one step, as this is a blind screen)
4. [Defender 2] Follow on the heels of the screener
5. [Player 1] Fake (jab step) toward the middle of the court, and make a backdoor cut to the basket
6. [Defender 1] Cut the screen to the inside (toward the lane); cut off the passing lane between the coach and player 1
7. Put your left hand up and try to deflect the pass

• Switch sides of the court

Variations of the Back Screen Drill:
- Move the coach to the left wing
- [Player 1] If defender 1 overplays the backdoor cut, make a cut to the foul line for a jump shot
- [Player 2] If player 1 makes a backdoor cut, cut to the foul line for a jump shot
- Defender 2 can switch on the screen to defend player 1

DRILL 10.4 FIGHT OVER THE TOP DRILL

1. Three offensive players line up around the perimeter, the player at the top of the key has a ball; three defenders match up
2. [Player 1] Pass to player 2; screen away for player 3
3. [Defender 1] Call out the screen and step back; allow defender 3 room to get through
4. [Defender 3] Take a step toward player 3 with your right foot; push that right foot over top (outside) of the screener, when she gets set
5. Step through and fight over screen; defend the cut to basket
6. [Player 3] Cut to basket after using the screen
7. [Player 2] Pass to player 3 for a layup

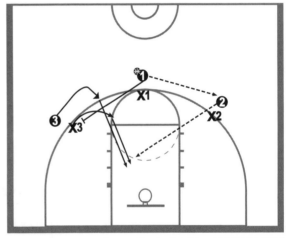

- If player 3 scores the layup, she moves out to the left wing; player 1 becomes the cutter, player 2 the passer
- If there's a turnover or a rebound, the defense goes to offense

Fight Over the Top Drill

DRILL 10.5 LOW POST SCREENING DRILL

1. Two offensive players set up on the right and left blocks; two defenders match up; the coach has a ball on the right wing
2. [Player 1] Set a cross screen on defender 2
3. [Defender 1] Call the screen
4. [Player 2] Cut hard across the lane to the ball
5. [Defender 2] Pull your left foot through the screen
6. Stay with player 2 as she cuts across the lane; assume 3/4 defensive stance on the right side of the lane
7. [Coach] Pass the ball to player 2 (who should attempt to score)

- After a few times through, switch offense and defense

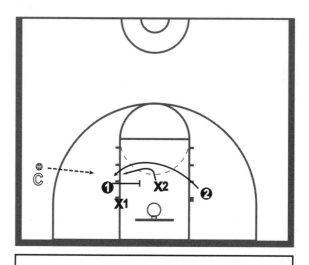

Low Post Screening Drill

DRILLS 11
Breakdown of Team Defense

DENYING THE PASS

These next drills are designed to teach players how to deny passing lanes.

DRILL 11.1 DENY THE WING DRILL

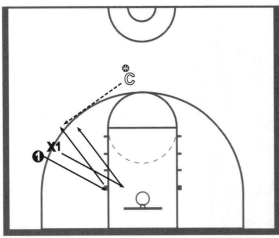

Deny the Wing Drill

1. One offensive player starts on the wing; one defender matches up; the coach stands at the top of the key with a ball
2. [Player 1] Make V-cuts and backdoor cuts to get open
3. [Defender 1] Slide and defend the offensive player; keep your back turned to the ball; look over your shoulder (with your chin on your shoulder) to keep track of the ball
4. If player 1 cuts backdoor, head snap and slide in the opposite direction; try to deflect the ball
5. [Player 1] When you catch a pass from the coach on the wing, pivot into triple-threat position
6. [Defender 1] Jump stop in front of player 1 (into good on-ball defensive position)

- Switch sides of the court

Variations of the Deny the Wing Drill:
- Allow the wing player to cut across the lane to the other side of the court; the defender must open up her stance and deny on the opposite side of the lane (all the while, keeping sight of the ball)
- Play live when player 1 catches the ball on the wing (the drill ends when player 1 scores or when defender 1 gets a defensive stop or rebound)
- Move the line to the top of the key and pass from the wing; work on making backdoor cuts down the middle of the lane

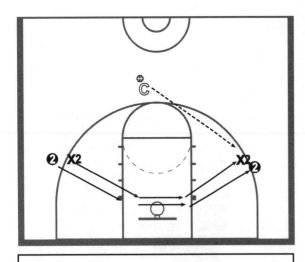

Variation of Deny the Wing Drill

DRILL 11.2 SUPER WING DENIAL DRILL

1. Identical to the Deny the Wing Drill, but add an extra offensive player at the block; the coach stands at the top of the key with three basketballs
2. The coach passes the ball to player 2
3. [Defender 2] Try to deflect the ball; once you have touched it (or player 2 has caught it), slide back to the block
4. The coach passes the ball to player 1
5. [Defender 2] Try to deflect the ball; once you have touched it (or player 1 has caught it), slide out to the wing

- Repeat for three passes (or more)
- Switch sides of the court and repeat

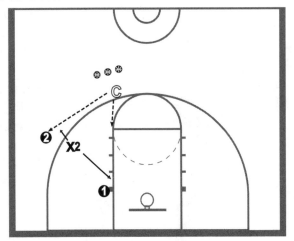

Super Wing Denial Drill

DRILL 11.3 POST DENIAL DRILL

1. Form one line on the baseline; the first player goes to the left wing with a ball, the second player plays defense at the block, the third player plays offense in the right corner
2. [Player 2] Cut hard to the high post
3. [Player 1] Look to make a pass to player 2
4. [Defender 2] Deny the pass into the high post; keep your body in the passing lane
5. [Player 2] If the defender overplays too much, make a backdoor cut to the hoop
6. If you catch the ball at the high post, pivot into triple-threat position, square to the basket

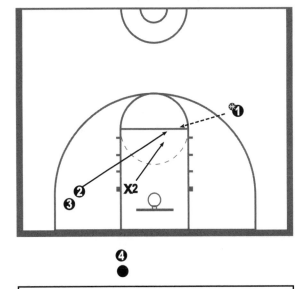

Post Denial Drill

- Play live when player 2 catches the ball at the high post
- The defender becomes the passer, the cutter becomes the defender, and a new offensive player steps in

DRILL 11.4 CUTTER DENIAL DRILL

1. Two offensive players start on the perimeter, one on the block; three defenders match up
2. [Defender 1] Play on-ball defense
3. [Defender 2] Play help-defense
4. [Player 3] Make a hard cut across the lane to the ball
5. [Defender 3] Deny the pass
6. [Player 3] If you don't catch the pass, slide down to the block
7. [Defender 3] Shift into 3/4 post defense
8. [Player 1] If you don't pass the ball into the post, skip pass it to player 2
9. [Defender 2] Move into on-ball defensive position
10. [Defender 1] Move to the ball by sliding into the passing lane, into help-defense position
11. [Defender 3] Step into the lane, into help-defense position

- Repeat for five ball-reversals

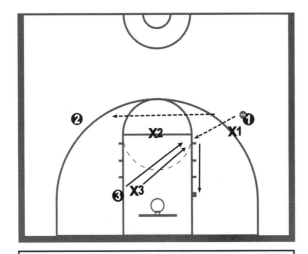

Cutter Denial Drill, Part 1

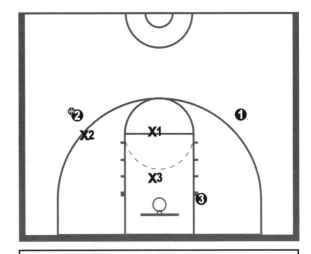

Cutter Denial Drill, Part 2

Variation of the Cutter Denial Drill:
- Have a wing player cut to the ball at the high post, instead of the post player; wing defenders deny the pass

DRILL 11.5 WEAK-SIDE DRILL

1. Three offensive players start on the perimeter, two at the blocks; four defensive players form a diamond around the key
2. [Offensive Players] Pass the ball around the perimeter and into the post
3. [Defenders 1–4] Always have one defender on the ball; deny the two players that are closest to the ball (one pass away on the strong-side of the court)
4. [Weak-side defender] Get into help-defense position; you must keep track of the weak-side players; you are responsible for closing out if the ball gets passed to one of them

- The offense shouldn't try to score, but should make crisp passes around the perimeter and into the post

CLOSING OUT

These next drills illustrate how to close out properly: take away the shot, force the offensive player to use her weak hand, and take away the sideline and the baseline.

DRILL 11.6 FOUL-LINE CLOSE OUT DRILL

1. Form two lines at half-court; first two players out are offense (with basketballs); two defenders start near the blocks
2. [Players 1 and 2] Control dribble toward the foul line area
3. [Defenders 1 and 2] Close out on the dribbler; turn her 45 degrees to the sideline
4. After the close out, play the ball live
5. [Defenders 1 and 2] Don't let your offensive player go over the middle (but don't let her beat you to the sideline or the baseline, either!)
6. [Players 1 and 2] Try to score a layup

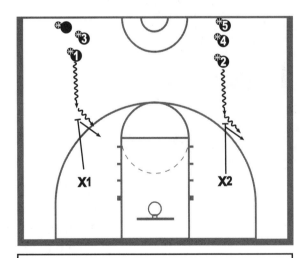

Foul-Line Close Out Drill

- Repeat until every player has closed out on the right and left sides

DRILL 11.7 WING CLOSE OUT DRILL

1. Form one line on the sideline; first player out goes to the left wing, the second player plays help defense in the middle of the key, the third plays offense on the right wing with the ball
2. [Player 1] Throw a skip (cross-court) pass to player 2
3. [Defender 2] Out of your help defense position close out on player 2
4. Try to breakdown into defensive stance in front of player 2 just as she receives the ball
5. Play the ball live from the wing

• Defender 2 should close out properly by approaching player 2 under control: jump-stopping into proper defensive stance within one arms-length of her opponent; taking away the shot; and taking away the sideline and baseline to force player 2 into the middle of court, where her help would be in a game

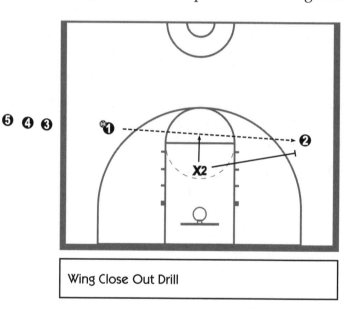

Wing Close Out Drill

DRILL 11.8 TWO-SIDED CLOSE OUT DRILL

1. Two offensive players line up on the right wing and two on the left wing; two defenders match up in the lane; the coach starts with a ball at the top of the key
2. Coach throws a pass to player 1, 2, 3, or 4 (in this diagram, player 1)
3. [Defender 1] Close out with one hand raised to take away the shot

4. In your defensive stance, angle your body slightly to take away the sideline and baseline
5. [Player 1] Catch the ball and get into your triple-threat position before you pass the ball back to the coach
6. [Defender 2] Jump stop into wing deny position

- On each pass, the corresponding defender closes out (defender 1 for players 1 and 3, defender 2 for players 2 and 4)
- Do not pass the ball back to the coach until both defenders close out

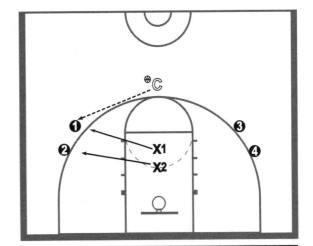

Two-Sided Close Out Drill

TAKING AWAY THE BASELINE

DRILL 11.9 TAKE AWAY THE BASELINE DRILL

1. One offensive player starts in the right corner; one defender matches up in help defensive position
2. The coach starts with the ball on the left wing and passes to offensive player in the right corner
3. [Defender] On the pass to the offensive player, close out with your inside hand up
4. When you break down into defensive stance, take away the baseline (shift your stance one step toward the baseline side); force the offensive player to drive into the middle of the court
5. [Offensive player] Try to drive baseline; keep attacking until you score or the defender gets a steal or rebound

- Switch sides of the court and repeat

DEFENDING SCREENS

DRILL 11.10 THREE-SCREEN DRILL

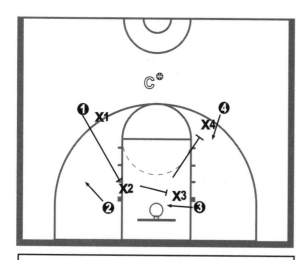

Three-Screen Drill

1. Two offensive players set up on the perimeter, two on the blocks; four defenders match up
2. [Player 1] Set a down-screen on defender 2; hold for one count
3. [Defender 1] Give your teammate room to get through the screen
4. [Player 2] Make a hard cut out to the wing
5. [Defender 2] Run between the screener and defender 1; try to deny player 2 as she cuts out to the wing
6. [Player 1] Set a cross-screen on defender 3; hold for one count
7. [Defender 1] Force player 3 to go behind the screen, rather than over the top
8. [Player 3] Make a hard cut across the lane
9. [Defender 3] Recover on the opposite side of the lane and play 3/4 deny defense
10. [Player 1] Set a back screen for player 4; hold for one count
11. [Defender 1] Follow on player 1's heels
12. [Player 4] Make a hard backdoor cut to the basket; catch the coach's pass and try to score a layup
13. [Defender 4] Come off the screen; try to deflect the pass; if you can't, recover at the block

• The drill ends after player 1 sets three screens and player 4 makes a layup

DEFENDING THE POST

DRILL 11.11 POST DENIAL DRILL

1. One offensive post player lines up at the left block; one defender matches up
2. One player lines up on the left wing; one player in the left corner; player 1 has a ball
3. [Defender 3] Start in 3/4 high deny defense with your left hand in passing lane
4. [Player 1] Pass the ball to player 2
5. [Defender 3] Step in front of player 3 with your right foot; front her for a moment
6. Reverse pivot on your right foot, bringing your left foot behind and through; play 3/4 low deny defense with your right hand in passing lane

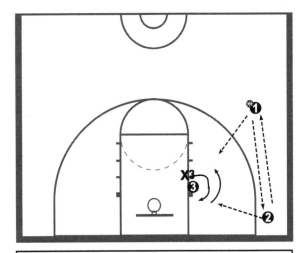

Post Denial Drill

7. Keep one hand in the passing lane at all times
8. [Player 3] Post up hard; try to seal defender 3 whenever you can
9. Play live as the players pass the ball back and forth
10. [Defender 3] Step through and switch defensive sides on every pass
11. [Player 3] When you catch a pass, make a move and try to score

- Switch sides of the court
- Switch offense and defense

FAST BREAK DEFENSE

DRILL 11.12 TRANSITION DEFENSE DRILL

1. Five offensive players line up across the baseline
2. Five defensive players match up across the foul line extended
3. The coach stands at a wing or the top of the key, with a ball
4. The coach passes the ball to one offensive player on the baseline (in this diagram, player 1)
5. [Player 1] Catch the pass
6. [Players 1–5] Run a fast break down the court

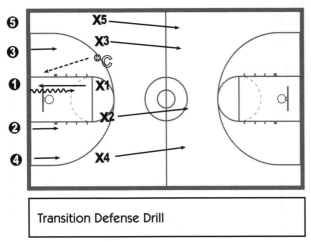

Transition Defense Drill

7. [Defender 1] Sprint to the baseline, touch it with your foot, and sprint down the court to recover on defense
8. [Defenders 2–5] Get back on defense; talk and find a way to cover the open player until defender 1 gets back

• The drill ends when the offense scores or the defense gets a rebound or a steal
• The defender guarding the offensive player that receives the pass from the coach must touch the baseline before sprinting down the court

Variation of the Transition Defense Drill:
• After the basket or rebound, fast break to the other end five-on-five

DRILL 11.13 "SIXER" DRIBBLING DRILL

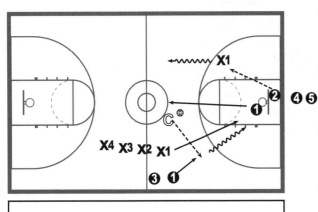

"Sixer" Dribbling Drill

1. Form three lines: two near half-court (one at the sideline and one further inside), and one on the baseline
2. The line at the sideline is offense, the line on the inside is defense, and the players on the baseline are the outlets
3. The coach, standing at the half-court circle, passes the ball to player 1 cutting to the basket
4. [Player 1] Attack the basket; read the defense to determine whether to drive for a layup or to pull up for a shot
5. [Defender 1] Sprint to the basket; try to stop the offensive player from scoring
6. [Player 2] Rebound after the shot, made or missed; pass the ball to defender 1, who is now on offense
7. [Player 2 and Defender 1] Break down the court two-on-one against player 1, who is now on defense

Special note: If defender 1 can't get in front of player 1 as she drives to the basket, then she should try to make player 1 alter her shot in some way—either by vocally distracting her, or running close along side her with hands up. But she must remember not to touch her in the act of shooting! Many referees will call even the slightest contact in a break-away layup situation.

RECOVERY DEFENSE

DRILL 11.14 FULL COURT CHASE DRILL

1. Split up into two even groups; start on opposite baselines (to the left of both baskets)
2. The first player steps out about five feet from the baseline with a ball; the second player stays on the baseline, as defense
3. [Offensive players] On the coach's whistle, speed dribble down the court using your right hand
4. [Defenders] Try to catch up with the dribbler and knock the ball away from behind

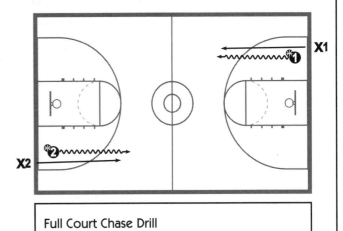

Full Court Chase Drill

- The starting distance between the players can vary depending on their speed
- Initially, the dribbler should not go full speed (to let the defender learn how to tip the ball from behind)
- Switch sides of the court (dribble with your left hand)

DRILL 11.15 DEFENDING THE BREAKAWAY LAYUP DRILL

1. Form two lines near half-court; the players on the outside are offense, the players on the inside are defense
2. [Player 1] On the coach's whistle, speed dribble to the basket
3. [Defender 1] Attempt to sprint to a point ahead of the dribbler; beat her to a spot in the lane and force her to pick up her dribble, or change directions to shoot with her weak hand
4. [Player 1] Try to score

- As soon as the first pair stops, the second pair should be ready to go
- Switch sides of the court and repeat

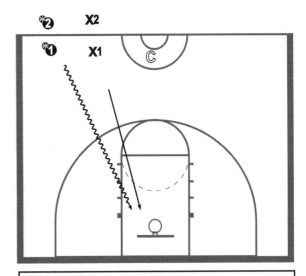

Defending the Breakaway Layup Drill

Variation of the Defending the Breakaway Layup Drill:
- [Defender 1] Sprint along side the dribbler in an attempt to make her shoot an off-balance layup

TAKING THE CHARGE

DRILL 11.16 TAKE THE CHARGE DRILL

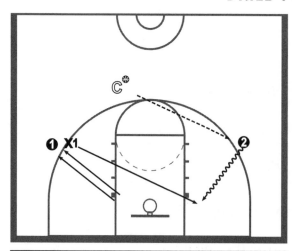

Take the Charge Drill

1. Starts off identical to the Deny the Wing Drill (Drill 11.1), with the exception of an additional offensive player on the left wing
2. As player 1 and defender 1 are cutting on the wing, the coach passes to player 2
3. [Player 2] Catch the pass from the coach; immediately drive to the basket
4. [Defender 1] On the coach's pass, rotate off player 1 and sprint to outside the left block; plant your feet and try to take a charge
5. [Player 2] Finish your drive to the basket

- Switch sides of the court and repeat

DEFENDING THE GIVE AND GO

DRILL 11.17 GIVE-AND-GO DEFENSE DRILL

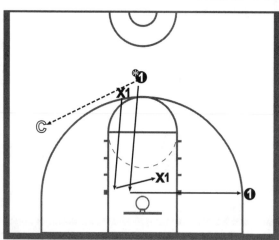

Give-and-Go Defense Drill

1. One offensive player starts at the top of the key with a ball, one defender matches up; the coach stands on the right wing
2. [Player 1] Pass to the coach; try to make a give-and-go cut to the basket
3. [Defender 1] On the pass, move toward the ball as player 1 tries to cut in front of you
4. Stay between the ball and player 1; keep a hand in the passing lane as player 1 continues down the lane; as she cuts out to the left wing, get into good help-defensive position with one foot in the lane

- Switch sides of the court and repeat

Variation of the Give-and-Go Defense Drill:
- Coach should make bounce pass to player 1 as she cuts to the basket; defender 1 should attempt to deflect or steal the pass
- Have the players cut to the strong-side block and post up; defender 1 must play 3/4 high deny defense

JUMPING TO THE BALL

This next drill emphasizes the importance of moving quickly on every pass.

DRILL 11.18 JUMP TO THE BALL DRILL

1. One offensive player is at the top of the key, and another is on the left wing
2. Player 1 starts with the ball, defender 1 plays on-ball defense, defender 2 plays deny defense on the left wing
3. [Player 1] Make a game-speed pass to player 2 (to the outside hand away from the defender)
4. [Defender 1] Jump to (move toward) the ball (slide to your right, and drop down to a level even with the ball to follow the ball-line principle)
5. [Defender 2] Play on-ball defense
6. [Player 2] Pass the ball back to player 1 (to the outside hand away from the defender)
7. [Defender 1] Recover to on-ball defensive position
8. [Defender 2] Jump to the ball (slide to your left, with a hand in the passing lane between players 1 and 2) and play deny defense

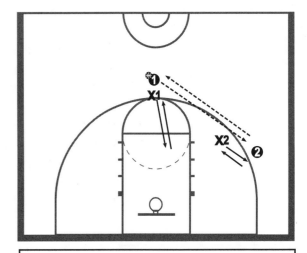

Jump to the Ball Drill

- Repeat continuously for 30 seconds; switch offense and defense
- Defenders should focus on moving when the ball is in the air

PLAYING ON-BALL AND HELP DEFENSE

DRILL 11.19 TWO-PLAYER ROTATION DRILL

1. Offensive players set up on the right and left wings; two defenders match up
2. The ball starts with the coach at the top of the key
3. [Defenders 1 and 2] Start in wing-deny defensive position
4. The coach passes to player 1 or player 2 (in this diagram, player 1)
5. [Defender 1] Jump into good on-ball defensive position
6. [Defender 2] Jump into help defensive position
7. [Player 1] Pass the ball back to the coach
8. [Defenders 1 and 2] Jump back into wing-deny defensive position
9. The coach passes to player 2
10. [Defender 2] Jump into good on-ball defensive position
11. [Defender 1] Jump into help defensive position

- Switch offense and defense and repeat
- Help defenders should follow the ball-line and mid-line principles (by dropping down in line with the ball, and shifting to the same side of the court as the ball)
- On-ball defenders should work on taking away the baseline

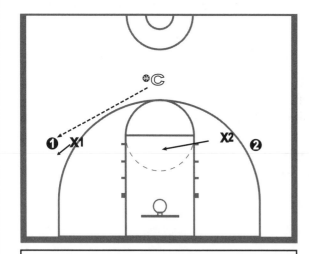

Two-Player Rotation Drill, Part 1

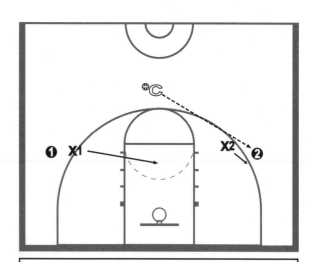

Two-Player Rotation Drill, Part 2

HELP AND RECOVER DEFENSE

This drill teaches players how to recover out of help defense.

DRILL 11.20 THREE-ON-THREE HELP AND RECOVER DRILL

1. Three offensive players line up around the perimeter; three defenders match up
2. [Player 1] Pass to a wing player (in this diagram, player 3)
3. [Defenders 1-3] Rotate accordingly
4. [Player 3] Skip pass to player 2
5. [Player 2] Catch the ball and immediately drive to the basket
6. [Defender 2] Jump out of help defense; sprint and attempt to stop the driving player 2
7. [Defenders 1 and 3] Drop down into help position and stop player 2 from driving to the basket (in this example, player 2 is beating defender 2)
8. [Player 2] If you don't have a shot, turn and dribble out to the wing; skip pass back to player 3
9. [Player 3] Drive immediately to the basket as defenders rotate, etc.

- Help defenders should slide and drop down to a level even with the ball to follow the ball-line principle
- On-ball defenders should work on taking away the strong hand and baseline

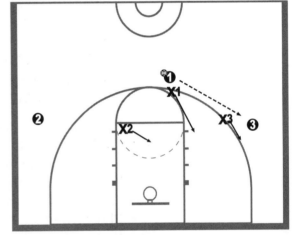

Three-on-Three Help and Recover Drill, Part 1

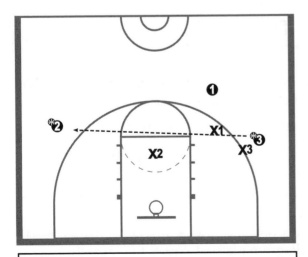

Three-on-Three Help and Recover Drill, Part 2

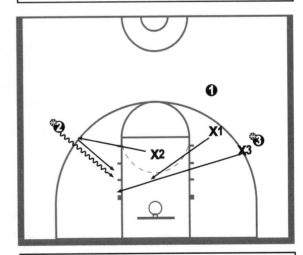

Three-on-Three Help and Recover Drill, Part 3

POSITIONING ON DEFENSE

DRILL 11.21 BALL-LINE, MID-LINE DRILL

1. Five players line up on offense on the perimeter; five defenders match up
2. [Offensive players] Pass the ball around the perimeter
3. [Defenders] If the ball is in the right corner, rotate so that you are below the foul line extended (ball-line principle) and on the same (right) side of the court (mid-line principle)
4. When the ball goes to the left corner, rotate accordingly: below the foul line extended (ball-line principle) and on the same (left) side of the court (mid-line principle)
5. When the ball is on the right wing, you should be positioned on right side of the court either in on-ball or help defense (if in help, at a level at or below that of the ball)
6. When the ball is on the left wing, you should be positioned on the left side of the court either in on-ball or help defense (if in help, at a level at or below that of the ball)

- Emphasize the ball-line principle: each defensive player should drop to the level of the ball
- Emphasize the mid-line principle: each defensive player should be positioned on the same side of the court as the ball when the ball is on the wing or corner
- Players that are one pass away should play deny defense; players that are two passes away should be in help defensive position
- After five rotations, switch offense and defense and repeat

TRAPPING

This drill teaches guards how to collapse on the ball in a double-team, trap properly, and rotate out of the trap.

DRILL 11.22 WEAK-SIDE DOUBLE DRILL

1. Three offensive players start on the perimeter, one in the post; four defenders match up
2. [Players 1–3] Work the ball around the perimeter; try to pass the ball into the post
3. [Player 4] Make cuts around the lane; seal your defender whenever you can (in this diagram player 1 passes to player 4)

4. [Defenders 2 and 3] When the ball goes into the post, send a player from the weak-side to double-team; you must communicate to determine which of you it should be (in this diagram, player 3 doubles)
5. [Defender 1] Stay in the passing lane
6. [Defender 2] Drop into help defense; you are now responsible for covering the first cross-court pass out of the double team, whether it be to player 2 or player 3
7. [Defenders 1–4] When the ball goes out of the post, rotate out of the double team; recover into good defensive position on your matchup

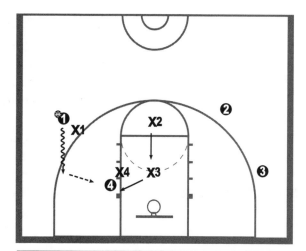

Weak-Side Double Drill

- Play the ball live if the post player kicks the ball out of the trap; double-team again if ball is passed back to the post
- Switch offense and defense and repeat

DRILL 11.23 STRONG-SIDE DOUBLE DRILL

1. Identical to the Weak-Side Double Drill, except that on the pass into the post, the defender guarding the passer (in this diagram, defender 1) drops down to double with defender 4
2. [Defenders 2 and 3] Drop into help defense—you are responsible for covering kick-out passes to your player
3. [Defenders 1–4] When the ball goes out of the post, rotate out of the double team; recover into good defensive position on your matchup

- Play the ball live if the post player kicks the ball out of the trap; double-team again if ball is passed back to the post
- Switch offense and defense and repeat

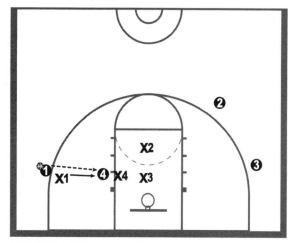

Strong-Side Double Drill

DRILL 11.24 WING TRAP DRILL

1. Five defenders set up in a 2-3 shell defense; offensive players set up on the right and left wings; coach starts at the top of the key with a ball
2. [Guard defender on right] When the coach passes to the right wing, run out and trap with the strong side baseline defender
3. [Weak-side guard defender] On the pass, rotate to take away the passing lane back to the coach
4. After 3 seconds, return to your normal positions; throw the ball back to the coach
5. Repeat on the left side of the court

- Practice getting into good trap position; form a "V" facing away from the basket, keep your hands up and active, don't make any contact with the defensive player (trappers don't worry about stealing the ball!)
- Practice trapping out of a 1-3-1 zone defense alignment, as well as a 2-3

Variation of the Wing Trap Drill:
- Put an offensive player in the post; on the pass in, have the strong-side guard defender drop down to trap with the center defender

DRILL 11.25 LANE TRAP DRILL

1. One offensive player (player 1) lines up at the foul line with a ball, one on the right block (player 2), and one on the left block (player 3)
2. Two defenders match up to player 1; one defender splits the low players
3. [Defenders 1 and 2] Trap player 1
4. [Player 1] Try to make a pass to player 2 or 3; use pivots, fakes, and step-through moves to break the trap
5. [Defender 3] Try to intercept the pass coming out of the trap

DRILL 11.26 TWO-MAN WING TRAP DRILL

1. One offensive player starts near half-court with a ball, another on the right wing; two defenders match up
2. [Player 1] Dribble up the sideline; pass to player 2
3. [Defender 1] Follow the pass and trap player 2 with defender 2
4. [Player 2] Try to pass the ball out of the trap to player 1; use pivots, fakes, and step-through moves to break the trap

• Switch sides of the court and repeat

Variation of the Two-Man Wing Trap Drill:
• Send defender 2 up the sideline to trap player 1 as she dribbles up the court (player 1 tries to pass to player 2 out of the trap)

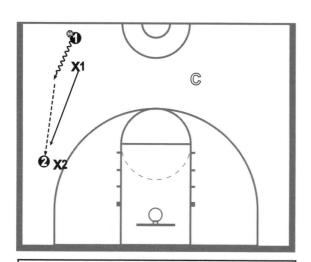

Two-Man Wing Trap Drill, Part 1

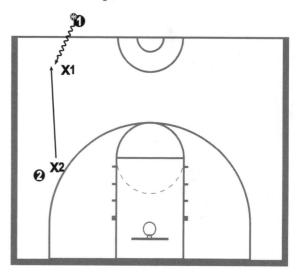

Two-Man Wing Trap Drill, Part 2

DRILL 11.27 HERDING DRILL

1. Form one line on the baseline
2. The first two players out are defense: one just in front of the half-court line, the other just behind
3. [Player 1] Start to dribble up the court
4. [Defender 1] Pressure the ball-handler toward the sideline; don't let her dribble up the middle
5. [Defender 2] Trap the dribbler with defender 1; time your move—trap just after player 1 crosses half-court; if possible, plant your outside foot on the sideline just as the dribbler arrives at the same point
6. [Player 1] Allow the defenders to trap you the first time; next time avoid the trap (or, better, split the defense); back dribble and reverse the ball, if you can

• The dribbler becomes defender 1, defender 1 becomes defender 2, defender 2 goes to the end of the baseline line

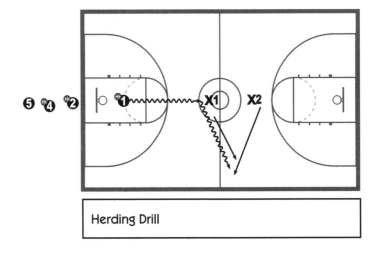

Herding Drill

RECOVERING OFF THE PRESS

DRILL 11.28 PRESS RECOVERY DRILL

1. Three defensive players line up facing the basket, as if they were playing the top of a 1-2-1-1 zone press
2. Three offensive players line up as though they were attempting to bring the ball up the court against a press: one on the near right wing below the foul line extended, another on the near left wing below the foul line extended; one positioned between the half-court and top of the key
3. The coach stands under the basket, facing the three defenders and offensive players, and passes to one of the offensive players
4. [Defenders] If the coach passes to an offensive player at a wing, trap her
5. If the coach passes to one of the offensive players beyond the top of the key, sprint back into half-court defense

• Defenders must sprint back immediately once the ball is passed beyond the initial line of defense

Variation of the Press Recovery Drill:
• Use all five defenders (in a full 1-2-1-1 setup)
• Switch offense and defense and repeat

DRILLS SECTION 4
Team Offense and Defense

ONE-ON-ONE

DRILL 12.1 CONTINUOUS ONE-ON-ONE DRILL

1. Form one line on the baseline; the first player steps out to the top of the key, with a ball; the second player matches up
2. [Player 1] Attack the basket; use as many dribbles as you need
3. If you score, stay on offense; take the ball back to the top of the key
4. [Defender 1] If you get the rebound, dribble to the top of the key
5. [Player 2] Step in and play defense (on either player 1 or defender 1)

• Repeat continuously for 3–4 minutes; keep track of each player's score

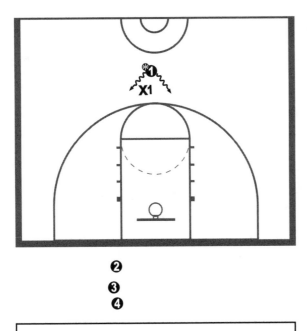

Continuous One-on-One Drill

DRILL 12.2 GET ON THE FLOOR DRILL

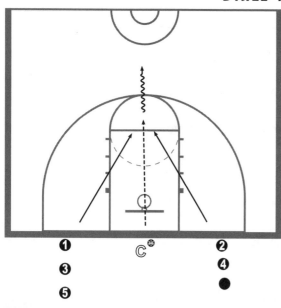

1. Form two lines on the baseline, to the right and left of the basket; the coach stands near the basket with basketballs
2. The coach rolls a ball down the court
3. [Players 1 and 2] Sprint and fight for the ball; dive on the floor if you need to
4. The player that picks up the ball is on offense, the other player on defense; play one-on-one, one time down the court

• Once the first pair crosses the half-court line, the second pair starts

Get on the Floor Drill

DRILL 12.3 FULL COURT ONE-ON-ONE DRILL

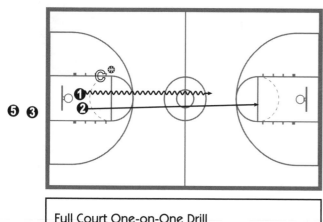

Full Court One-on-One Drill

1. Two players start in the lane
2. The coach throws a ball off the backboard
3. [Players 1 and 2] Fight for the rebound (in this diagram, player 1 gets the board)
4. [Player 1] Turn and dribble down the court
5. [Player 2] Play full court defense; try to turn player 1 as many times as possible
6. Play full court one-on-one for 1 minute, or until one player scores

• After 1 minute runs out, the next pair starts

CLOSING OUT

DRILL 12.4 ROLL AND CLOSE OUT DRILL

1. Form one line on the baseline; the first player out goes to offense at the top of the key
2. The next player starts on the baseline, with a ball, as a defender
3. [Defender 1] Roll or pass the ball out to player 1; close out with your hands up
4. [Player 1] Attack the basket and try to score
5. [Defender 1] Box out after a shot

- Defense goes to offense; a new defender steps in and rolls the ball out
- Repeat continuously for 5 minutes

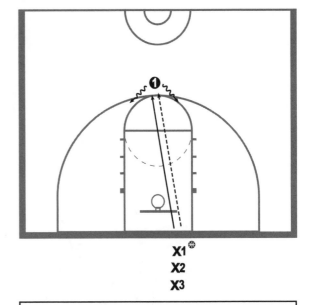

Roll and Close Out Drill

DRILLS 13
Drills for Forwards

BASIC POST MOVES

DRILL 13.1 SHELL POST DRILL

1. Form a line behind the right block; the coach stands on the left wing with ball
2. [Player 1] Make a cut across the lane; post up against an imaginary defender
3. Meet the pass from the coach
4. Make a post move and score: practice drop steps, pivots, pump fakes, crossover steps, up-and-under moves, spin moves, and turnaround jump shots
5. After you score the basket, grab your own rebound and outlet to the coach
6. [Player 2] Cut across the lane

- Switch sides of the court and repeat
- See Drill 3.7 for post moves

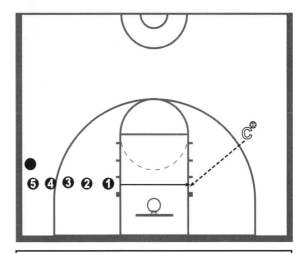

Shell Post Drill

DRILL 13.2 POWER DRIBBLE DRILL

1. Form one line on the baseline, behind the right block (each player with a ball)
2. [Player 1] Step to the block with your back to the basket; power dribble up the right side of the lane (a power dribble is a low, hard dribble that bounces no higher than the knees, performed in the middle of a slide step)
3. Pivot; with your back to basket, power dribble across the lane
4. Pivot; power dribble down the left side of the lane; make a shot
5. Return to the back of the line
6. [Player 2] As soon as post 1 gets to the left side of the lane, start your power dribble series

- Switch sides of the court and go in the opposite direction

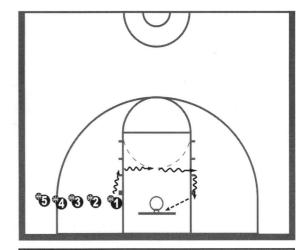

Power Dribble Drill

CLOSING OUT

This drill teaches players how to close out in the low post, rather than on the wing.

DRILL 13.3 POST CLOSE OUT DRILL

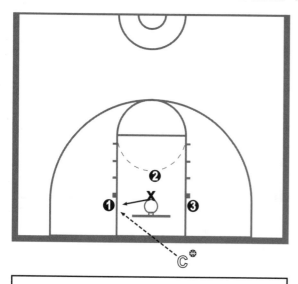

Post Close Out Drill

1. Three offensive players line up around the lane (on the two blocks and in the lane); one defender starts under the basket
2. The coach passes the ball to one of the offensive players (in this diagram, player 1)
3. [Defender] Close out with your hands up; pressure the shot and box out the shooter (if a shot is taken)
4. [Player 1] Shoot or drive; if you get an offensive rebound, shoot again
5. [Defender] Keep playing one-on-one until you get a defensive rebound; pass the ball back to the coach and get ready to close out again

• Run each defender through three times; then switch positions

LOW POST SCREENING

DRILL 13.4 CROSS SCREENING DRILL

1. One offensive player lines up on the right wing; one offensive player starts on the right block, another on the left block; two post defenders match up
2. [Player 5] Set a cross screen for the left post (player 4)
3. [Player 4] Run your defender off the screen shoulder-to-shoulder (foot-to-foot); cut off the screen high (to the foul line) or low (to the block)

4. [Player 5] Roll off the screen; fill the vacant position on the strong-side of the lane (if player 4 goes high then roll low, if player 4 goes low then roll high)
5. [Player 1] Pass the ball to the open player

• Switch offense and defense and repeat

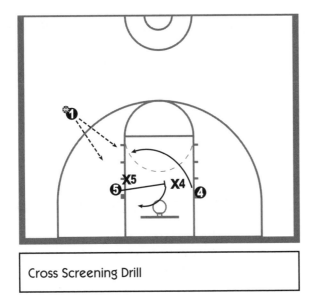

Cross Screening Drill

Variation of the Cross Screening Drill:
• Have one offensive player start at the foul line, the other on the block; practice back screens and down screens

POST DEFENSE

DRILL 13.5 GET OVER THE TOP DRILL

1. Two offensive players line up, one on the right wing and one on in right corner; one offensive post player starts on the left block; one post defender matches up
2. [Player 3] Make a cut to the right block
3. [Defender 3] Deny the pass during the cut and then play 3/4 high side deny defense
4. [Player 1] Pass the ball to player 2
5. [Defender 3] Step through over the top of the offensive post: step with your left foot and pull your right foot through
6. Assume 3/4 low side deny defensive stance on the baseline side

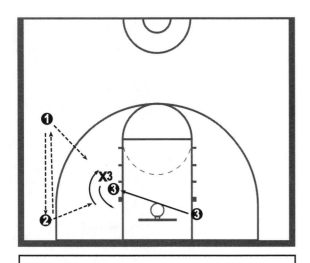

Get Over the Top Drill

7. [Player 2] Pass the ball back to player 1
8. [Defender 3] Step through over the top of the offensive post; step with your right foot and pull your left foot through
9. Assume 3/4 high side deny defensive stance

- Repeat continuously for 20 seconds
- Switch offense and defense; switch sides of the court and repeat

DRILL 13.6 GUARD DOUBLE-DOWN DRILL

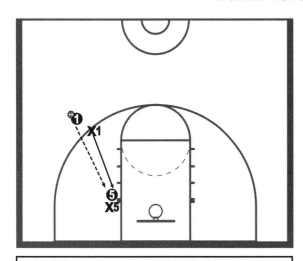

Guard Double-Down Drill

1. One player (guard) lines up on the right wing, one forward on the right block; two defenders match up
2. [Player 5] Post up; try to get open
3. [Defender 5] Play 3/4 low side deny defense
4. [Defender 1] On the pass into the post, collapse and double-team on the high side of the offensive post player (player 5)
5. On the pass back out of the post, close out on player 1

- Switch offense and defense
- Switch sides of the court and repeat

POST OFFENSE AND DEFENSE

DRILL 13.7 HIGH POST FLASH DRILL

1. Two offensive players line up on the perimeter, one offensive post on the left block; one post defender matches up
2. [Player 5] Cut to the right elbow; if you catch the pass from player 1, pivot to the basket and shoot, or drive to the basket
3. [Defender 5] As the cutter comes across the lane; try to deflect the pass
4. After a deflection, score or defensive rebound, pass the ball out to player 2
5. [Player 5] Jog to the right block; make a cut to the left elbow to receive pass from player 2

Variation of the High Post Flash Drill:
- Put two offensive players on the left and right wings, two players in the left and right corners; one post defender starts in the middle of the lane
- The coach starts at the top of the key with three basketballs
- When the ball goes to player 1, player 4 cuts to the elbow; the defender must deny the pass from the corner
- As soon as player 4 clears, another ball goes to player 2; player 3 cuts to the elbow; the defender must deny the pass
- Play the ball live when the pass goes into the post

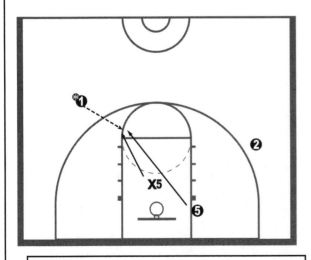

High Post Flash Drill

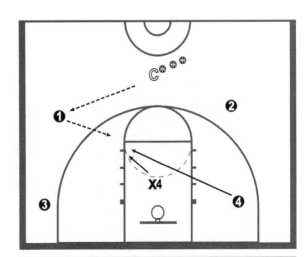

Variation of the High Post Flash Drill

DRILLS 14
Team Offense and Defense

COMBINATION OFFENSIVE AND DEFENSIVE DRILLS

DRILL 14.1 SHELL DRILLS

1. Four (or five) offensive players start on the perimeter; four (or five) defenders match up in man offense
2. [Players 1–5] Pass the ball around the perimeter
3. [Defenders 1–5] Play half-court defense: maintain good on-ball position, jump to the ball on a pass, get into good help defense position when the ball is on the opposite side of the court
4. Emphasize the ball-line principle: each defensive player should drop to the level of the ball
5. Emphasize the mid-line principle: each defensive player should be positioned on the same side of the court as the ball
6. Players that are one pass away should deny the pass; players that are two passes away should be in help defensive position

- Pass continuously for 1 minute, then switch offense and defense
- Defenders should practice getting into proper position, instead of trying to steal the ball
- At first, the offense should not shoot

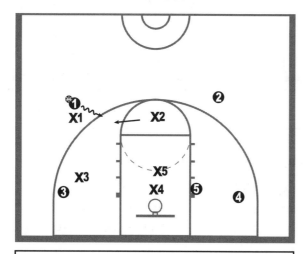

Shell Drill

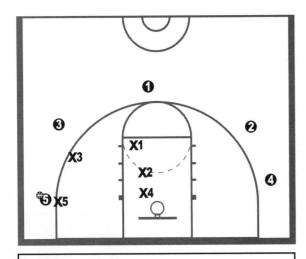

Shell Drill: Ball in Right Corner

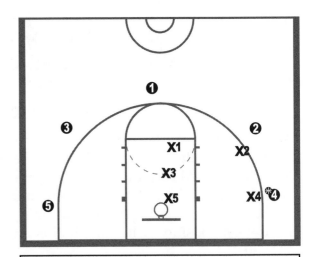

Shell Drill: Ball in Left Corner

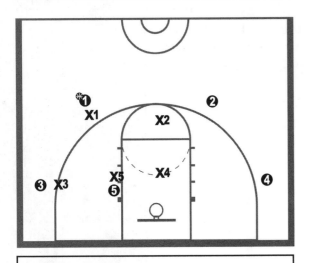

Shell Drill: Ball on Right Wing

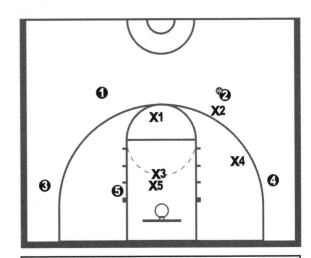

Shell Drill: Ball on Left Wing

Variations of the Shell Drill:

Shell Drill with Cuts:
- Have the offensive players make V-cuts, backdoor cuts, cuts to the high post, etc.; the defense should rotate to deny passes (but not steal the ball)

Shell Drill with Screens:
- Have the offensive players screen for their teammates, using on-ball pick-and-rolls, diagonal screens, down screens, back screens, and cross screens

Shell Drill with the Dribble:
- Have the offensive players penetrate the gaps with the dribble; the defense should rotate (step in) to stop the penetration and then recover back

Shell Drill with a Post Player:
- Put two players in the post; the offensive post players should make hard cuts across the lane as the ball moves around the perimeter; the defensive post players should play tough post defense

DRILL 14.2 SCRIMMAGING

Setting certain scrimmage criteria is a great way to get players to focus on specific concepts. For example, sometimes I make a rule that no shot can go up until at least one screen has been set. If an offensive player manages to drive all the way to the basket without facing help defense, the defensive team runs a sprint. These kinds of specific rules help players focus in on the tasks at hand. Other examples of how the rules can be modified are provided below:

- No shot can be taken until three passes have been made
- No shot can be taken until the ball goes into the post at least two times
- If a defender doesn't drop to the level of the ball as she rotates, she does five push-ups
- If a defender allows her opponent to drive baseline (away from her help) she does five push-ups
- Every offensive player must take at least two hard steps toward the basket to rebound when a shot goes up (no fast breaks are allowed when this crash-the-boards rule is in effect). If one player doesn't move toward the basket, the entire offensive team runs a sprint

MAN-TO-MAN AND ZONE OFFENSE

DRILL 14.3 MOTION OFFENSE DRILL

1. Five offensive players line up around the perimeter with no defenders
2. [Players 1–5] Run through basic motion offense cuts: pass and screen away, pick-and-roll, give-and-go, etc.; use V-cuts and backdoor cuts to simulate getting open on the wing

Variation of the Motion Offense Drill:
- Have the offensive players shell through the team's offenses with no defense

DRILL 14.4 SHOT CLOCK PASSING DRILL

1. Set up in the front court as if in the team offense
2. On the whistle by the coach, pass the ball quickly around the perimeter and into the post
3. Count the number of passes the players can make in 30 seconds

- A "pass" only counts if the passer first squares and looks to basket or looks inside to see if a post player is open

PRIMARY FAST BREAK

DRILL 14.5 RECOGNITION DRILL

1. Five offensive players start near one basket
2. Four defenders start on the sideline near the half-court line, with an assistant
3. On the coach's missed shot, players 1–5 grab the rebound and fast break down the court
4. The assistant sends one, two, three or all four defenders onto the court to defend the opposite basket
5. [Players 1–5] Find the open player(s) and score

6. [Defenders 1–4] Communicate with each other, rotate and defend the basket

• Switch offensive and defensive teams and repeat

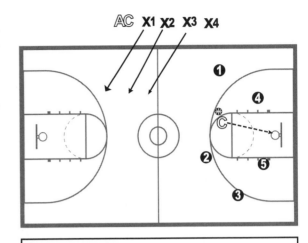

Recognition Drill

DRILL 14.6 THREES AND TWOS

1. Three players start on one baseline, two players on the other
2. [Three offensive players] Attack the opposite basket in a three-on-two break
3. [Two defenders] Communicate and defend
4. On a defensive rebound, break back down the court in a two-on-three situation
5. [Three defenders] Defend
6. [Three offensive players] After the rebound, break down the court in a three-on-two, etc,

• Run continuously for 2 minutes; send new teams of three and two onto the court

SECONDARY FAST BREAK

DRILL 14.7 TRANSITION POST DRILL

1. One player starts on offense, one on defense, near the basket
2. [Player 1] Throw the ball off the backboard; rebound and outlet to the coach on the right wing
3. Sprints to the free-throw line, touch the line with your foot, and sprint back to the right block

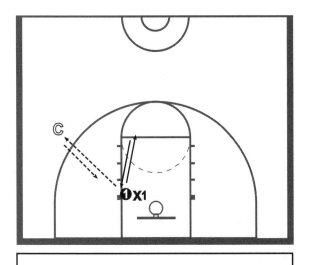

Transition Post Drill

4. Post up against defender 1
5. [Defender 1] Wait above the block; play tough post defense
6. [Player 1] Catch a pass from the coach; make a post move to the basket and score
7. Catch the ball out of the net; pivot and outlet to the coach
8. Sprint to the half-court line; touch the line with your foot and sprint back to the block; post up and score
9. Repeat, touching the far foul line and baseline

• Switch offensive and defensive players and repeat

THREE-ON-THREE

DRILL 14.8 THREE-ON-THREE DRILL

1. Three offensive players line up around the perimeter; three defenders match up
2. [Offensive players] Play three-on-three basketball; use down screens, back screens, cross screens, pick-and-rolls and give-and-go's to get open for shots; use proper spacing
3. [Defensive players] Use your defensive principles of on-ball defense, help defense (ball-line and mid-line principles); don't let the offensive players score

•Repeat continuously for 3 minutes

Variations of the Three-on-Three Drill:
• Start the offense at half-court; have the defenders play a half-court trap zone defense
• Don't allow the offensive players to dribble
• Count the number passes the offensive team can complete in 30 seconds

DRILLS 15
Special Situation Drills

COMING FROM BEHIND

This drill allows players to simulate a true game situation: coming back from a deficit late in the game.

DRILL 15.1 COUNT DOWN DRILL

1. Five offensive players line up in the front court; five defenders match up
2. The offense is down by a given number of points (for example, three)
3. The offense has 30 seconds to scrimmage live and take the lead

- The coach tells the offense how many timeouts they have left and if either team is in the bonus foul situation

Variation of the Count Down Drill:
- Put more time on the clock and make the offense score more points

CONFUSING THE OPPONENT

DRILL 15.2 SWITCH THE DEFENSE DRILL

1. Five offensive players (positions 1–5) line up at the far foul line; five defenders line up in a 2-3 zone around the near basket
2. [Offensive players] On the coach's whistle, attack the zone
3. [Defensive players] As soon as the offense crosses half-court, jump into a man-to-man defense
4. Communicate so that every defender knows which player to pick up

Variation of the Switch the Defense Drill:
- As soon as the offense crosses half-court, have the two top defenders jump into a half-court trap

DRILL 15.3 DISGUISE THE DEFENSE DRILL

1. Five defenders match up to five offensive players at the far end of the court
2. Scrimmage; the offense keeps the ball until it scores
3. [Defensive team] Inbound the ball and head down the court on offense
4. [Offensive team] Start to retreat on defense; as soon as you see the ball beyond the foul line, turn and jump into a 3/4 court trap

Variation of the Disguise the Defense Drill:
- Don't trap, but have the coach call out the half-court defensive set (zone or man-to-man) as the defenders get back

DRILL 15.4 ROTATING DEFENSES DRILL

1. Five defenders match up to five offensive players on the far end of the court
2. Scrimmage; play the ball live
3. [Offensive team] After you lose possession of the ball (through a made or missed basket or turnover), switch to defense
4. Automatically choose your defensive set based on the events on the court:

- After a made basket or free throw, set up in a full court zone press
- After a missed basket or free throw, or a steal, drop back into half-court man-to-man defense
- After a time-out or dead ball, set up in a half-court trap defense press
- Run the drill continuously for 3 minutes
- Switch offense and defense and repeat

DRILLS SECTION 5
Concluding Practice

DRILLS 16
Fun Drills

These drills are designed to be fun, but at the same time, to develop skills and improve conditioning.

DRILL 16.1 PARTNER ATTACK DRILL

1. Pair up, spread out around the entire court (one member of each pair with a ball)
2. [Offensive players] On the coach's whistle, start to dribble with your strong hand, keeping the ball very low
3. [Defenders] Try to tip the ball away from your opponent
4. [Offensive players] On the coach's second whistle, switch to your weak hand

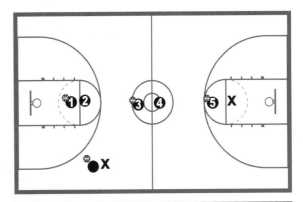

Partner Attack Drill

- After 30 seconds, switch offense and defense

Variation of the Partner Attack Drill:
- Use two defenders against one dribbler

DRIBBLING

DRILL 16.2 DRIBBLE TAG DRILL

1. Spread out on one half of the court, every player with a ball
2. On the coach's whistle, start dribbling
3. Try to knock each teammate's basketball away (out of their control) while keeping your own dribble alive

- A player is out if her ball gets tipped out of bounds or to the half-court line; the drill continues until only one player is left
- The last player in control of her dribble wins the drill

Variation of the Dribble Tag Drill:
- Have each player use two basketballs; both balls must be knocked away before the player is out
- Confine the dribbling area to the inside of the three-point line

DRILL 16.3 CRAZY CONE DRIBBLING DRILL

1. Place cones randomly around the court
2. Split up evenly; line up on each baseline, to the left of a basket
3. [First players in line] Dribble out to the first cone and listen as the coach calls out a dribbling move (crossover, spin, etc.)
4. [Next players in line] Begin dribbling as soon as the first player passes the first cone

• Run continuously for 2–3 minutes

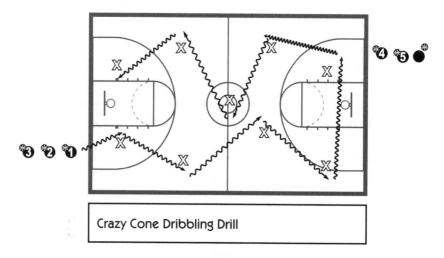

Crazy Cone Dribbling Drill

Variation of the Crazy Cone Dribbling Drill:
• Circle each cone before moving to the next one
• Dribble two basketballs

SHOOTING

DRILL 16.4 KNOCKOUT DRILL

1. Form one line at the foul line; the first two players have basketballs
2. [First player in line] Shoot a foul shot
3. [Second player in line] Shoot after the first player releases the ball
4. Try to make a basket or a put-back before the first player in line can do the same; if you do, she's out
5. [First player] As soon as you make a basket (or as soon as you're "knocked out") pass the ball back to the third player in line

6. [Second player] As soon as you make your shot (or are knocked out), pass the ball to the next player in line
7. [Third player in line] Shoot a foul shot
8. [Fourth player in line] Shoot as soon as the third player releases the ball, etc.

• Run the drill continuously until only one player is left standing

Variation of the Knockout Drill:
• Shoot three-pointers from the top of the key

DRILL 16.5 TWENTY-ONE DRILL

1. Split up into groups of two or three, each group to a basket
2. One player starts with the ball at the foul line, as a shooter
3. [Shooter] Shoot a maximum of three foul shots, each worth 1 point
4. If you make all three, take the ball to the top of the key; attack the basket against the two defenders
5. [Defenders] If the shooter misses one of her foul shots, fight for the ball; rebound and put it back up
6. The player that scores a 2-point basket (whether off of a rebound or a drive to the basket) takes the ball to the foul line to shoot a maximum of three foul shots

• The first player to score 21 points wins

Variation of the Twenty-One Drill:
• Run the drill (game) with four or five players
• Require any player that goes *over* 21 points to drop back to 15 and try again

ONE-ON-ONE

DRILL 16.6 HALF-COURT ONE-ON-ONE DRILL

1. Form two lines, to the right and left of the top of the key
2. The first players out are on defense, the second players offense with basketballs
3. [Offensive players] Attack the basket, staying on your side of the court (don't cross over the imaginary line that divides the lane)
4. Incorporate crossover dribbles, spin moves, behind-the-back dribbles, etc., into your drive
5. [Defenders] Force the dribblers to change directions at least twice before they shoot
6. Play the ball live on each side of the court until a made basket or a rebound

- First player to score 6 points wins

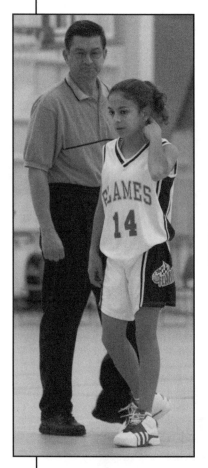

ONE-ON-ONE FULL COURT

DRILL 16.7 FULL COURT ONE-ON-ONE DRILL

1. Form one line on the baseline, to the left of the basket; the first player out is defense, the next player out is offense with a ball
2. [Offensive player] Dribble the length of the court; use as many dribbling moves as you need, but stay within the drill boundaries (the sideline and the lane line extended)
3. [Defender] Play full court on-ball defense; force the dribbler to turn and use her weak hand as much as possible

- The next dribbler and defender should start as soon as the first pair crosses the half-court line
- On the return trip down the court (on the opposite side), switch offensive and defensive players
- Repeat the drill starting from the right of the basket

REBOUNDING

DRILL 16.8 SINGLE LINE REBOUNDING DRILL

1. Form one line facing the left side of the backboard; the first player has a basketball
2. [First player in line] Toss the ball of the backboard; move to the end of the line
3. [Second player in line] Catch ball as you leap and release it near the peak of your jump (tip the ball off the backboard before you land)
4. Run to the end of the line
5. [Third player in line] Catch ball as you leap and release it near the peak of your jump (tip the ball off the backboard before you land)
6. Run to the end of the line

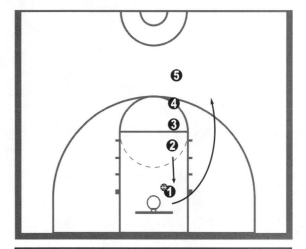

Single Line Rebounding Drill

• Try to rebound or tip continuously as a team for 30 seconds, without letting the ball hit the floor

DRILL 16.9 OFF THE BACKBOARD TRICK PLAY

1. Have a wing player shoot the ball off the backboard so that it bounces cleanly to the weak-side of the basket; have your posts work on getting weak-side position, rebounding, and putting the ball back in the basket off a tip.

Practicing the Off-the Backboard Trick Play is a good way to inject some life into a practice (as well as going over a play that just might come in handy sometime).

PART SIX
Appendices

Appendix 1
Rules of the Game

The following are excerpts of women's basketball rules and interpretations from the official NCAA rulebook. Men's rules are sometimes included for comparison purposes.

Reprinted with permission by the NCAA. Rules subject to change annually.

RULES AND INTERPRETATIONS

2004 NCAA Men's and Women's Basketball
Rules and Interpretations

National Collegiate Athletic Association
[ISSN 1042-3877]

The National Collegiate Athletic Association
P.O. Box 6222
Indianapolis, Indiana 46206-6222
317/917-6222 • www.ncaa.org

September 2003

POINTS OF EMPHASIS

In each edition of the NCAA Men's and Women's Basketball Rules and Interpretations, there are several areas that are given special attention. These are identified as points of emphasis. While they may not represent any rules changes, their importance must not be overlooked. In some cases, the points of emphasis are more important than some of the rules changes. When a topic is included in the points of emphasis, there has been evidence during the previous year(s) that there has been inconsistency in administering the area.

POINTS OF EMPHASIS FOR WOMEN

DISPLACEMENT

Eliminating displacement of an opponent, regardless of where she is on the court, will bring basketball back to a more skillful game that allows freedom of movement. If a player is displaced and cannot continue to cut, screen, post-up, dribble or rebound, a foul shall be called.

For the past five years, guidelines have been published in this section for the proper officiating of post play and hand-checking. These guidelines, which are listed in Appendix III of this book (sections 6 and 7), must continue to be followed. Officials must continue to enforce these guidelines to ensure that freedom of movement is allowed in the game.

1. **Displacement as it relates to hand-checking:**
    a. The dribbler may not be moved off her path by the use of the forearm by the defender.
    b. The dribbler may not be held, pushed or bumped by the body of the defender.

    c. The defender may not be pushed away by the use of the body or forearm of the dribbler.

    d. Displacement by either the offensive or defense player is a foul.

2. Displacement as it relates to post play:

    a. The defensive post player may not hold or push the offensive post player from her established position with the forearm, body or leg.

    b. The offensive post player may not hold or push the defensive post player from her established position with the forearm, body or leg.

    c. Displacement by either the offensive or defensive player is a foul.

3. Displacement as it relates to screening:

    a. The screener may not use arms, legs or body to hold or push the defensive player off of her intended path around the screen.

    b. The defensive player may not hold or push through the screen with her arms, legs or body to gain an advantage.

    c. Displacement by either the offensive or defensive player is a foul.

4. Displacement as it relates to cutting:

    a. Cutters must be allowed the freedom to move if they get to the path before the defender. Defensive players may not hold or push cutters off of their intended path by using their arms, legs or body.

    b. Cutters may not displace a defensive player in any way by using their arms, legs or body.

    c. Displacement by either the offensive or defensive player is a foul.

5. Displacement as it relates to rebounding:

    a. The use of the arms or body to hold or push by either the offensive or defensive player to get a good position to rebound is a foul.

    b. Backing a player away from the basket with the body and displacing her is a foul.

RULE 1—COURT AND EQUIPMENT

SECTION 1. THE GAME

Art. 1. Basketball is played by two teams of five players each. The objective is for each team to throw or tap the ball into its own basket and to prevent the other team from scoring.

Art. 2. The ball may be thrown, batted, rolled or dribbled in any direction, subject to the restrictions that follow.

SECTION 2. THE PLAYING COURT—DIMENSIONS

Art. 1. The playing court shall be a rectangular surface free from obstructions with sidelines of 94 feet in length and end lines of 50 feet in length, measured from the inside edges.

SECTION 8. COACHING BOX

Art. 1. The coaching boxes shall extend from the sideline to the back of the team benches.

SECTION 15. THE BALL

Art. 1. The ball shall be spherical.

Art. 2. The ball's color shall be the approved orange shade.

Art. 3. The ball shall have a deeply pebbled leather cover or a composite cover.

Art. 4. The ball shall have the traditionally shaped eight panels, bonded tightly to the rubber carcass.

Art. 5. The width of the black rubber rib (channels and/or seams) shall not exceed ¼ inch.

Art. 6. When dribbled vertically, without rotation, the ball shall return directly to the dribbler's hand.

Art. 7. The air pressure that will give the required reaction shall be stamped on the ball. The ball shall be inflated to an air pressure such that when it is dropped to the playing surface from a height of 6 feet measured to the bottom of the ball, it will rebound to a height, measured to the top of the ball of:

　a. **(Men)** Not less than 49 inches when it strikes its least resilient spot nor more than 54 inches when it strikes its most resilient spot.

　b. **(Women)** Not less than 51 inches when it strikes its least resilient spot nor more than 56 inches when it strikes its most resilient spot.

Art. 8.

　a. **(Men)** The circumference of the ball shall be within a maximum of 30 inches and a minimum of 29 ½ inches.

　b. **(Women)** The circumference of the ball shall be within a maximum of 29 inches and a minimum of 28 ½ inches.

Art. 9.

　a. **(Men)** The weight of the ball shall not be less than 20 ounces nor more than 22 ounces.

　b. **(Women)** The weight of the ball shall not be less than 18 ounces nor more than 20 ounces.

Art. 10. The home team shall provide a ball that meets the specifications listed in this Section. The referee shall judge the legality of the ball and may select for use a ball provided by the visiting team when the home team cannot provide a legal ball.

RULE 2—OFFICIALS AND THEIR DUTIES

SECTION 10. CORRECTABLE ERRORS

Art. 1. The correctable errors are listed in this Section. In order to correct any of them, such errors must be recognized by an official during the first dead ball after the game clock has been started properly.

　a. Failing to award a merited free throw.

　b. Awarding an unmerited free throw.

　c. Permitting a wrong player to attempt a free throw.

　d. Permitting a player to attempt a free throw at the wrong basket.

　e. Erroneously counting or canceling a score.

RULE 3—PLAYERS, SUBSTITUTES AND PLAYER EQUIPMENT

SECTION 1. THE TEAM

Art. 1. At the start of the game, each team shall consist of five players, one of whom shall be the captain.

A.R. 1. Teams A and B each have co-captains. At the pre-game conference, one of the co-captains requests permission from the referee that both co-captains be allowed to confer with officials on interpretations. **RULING:** Co-captains may participate in the pre-game conference, but only one co-captain of each team may confer with the officials during the game. During the pre-game conference, the referee shall be informed which co-captain of each team shall be the speaking co-captain during the game.

Art. 2. Each team may continue to play with fewer than five players when all other squad members are not eligible or able to play.

Art. 3. When there is only one player participating for a team, that team shall forfeit unless the referee believes that both teams have an opportunity to win.

SECTION 2. THE CAPTAIN

Art. 1. The captain is the representative of the team and may address an official on matters of interpretation or to obtain essential information, when it is done in a courteous manner. Dialogue between coaches and officials should be kept to a minimum.

Art. 2. Any player may address an official to request a timeout or permission to leave the playing court.

SECTION 5. UNIFORMS

Art. 12. Each team member's game jersey shall be numbered on the front and back with plain Arabic numerals.
    a. The following numbers are legal: 0, 1, 2, 3, 4, 5, 00, 10, 11, 12, 13, 14, 15, 20, 21, 22, 23, 24, 25, 30, 31, 32, 33, 34, 35, 40, 41, 42, 43, 44, 45, 50, 51, 52, 53, 54, 55. Team rosters can include 0 or 00 but not both. The numbers on the front and back of the game jersey shall be of the same color and style.
    b. The number shall be at least 6 inches high on the back and at least 4 inches high on the front and not less than ¾ inch in width.
    c. Numbers shall be centered on the front and back of game jerseys.
    d. No more than three colors may be used on uniforms. The style used for the uniform number shall allow for the uniform number to be clearly visible and shall conform to one of the following:
        1. A solid contrasting color with no more than two solid ¼-inch borders. A solid contrasting "shadow" trim, not to exceed ½ inch in width, may be used on part of the uniform number. When the game-jersey color is used as a border, it shall be counted as one of the allowed colors.
        2. The game-jersey color itself shall be counted as one of the allowable colors when bordered with not more than two ¼-inch solid border(s) contrasting with the game-jersey color.

Art. 13. Members of the same squad shall not wear identical numbers.
    a. When such an infraction occurs, the second-listed squad member in the official scorebook (and any following member) wearing an identical number shall be charged

with an indirect technical foul. The penalty shall be imposed when the infraction is discovered.

    b. When there is duplication, only one squad member shall be permitted to wear a given uniform number. All others must change to a uniform number not already in use before they may participate.

Art. 14. Opposing team uniforms shall be of contrasting colors. The home team should wear light game jerseys and the away team should wear dark game jerseys.

RULE 4—DEFINITIONS

SECTION 4. BASKET INTERFERENCE

Art. 1. Basket interference occurs when a player:
    a. Touches the ball or any part of the basket while the ball is on or within the basket,
    b. Touches the ball while any part of it is within the cylinder that has the ring as its lower base, or
    c. Reaches through the basket from below and touches the ball before it enters the cylinder.

Art. 2. Basket interference also occurs when a movable basket ring is pulled down by a player so that it contacts the ball before the ring returns to its original position.

Art. 3. Batting the ball is intentionally striking the ball or intentionally changing its direction with the hand or arm.

SECTION 6. BENCH PERSONNEL

Art. 1. Bench personnel includes anyone in the team bench area and substitutes.

SECTION 7. BLOCKING

Art. 1. Blocking is illegal personal contact that impedes the progress of an opponent.

SECTION 8. CHARGING

Art. 1. Charging is illegal personal contact by pushing or moving into an opponent's torso.

SECTION 9. BONUS FREE THROWS

Art. 1. One type of bonus free throw is a second free throw that is awarded for each common foul (except a player-control or team control foul) committed by a player of a team, beginning with that team's seventh foul in a half, which is a combination of personal fouls, direct technical fouls, intentional technical fouls and flagrant technical fouls, provided that the first free throw for the foul is successful.

Art. 2. The other type of bonus free throw occurs starting with the offending team's 10th team foul in a half, which is a combination of personal fouls, direct technical fouls, intentional technical fouls and flagrant technical fouls. From this point, two free throws shall be awarded for each common foul (except a player-control or team-control foul).

Art. 3. Player-control fouls and team-control fouls shall count as team fouls for reaching the bonus.

Art. 4. All direct technical fouls charged to bench personnel shall count toward the team-foul total and bonus.

SECTION 10. BOUNDARY LINES

Art. 1. Boundary lines of the playing court shall consist of end lines and sidelines. The inside edges of these lines define the inbounds and out-of-bounds areas.

SECTION 11. CLOSELY GUARDED

Art. 1. (Men) A player in control in the front court only while holding or dribbling the ball is closely guarded when his opponent is in a guarding stance at a distance not exceeding 6 feet.

Art. 2. (Women) A player in control anywhere on the playing court while holding (not dribbling) the ball is closely guarded when her opponent is in a guarding stance at a distance not exceeding 3 feet.

Art. 3. After the start of a five-second closely guarded count, in order for a closely guarded violation to occur, there shall be continuous guarding by the same opponent.

Art. 4. When a player is positioned between the player in control of the ball and his or her opponent, who is within 6 feet **(men)** or 3 feet **(women)**, a closely guarded situation does not exist.

SECTION 12. CONTINUOUS MOTION

Art. 1. Continuous motion applies to a try for field goal or free throw, but shall have no significance unless there is a foul by the defense during the interval that begins when the habitual throwing movement starts a try or with the touching on a tap and ends when the ball is clearly in flight.

SECTION 13. IN CONTROL—PLAYER, TEAM

Art. 1. A player shall be in control when:
    a. Holding a live ball; or
    b. Dribbling a live ball while in bounds.

Art. 2. A team shall be in control when:
    a. A player of the team is in control;
    b. While a live ball is being passed between teammates; or
    c. When a player of that team has disposal of the ball for a throw-in.

Art. 3. Team control shall continue until the ball is in flight during a try for goal, an opponent secures control or the ball becomes dead.

Art. 4. There shall be no team control during:
    a. A jump ball;
    b. The tapping of a rebound (unless it is a try for goal);
    c. A try for goal after the ball is in flight;
    d. The period that follows any of these acts (a–c) while the ball is being batted (from the vicinity of other players) in an attempt to secure control;
    e. A dead ball.

Art. 5. Team control is re-established in Article 4 of this Rule when a player secures control.

Art. 6. "Control" for purposes of establishing the alternating-possession procedure occurs when:
    a. A player is in control;
    b. The ball is handed/bounced to or placed at the disposal of the free-thrower after a common foul or placed at the disposal of a thrower-in.

SECTION 14. CYLINDER

Art. 1. The cylinder is the imaginary geometric figure that has the ring as its base and is formed by the upward extension of that ring.

SECTION 15. DESIGNATED SPOT

Art. 1. A designated spot is the location at which a thrower-in is presented disposal of the ball out of bounds nearest to where the ball was located and from which he or she cannot move until releasing the ball. **(Men)** For a flagrant technical foul or an intentional technical foul, the designated spot is at the out-of-bounds location at the division line.

Art. 2. A designated spot shall be 3 feet wide with no depth limitation.

SECTION 16. DISPOSAL OF BALL

Art. 1. The ball is at the disposal of a player when it is:
   a. Handed to the thrower-in or free-thrower;
   b. Caught by the thrower-in or the free-thrower after it is bounced to him or her;
   c. Placed at a spot on the floor; or
   d. Available to a player after a goal.

SECTION 17. DISQUALIFIED PLAYER

Art. 1. A disqualified player is one who is barred from further participation in a game because of:
   a. Committing a fifth foul, including personal fouls, direct technical fouls and intentional technical fouls;
   b. Ejection.

Art. 2. A team member who leaves the bench area during a fight shall be disqualified and ejected.

Art. 3. The officials shall notify the player and coach of any disqualification.

Art. 4. When the coach is notified by an official that a player is disqualified, that player becomes bench personnel, except when the disqualified individual is ejected.

SECTION 18. DRIBBLE

Art. 1. A dribble is ball movement caused by a player in control who bats, pushes or taps the ball to the playing court once or several times.

Art. 2. The dribble may be started by pushing, throwing, tapping or batting the ball to the playing court.

Art. 3. During a dribble, the ball may be batted into the air, provided that it is permitted to strike the playing court one or more times before the ball is touched again with either hand.

Art. 4. The dribble ends when:
   a. The dribbler catches or carries/palms the ball by allowing it to come to rest in one or both hands.
   b. The dribbler touches the ball with both hands simultaneously.
   c. An opponent bats the ball.
   d. The ball becomes dead.

Art. 5. An interrupted dribble occurs when the ball is loose after deflecting off the dribbler or after it momentarily gets away from the dribbler.

Art. 6. During an interrupted dribble, there shall be no player control and the following cannot occur:
   a. Player-control foul.
   b. Acknowledgment of a timeout request.
   c. **(Men)** Five-second closely guarded dribbling violation.

SECTION 26. FOUL

A foul is an infraction of the rules that is charged to a squad member or a coach and is penalized in various ways. Following are the types of fouls:

Art. 1. **Personal foul.** A personal foul shall be a foul committed by a player that involves illegal contact with an opponent while the ball is live.

Art. 2. **Common foul.** A common foul shall be a personal foul that is neither flagrant nor intentional, nor committed against a player trying for a field goal, nor part of a double, multiple or simultaneous foul.

Art. 3. **(Women) Indirect and direct technical foul.** A technical foul that is direct or indirect shall be a foul by any player, squad member, coach, bench personnel or follower that neither involves contact nor causes contact with an opponent while the ball is dead.
   (Women) A direct technical foul is also a non-flagrant foul by any player that involves contact or causes contact with an opponent while the ball is dead.
   Examples of indirect and direct technical fouls include:
   a. Unsporting conduct (direct);
   b. Requesting an excessive timeout (indirect);
   c. Hanging on the ring, except when doing so to prevent an injury (indirect); and
   d. Making non-flagrant contact with an opponent while the ball is dead (direct).

Art. 4. **Flagrant personal foul, live ball.** A flagrant personal foul shall be a personal foul that involves severe or excessive contact with an opponent or involves contact that is extreme in nature while the ball is live.

Art. 5. **Flagrant technical foul, dead ball.** A flagrant foul shall be a technical foul when it involves either unsporting conduct that is extreme in nature, or severe, excessive contact against an opponent while the ball is dead.
a.An exception is a foul by an airborne shooter.

Art. 6. **Intentional personal foul.** An intentional foul shall be a personal foul that, on the basis of an official's observation of the act, is not a legitimate attempt to directly play the ball or a player. Determination of whether a personal foul is intentional shall not be based on the severity of the act. Examples include, but are not limited to:
   a. Fouling a player who is away from the ball and not directly involved with the play.
   b. Contact with a player making a throw-in.
   c. Holding or pushing an opponent in order to stop the game clock.
   d. Pushing a player from behind to prevent a score.
   e. Causing excessive contact with an opponent while playing the ball.

SECTION 27. FREE THROW

Art. 1. A free throw is the privilege given a player to score one point by an unhindered try for goal from within the free-throw semicircle and behind the free-throw line.

Art. 2. A free throw starts when the ball is placed at the disposal of the freethrower.

Art. 3. A free throw ends when:
   a. The try is successful;
   b. It is certain the try will not be successful;

c. The try touches the floor or any player; or

d. The ball becomes dead.

SECTION 28. FRONT COURT/BACK COURT

Art. 1. A team's front court shall consist of that part of the playing court between its end line and the nearer edge of the division line, including its basket and the inbounds part of its backboard.

Art. 2. A team's back court consists of the rest of the playing court, including its opponent's basket and inbounds part of the backboard and the division line, excluding the mathematical edge nearest the team's basket.

Art. 3. A live ball is in the front court or back court of the team in control as follows:

    a. A ball that is in contact with a player or with the playing court shall be in the back court when either the ball or the player (either player when the ball is touching more than one) is touching the back court. It shall be in the front court when neither the ball nor the player is touching the back court.

A.R. 22. As Team A advances the ball from its back court toward its front court, A1 passes the ball to A2. A2 catches the ball while both feet are on the playing court with one foot on either side of the division line. In this situation, either foot may be the pivot foot. (a) A2 lifts the foot that is in the back court and then puts it back on the floor in the back court; or (b) A2 lifts the foot that is in the front court, pivots and puts it on the floor in the back court. **RULING:** In (a), back-court violation. When A2, while holding the ball, lifts the foot that was in the back court, the ball is in the front court. When A2's foot touches in the back court, it shall be a violation. In (b), when A2 lifts the foot that is in the front court and places it down in the back court, the location of the ball has not changed. The ball is still in the back court and no violation has occurred. (See Rule 4-28.2.)

    b. A ball that is not in contact with a player or the playing court retains the same status as when it was last in contact with a player or the playing court.

    c. During a dribble from back court to front court, the ball shall be in the front court when both feet of the dribbler and the ball touch the playing court entirely in the front court.

SECTION 33. GUARDING

Art. 1. Guarding shall be the act of legally placing the body in the path of an offensive opponent.

Art. 2. There is no minimum distance required between the guard and opponent, but the maximum shall be **(men)** 6 feet or **(women)** 3 feet when closely guarded. These distances shall apply only when a player is holding the ball (for men, this distance also applies while dribbling).

Art. 3. Every player shall be entitled to a spot on the playing court, provided that such player gets there first without illegally contacting an opponent.

Art. 4. The guard may shift to maintain guarding position in the path of the dribbler, provided that the guard does not charge into the dribbler nor otherwise cause contact as in Rule 10-21.2 and 10-21.3.

Art. 5. The responsibility of the dribbler for contact shall not be shifted merely because the guard turns or ducks to absorb shock when contact caused by the dribbler is imminent.

Art. 6. To establish an initial legal guarding position on the player with the ball:

a. The guard shall have both feet touching the playing court. When the guard jumps into position initially, both feet must return to the playing court after the jump, for the guard to attain a guarding position.
b. The guard's torso shall face the opponent.
c. No time and distance shall be required.
d. When the opponent with the ball is airborne, the guard shall have attained legal position before the opponent left the playing court.

SECTION 34. HANDS AND ARMS, USE OF

Art. **1.** The arms may be extended vertically above one's shoulder and need not be lowered to avoid contact with an opponent when the action of the opponent causes contact.
    a. This legal use of the arms and hands usually occurs when guarding:
       1. The thrower-in
       2. The player with the ball in pressing tactics or
       3. A player with the ball who is maneuvering to try for goal by pivoting, jumping or hooking either a pass or try for goal.

Art. **2.** It shall be legal for a defender to accidentally hit the hand of a ball-handler when reaching to block or slap the ball when there is player control with that player's hand in contact with the ball and when that player is a:
    a. Dribbler
    b. Player attempting a try for field goal, or
    c. Player holding the ball.

Art. **3.** A player shall be permitted to hold his or her hands and arms in front of his or her face or body for protection in a recoil action rather than a pushing action:
    a. To absorb force from imminent contact by an opponent or
    b. When that player, who has set a blind screen, is about to be run into by the player being screened.

Art. **4.** A player shall not use the arms, hands, hips or shoulders
    a. To force his or her way through a screen or
    b. To hold the screener and then push the screener aside in order to maintain a guarding position relative to his or her opponent.

Art. **5.** It shall be illegal to extend one's arms fully or partially, other than vertically, so that the freedom of movement of an opponent is hindered when contact with the extended arms occurs.

Art. **6.** It shall be illegal to extend one's elbow(s) when one's
    a. Hands are on one's hips,
    b. Hands are held near one's chest or
    c. Arms are held approximately horizontal to the playing court.
    Note: These illegal positions are most commonly used when rebounding, screening or in the various aspects of post play.

Art. **7.** The following shall be considered excessive swinging:
    a. When arm(s) and elbow(s) are swung about while using the shoulders as pivots, and the speed of the extended arm(s) and elbow(s) exceeds that of the rest of the body as it rotates on the hips or on the pivot foot; or
    b. When the speed and vigor with which the arm(s) and elbow(s) are swung is such that injury could result if another player were contacted.

SECTION 35. HELD BALL

Art. 1. A held ball occurs when an opponent places his or her hand(s):
   a. So firmly on the ball that control cannot be obtained without undue roughness.
   b. On the ball to prevent an airborne player from throwing the ball or attempting a try.

SECTION 38. INCIDENTAL CONTACT

Art. 1. Contact shall not constitute a foul. When 10 players move rapidly in a limited area, some contact is certain to occur. Incidental contact shall be contact with an opponent that is permitted and does not constitute a foul.

Art. 2. Contact that is incidental to an effort by an opponent to reach a loose ball, or contact that results when opponents are in equally favorable positions to perform normal defensive or offensive movement, should be permitted even though the contact may be severe or excessive.

Art. 3. Contact that does not hinder the opponent from participating in normal defensive or offensive movements shall be considered incidental.

Art. 4. A player who is screened within his or her visual field shall be expected to avoid contact with the screener by stopping or avoiding the screener.

Art. 5. A player who is screened outside his or her visual field may make inadvertent contact with the screener. Such contact shall be incidental, provided that the screener is not displaced when he or she has the ball.

Art. 6. When a player approaches an opponent from behind or a position from which the player has no reasonable chance to play the ball without making contact with the opponent, the responsibility for contact shall be that of the player in the unfavorable position.

SECTION 40. JUMP BALL

Art. 1. A jump ball is a method of putting the ball into play at the beginning of the game or any extra period(s) by tossing it up between two opponents in the center circle.

Art. 2. A jump ball shall begin when the ball leaves the official's hand and shall end when it touches a non-jumper, the floor, basket or backboard.

SECTION 41. JUMPERS

Art. 1. Jumpers are the two opposing players vying for the tip during a jump ball.

SECTION 42. KICKING THE BALL

Art. 1. Kicking the ball is striking it intentionally with any part of the leg or the foot.

Art. 2. Accidentally striking the ball with the foot or leg shall not be a violation.

SECTION 43. LOCATION OF A PLAYER

Art. 1. The location of a player (or non-player) is determined as being:
   a. Where he or she is touching the floor, as far as being in bounds or out of bounds.
   b. In the front court or back court.
   c. Outside or inside the three-point line with at least one foot in contact with the playing floor behind the line and the other foot not contacting the line or the playing floor in front of the line.

Art. 2. When a player is in the air from a leap (except during a throw-in) or when a defensive player intercepts a ball while in the air, the player's status with reference to these two situations shall be the same as at the time the player was last in contact with the floor or an extension of the floor, such as a bleacher.

Art. 3. When the ball touches an official or a player who is on the playing court, play shall continue as if the ball touched the floor at that individual's location.

SECTION 46. PENALTY

Art. 1. A penalty for a foul is the charging of the offender with the foul and awarding one or more free throws, or awarding the ball to the opponent for a throw-in. For any flagrant foul, the penalty includes ejection of the offender.

Art. 2. The penalty for a violation is the awarding of the ball to the opponent for a throw-in, one or more points or a substitute free throw.

SECTION 47. PIVOT

Art. 1. A pivot takes place when a player who is holding the ball steps once or more than once in any direction with the same foot, while the other foot, called the pivot foot, is kept at its point of contact with the playing court.

SECTION 51. POST PLAYER

Art. 1. A post player is an offensive or defensive player with or without the ball with his or her back to the basket who is inside the free-throw lane or just outside the lane.

SECTION 52. REBOUND

Art. 1. A rebound is an attempt by any player to secure possession of the ball after a try for goal. In a rebounding situation, there is no player or team control.

Art. 2. To attain or maintain legal rebounding position, a player shall not:
    a. Displace, charge or push an opponent.
    b. Extend either or both shoulders, hips, knees or extend either or both arms or elbows fully or partially in a position other than vertical so that the freedom of movement of an opponent is hindered when contact with any of these body parts occurs.
    c. Bend his/her body in an abnormal position to hold or displace an opponent.
    d. Violate the principle of verticality.

Art. 3. Every player shall be entitled to a spot on the playing court, provided that such player gets there first without illegally contacting an opponent.

SECTION 56. SCREEN

Art. 1. A screen is legal action by a player who, without causing contact, delays or prevents an opponent from reaching a desired position.

Art. 2. In screening tactics, the screener shall not be required to face in any particular direction at any time.

Art. 3. The screener shall not lean into the path of an opponent or extend his or her hips into that path, even though his or her feet are stationary.

Art. 4. A player with the ball may be a screener and shall be subject to the principles of screening.

Art. 5. While most screening is by the offense, the principles of screening shall apply equally to the offense and defense.

SECTION 63. THREE-SECOND LANE

Art. 1. The three-second lane is the area in the front court that is bounded by the end line, the free-throw lane lines and the free-throw line, and includes such lines.

SECTION 64. THROW-IN/THROWER-IN

Art. 1. A throw-in is the method of putting the ball in play from out of bounds.
Art. 2. A thrower-in is the player attempting the throw-in.
Art. 3. A throw-in and the throw-in count shall begin when the ball is at the disposal of the player entitled to the throw-in.
Art. 4. A thrower-in shall have five seconds from receiving disposal of the ball to release the throw-in. The throw-in count shall end when the ball is released by the thrower-in so that the ball goes directly into the playing court.
Art. 5. A throw-in shall end when the passed ball is controlled by an inbounds player other than the thrower-in.
Art. 6. After a goal is scored by an opponent or awarded because of basket interference or goal-tending, the thrower-in may run along the end line.
Art. 7. A thrower-in shall be permitted to throw the ball to a teammate along the end line after a goal is scored by an opponent or awarded because of basket interference or goaltending.

SECTION 65. TRAVELING

Art. 1. Traveling occurs when a player holding the ball moves a foot or both feet in any direction in excess of prescribed limits described in this Rule.
    A.R. 35. A1 attempts a try at Team A's basket after having —completed the dribble. The try does not touch the backboard, the ring or the flange or any other player. A1 runs and catches the ball before it strikes the playing court. Is this traveling? **RULING:** When A1 recovered his or her own try, A1 could either dribble, pass or try again. There is no team control by either team when a try is in flight. However, when the shot clock expires and a try by A1 or a teammate has not struck the ring or the flange, it shall be a violation of the shot-clock rule.
Art. 2. A player who catches the ball with both feet on the playing court may pivot, using either foot. When one foot is lifted, the other is the pivot foot.
Art. 3. A player who catches the ball while moving or dribbling may stop and establish a pivot foot as follows:
    a. When both feet are off the playing court and the player lands:
        1. Simultaneously on both feet, either may be the pivot foot;
        2. On one foot followed by the other, the first foot to touch shall be the pivot foot;
        3. On one foot, the player may jump off that foot and simultaneously land on both; neither foot can be the pivot foot.
    b. When one foot is on the playing court:
        1. That foot shall be the pivot foot when the other foot touches in a step;
        2. The player may jump off that foot and simultaneously land on both; neither foot can then be the pivot foot.

Art. 4. After coming to a stop and establishing the pivot foot:
- a. The pivot foot may be lifted, but not returned to the playing court, before the ball is released on a pass or try for goal;
- b. The pivot foot shall not be lifted before the ball is released to start a dribble.

Art. 5. After coming to a stop when neither foot can be the pivot foot:
- a. One or both feet may be lifted, but may not be returned to the playing court, before the ball is released on a pass or try for goal;
- b. Neither foot shall be lifted, before the ball is released, to start a dribble.

A.R. 38. Is it traveling when a player (a) falls to the playing court while holding the ball; or (b) gains control of the ball while on the playing court and then, because of momentum, rolls or slides, after which the player passes or starts a dribble before getting to his or her feet? **RULING:** In (a), yes, because it is virtually impossible not to move the pivot foot when falling to the playing floor. In (b), no. The player may pass, shoot, start a dribble or call a timeout. Once the player has the ball and is no longer sliding, he or she may not roll over. When flat on his or her back, the player may sit up without violating. When the player puts the ball on the floor, then rises and is the first to touch the ball, it also is traveling. When a player rises to his or her feet while holding the ball, it is traveling. When a player falls to one knee while holding the ball, it is traveling if the pivot foot moves.

SECTION 66. TRY FOR FIELD GOAL/ACT OF SHOOTING

Art. 1. A try for field goal is an attempt by a player to score two or three points by throwing or tapping the ball into his or her basket.

Art. 2. The try shall start when the player begins the motion that habitually precedes the release of the ball on a try. The ball does not need to leave the player's hand. The arm might be held so that the player cannot throw; however, he or she may be making an attempt.

SECTION 69. VERTICALITY

Art. 1. Verticality applies to a legal position. The basic components of the principle of verticality are:
- a. Legal guarding position must be established and attained initially, and movement thereafter must be legal.
- b. From such position, the defender may rise or jump vertically and occupy the space within his or her vertical plane.
- c. The hands and arms of the defender may be raised within his or her vertical plane while the defender is on the playing court or in the air.
- d. The defender shall not be penalized for leaving the playing court vertically or having his or her hands and arms extended within the vertical plane.
- e. The offensive player, whether on the playing court or airborne, shall not "clear out" or cause contact that is not incidental.
- f. The defender may not "belly up" or use the lower part of the body or arms to cause contact outside his or her vertical plane.
- g. The player with the ball shall be given no more protection or consideration than the defender in the judging of which, if either, player has violated the principle of verticality.

RULE 6—LIVE BALL AND DEAD BALL
SECTION 2. HELD BALL—ALTERNATING PROCESS

Art. 1. In held-ball situations, teams shall alternate taking possession of the ball at a designated spot nearest to where the held ball occurred.

Art. 2. The team that does not obtain control of the initial jump ball shall start the alternating process when the next alternating-possession situation occurs by being awarded the ball at a designated spot nearest to where the held ball occurred.

    a. When the ball is last touched by two opponents, both of whom are in bounds or out of bounds, the alternating-possession procedure has not been established, so a jump ball shall take place between the two involved players.

    b. When the officials are in doubt as to who last touched the ball and the alternating-possession procedure has not been established, a jump ball shall take place between the two involved players.

SECTION 4. POSITION FOR JUMP BALL

Art. 1. For any jump ball, each jumper shall have both feet inside the half of the center circle that is farther from his or her team's basket.

Art. 2. Each jumper may face in either direction.

Art. 3. The referee shall toss the ball upward between the jumpers in a plane at right angles to the sidelines, to a height greater than either of them can jump and so that the ball will drop between them.

Art. 4. The ball shall be touched by one or both of the jumpers after it reaches its highest point.

Art. 5. When the ball touches the playing court without being touched by at least one of the jumpers, the official shall toss the ball again.

Art. 6. Neither jumper shall touch the tossed ball before it reaches its highest point, leave the center circle until the ball has been touched, catch the jump ball, nor touch it more than twice.

Art. 7. The jump ball and these restrictions end when the ball touches one of the eight non-jumpers, the playing court, the basket, the backboard or when the ball becomes dead.

Art. 8. When the referee or designated official is ready to make the toss, a non-jumper shall not move onto the center circle or change position around the center circle until the ball has left the official's hand.

Art. 9. None of the eight non-jumpers shall have either foot break the plane of the geometrical cylinder that has the center circle as its base, nor shall any player take a position in any occupied space until the ball has been touched.

Art. 10. Teammates shall not occupy adjacent positions around the center circle when an opponent indicates a desire for one of these positions before the referee is ready to toss the ball.

Art. 11. Players may move around the center circle without breaking the geometrical cylinder that has the center circle as its base after the ball has left the referee's hand(s) during the toss.

RULE 7—OUT OF BOUNDS AND THE THROW-IN
SECTION 5. OUT OF BOUNDS, BALL IN PLAY FROM

Art. 1. When the ball is out of bounds after any violation as outlined in Rules 9-3 through 9-15, an official shall place the ball at the disposal of an opponent of the player who committed the violation for a throw-in from a designated spot nearest to where the violation occurred.

SECTION 6. THROW-IN

Art. 1. The throw-in shall start and the throw-in team shall have team control when the ball is placed at the disposal of a player entitled to the throw-in.

Art. 2. The throw-in count shall end when the ball is released by the thrower-in so that the ball goes directly onto the playing court.

Art. 3. The thrower-in shall release the ball within five seconds so that the pass goes directly into the playing court, except as provided in Rule 7-5.6.

RULE 8—FREE THROW

SECTION 1. POSITIONS DURING ATTEMPT

Art. 1. When a free throw is awarded, an official shall take the ball to the free-throw line of the offended team.

Art. 2. After allowing reasonable time for players to take their positions, the official shall put the ball in play by placing it at the disposal of the free-thrower.

Art. 3. The same procedure shall be followed for each free throw of a multiple free throw.

Art. 4. For **men**, a maximum of six players (four opponents of the free-thrower and two teammates of the free-thrower) shall be permitted on the free-throw lane during a free throw. All other players shall be behind the free-throw line extended and behind the three-point field-goal line.

    a. **(Men)** Within this limit, opponents of the free-thrower may occupy the third lane space (with the spot closest to the end line being the first). If they opt not to, a teammate of the free-thrower may occupy the third space. No player shall occupy the fourth space.

Art. 5. (Women) A maximum of six players (four opponents of the free-thrower and two teammates of the free-thrower) shall be permitted on the lane. All other players shall be behind the free-throw line extended and behind the three-point field-goal line.

    a. The two lane spaces closest to the end line shall remain open.

    b. The first space on each side of the lane that is closer to the free-throw line after the block is designated for an opponent of the free-thrower. The next lane space on each side of the lane is designated for a teammate of the free-thrower. The next available space on each side of the lane is designated for an opponent of the free-thrower.

    c. Teammates of the free-thrower shall not occupy lane spaces designated for opponents of the free-thrower; opponents of the freethrower shall not occupy lane spaces designated for teammates of the free-thrower.

Art. 6. During a free throw for a personal foul, **(men)** each of the lane spaces adjacent to the end line shall be occupied by one opponent of the free-thrower unless the resumption-of-play method of placing the ball on the floor at the disposal of the free-thrower is in effect. **(Women)** Each of the first lane spaces closer to the free-throw line after the block shall be occupied by one opponent of the free-thrower unless the resumption-of-play method of placing the ball on the floor at the disposal of the free-thrower is in effect.

Art. 7. (Men) The opponents of the free-thrower occupying the lane spaces adjacent to the end line shall be permitted to position themselves up to the edge of the block that is farthest from the end line. **(Women)** Each opponent of the free-thrower occupying the lane space on each side of the lane that is closer to the free-throw line after the block shall be permitted to position themselves up to the edge of the block that is closer to the free-throw line.

Art. 8. (Men) A teammate of the free-thrower shall be entitled to the second adjacent lane space on each side and an opponent of the free-thrower shall be entitled to occupy the next lane space on each side.

    a. No player shall be permitted to occupy the last (fourth) space on either side of the free-throw lane.

    b. Players shall be permitted to move along and across the lane to occupy a vacant space within the limitations listed in this Rule.

A.R. 1. (Men) During the first of two free throws by A1, B2 does not occupy the third lane space and A3 takes it. Before the ball is handed to A1 for the second try, B2 requests permission to occupy the third space. **RULING:** Grant B2's request.

Art. 9. A player shall position one foot at the near proximity of the outer edge of the free-throw lane line. The other foot may be positioned anywhere within the designated 3-foot lane space.

Art. 10. Only one player shall occupy any part of a designated lane space. **(Women)** Only the first lane space above the block closer to the free-throw line on each side must be occupied.

Art. 11. When the ball is to become dead regardless of whether the last free throw for a specific penalty is successful, players shall not take positions along the free-throw lane.

SECTION 3. 10-SECOND LIMIT

Art. 1. The try for goal shall be attempted within 10 seconds after the ball has been placed at the disposal of the free-thrower at the free-throw line.

RULE 9—VIOLATIONS AND PENALTIES
SECTION 1. FREE THROW

Art. 1. The try shall be attempted from within the free-throw semicircle and behind the free-throw line.

Art. 2. After the ball is placed at the disposal of a free-thrower:

    a. The free-thrower shall release the try within 10 seconds and in such a way that the ball enters the basket or touches the ring or flange before the free throw ends.

    b. The free-thrower shall not purposely fake a try nor shall the free-thrower's teammates nor opponents purposely fake a violation.

    c. The free-thrower shall not break the vertical plane of the free-throw line with either foot until the ball strikes the ring, flange or backboard or until the free throw ends.

    d. The free-thrower shall not enter the semicircle. The free-thrower shall not leave the semicircle before releasing the free throw.

    e. No player shall enter or leave a marked lane space.

    f. No opponent shall disconcert (e.g., taunt, bait, gesture or delay) the free-thrower.

    g. Players not in a legal marked lane space shall remain behind the free-throw line extended and behind the three-point field-goal line until the ball strikes the ring, flange or backboard, or until the free throw ends.

    h. Players occupying any of the legal marked lane spaces on each side of the lane may break the vertical plane of a lane-space boundary once the free-thrower has released the ball. (See Rule 8-1.)

    i. Players occupying a legal marked lane space may not have either foot beyond the vertical plane of the outside edge of any legal lane boundary or beyond the vertical plane of any edge of space (2 x 36 inches) designated by a legal lane space mark or beyond the vertical plane of any edge of the lane until the ball is released by the free-thrower.

    j. Neither team shall have more than the maximum number of players permitted on the free-throw lane.

    k. **(Men)** No player shall occupy the fourth lane space on either side of the free-throw lane.

    l. **(Women)** An opponent of the free-thrower shall occupy each lane space above and adjacent to the block.

Art. 3. No teammate of the free-thrower may occupy either of the legal lane spaces nearest the basket.

SECTION 8. THREE-SECOND RULE

Art. 1. A player shall not be permitted to have any part of his or her body remain in the three-second lane for more than three consecutive seconds while the ball is in control of that player's team in his or her front court.

    a. A team in control of the ball for a throw-in adjacent to a front-court boundary line may not be called for a three-second violation.

A.R. 13. The ball is loose or there is an interrupted dribble. **RULING:** The three-second count shall be in effect. The team that had control before the loose ball or during an interrupted dribble shall maintain team control until the opponent secures control.

Art. 2. Allowance shall be made for a player who, having been in the three second lane for less than three seconds, dribbles or moves in to try for field goal.

    a. The player shall not pass the ball instead of trying for goal.

SECTION 11. BALL IN BACK COURT

Art. 1. A player shall not be the first to touch the ball in his or her back court when the ball came from the front court while the player's team was in team control and the player or a teammate caused the ball to go into the back court.

A.R. 20. A1 receives a pass in Team A's front court and throws the ball to his or her back court where the ball (a) is touched by a teammate, (b) goes directly out of bounds or (c) rests, rolls or bounces with all players hesitating to touch it. RULING: Violation when touched in (a). In (b), it is a violation for going out of bounds. In (c), the ball is live so that Team B may secure control. When Team A touches the ball first, it shall be a violation. The ball continues to be in team control of Team A. For men, the 10-second count shall start when the ball goes in the back court, while the 35-second shot clock shall continue to run. For women, the 30-second clock shall continue.

Art. 2. A player meets the conditions of Article 1 of this Rule by having the ball touch any part of his or her body voluntarily or involuntarily.

Art. 3. A pass in the front court that is deflected by a defensive player so that the ball goes into the back court may be recovered by either team.

Art. 4. When the throw-in spot is located adjacent to a front-court boundary line, the throw-in team may cause the ball to go into the back court.

Art. 5. A defensive player shall be permitted to secure control of the ball while both feet are off the playing court and land with one or both feet in the back court.

A.R. 21. B1 (a) secures possession of a rebound from Team A's basket or (b) has the ball for a throw-in under Team A's basket. B1 is in the front court of Team A (in other words, the back court of Team B). B1 attempts a long pass down the playing court to teammate B2. A2, standing in Team A's front court close to the division line, leaps and intercepts a pass by B1, then lands in the back court of Team A with player control. **RULING**: In both (a) and (b), no violation has occurred. These are exceptions to the back-court rule. (See Rule 9-11.6.)

Art. 6. A player shall be permitted to be the first to secure control of the ball after a jump ball or throw-in while both feet are off the playing court and the player lands with one or both feet in the back court.

SECTION 12. ELBOW(S)

Art. 1. A player shall not excessively swing his or her arm(s) or elbow(s), even without contacting an opponent.

SECTION 13. CLOSELY GUARDED

Art. 1. Closely guarded violations occur when:

    a. A team in its front court (men) or on the playing court (women) controls the ball for five seconds in an area enclosed by screening teammates.

A.R. 23. Team A, while in possession of the ball, lines up four of its players side by side, just in bounds at a boundary line. The four players pass the ball back and forth to one another with their arms reaching out beyond the plane of the boundary line. The players are in (a) the front court or (b) the back court. **RULING**: In (a), after five seconds, a violation shall be called when a defensive player is within **(men)** 6 feet or **(women)** 3 feet of one of the offensive players. In (b), the 10-second rule applies for men.

    b. (1) **(Men)** A closely guarded player anywhere in his front court holds or dribbles the ball for five seconds. This count shall be terminated during an interrupted dribble.

    (2) **(Women)** A player in control of the ball, but not dribbling, is closely guarded when an opponent is in a guarding stance within 3 feet. A closely guarded violation shall occur when the player in control of the ball holds the ball for more than five seconds.

RULE 10—FOULS AND PENALTIES

PERSONAL FOULS

SECTION 20. BY PLAYERS

Art. 1. A player shall not hold, push, charge, trip or impede the progress of an opponent by extending arm(s), shoulder(s), hip(s) or knee(s) or by bending his or her own body into other than a normal position; nor use any unreasonably rough tactics.

Art. 2. A player shall not contact an opponent with his or her hand unless such contact is only with the opponent's hand while it is on the ball and is incidental to an attempt to play the ball.

Art. 3. A player shall not use his or her hand(s) on an opponent to inhibit the freedom of movement of the opponent in any way or to aid an opponent in starting or stopping.

Art. 4. A player shall not extend the arm(s) fully or partially other than vertically so that freedom of movement of an opponent is hindered when contact with the arm(s) occurs.

Art. 5. A player shall not use the forearm and hand to prevent an opponent from attacking the ball during a dribble or when trying for goal.

Art. 6. A player may hold his or her hand(s) and arm(s) in front of his or her own face or body for protection and to absorb force from an imminent charge by an opponent.

Art. 7. Contact caused by a defensive player approaching the player with the ball from behind is pushing; contact caused by the momentum of a player who has tried for goal is charging.

SECTION 21. BY DRIBBLER

Art. 1. A dribbler shall neither charge into nor contact an opponent in the dribbler's path nor attempt to dribble between two opponents or between an opponent and a boundary, unless the space is sufficient to provide a reasonable chance for the dribbler to pass through without contact.

Art. 2. When a dribbler, without contact, passes an opponent sufficiently to have head and shoulders beyond the front of the opponent's torso, the greater responsibility for subsequent contact shall be that of the opponent.

Art. 3. When a dribbler has obtained a straight-line path, the dribbler may not be crowded out of that path; when an opponent is able to legally obtain a defensive position in that path, the dribbler shall avoid contact by changing direction or ending the dribble.

SECTION 22. BY SCREENER

Art. 1. A player shall not cause contact by setting a screen outside the visual field of a stationary opponent that does not allow this opponent a normal step to move.

Art. 2. A screener shall not make contact with the opponent when setting a screen within the visual field of that opponent.

Art. 3. A screener shall not take a position so close to a moving opponent that this opponent cannot avoid contact by stopping or changing direction.

Art. 4. No player, while moving, shall set a screen that causes contact or delays an opponent from reaching a desired position.

Art. 5. When both opponents are moving in exactly the same path and direction and the screener slows down or stops and contact results, the trailing player shall be responsible for such contact.

Art. 6. No player shall use arm(s), hand(s), hip(s) or shoulder(s) to force through a screen or to hold or push the screener.

Art. 7. Screeners shall not line up next to each other within 6 feet of a boundary line and parallel to it so that contact occurs.

    a. Screeners shall be permitted to line up parallel to a boundary line and next to each other without locking arms or grasping each other, provided that the screen is set at least 6 feet from that boundary line.

APPENDIX I TO NCAA RULES

BOTH MEN AND WOMEN

SECTION 1. COACH AND BENCH DECORUM

Coaches and/or other bench personnel who engage in the following actions are in violation of the bench-decorum rules and should be assessed a direct technical foul for:

a. Questioning the integrity of an official by words or gestures.

b. Physically charging toward an official.

c. Directing personal, vulgar or profane remarks or gestures toward an official.

d. Excessively demonstrating officiating signals (e.g., traveling, holding, verticality) or excessively demonstrating by use of gestures or actions that indicate displeasure with officiating. When not excessive, a warning should be given to keep such behavior from becoming excessive.
e. Voicing displeasure about officiating through continuous verbal remarks. A warning could be given initially to keep it from becoming continuous.
f. Using disrespectful or unsporting words, gestures or actions toward an opposing player or coach.
g. Leaving the coaching box for an unauthorized reason.

APPENDIX III TO NCAA RULES
OFFICIATING GUIDELINES
SECTION 2. SCREENING

Officials responsible for coverage away from the ball must be diligent in detecting and penalizing illegal screens. Some guidelines for officials to use when officiating screening situations:
a. When a player uses arm(s), hand(s), hip(s) or shoulder(s) to force through a screen or to hold or push the screener, it is a personal foul.
b. When contact results because a player sets a screen while moving, the screener commits a personal foul.
c. When a screener takes a position so close to a moving opponent that this opponent cannot avoid contact by stopping or changing direction, it is a personal foul.
d. When a player sets a screen outside the visual field of a stationary opponent and does not allow this opponent a normal step to move, it is a personal foul.
e. In cases of blind screens, the opponent may make inadvertent contact with the screener; and, if the opponent is running rapidly, the contact may be severe. Such a case is to be ruled as incidental contact, provided that the opponent stops (or attempts to stop) on contact and moves around the screen, and provided that the screener is not displaced if he or she has the ball.
f. A player who is screened within his or her visual field is expected to avoid contact by going around the screener.
g. A player may not use the arm(s), hand(s), hip(s) or shoulder(s) to force his or her way through a screen or to hold the screener and then push the screener aside in order to maintain a guarding position relative to his or her opponent.

SECTION 4. INTENTIONAL PERSONAL FOULING

Guidelines for calling the intentional personal foul are:
a. Any personal foul that is not a legitimate attempt to directly play the ball or a player is an intentional personal foul.
b. Running into the back of a player who has the ball, wrapping the arm(s) around a player and grabbing a player around the torso or legs are intentional personal fouls.
c. Grabbing a player's arm or body while initially attempting to gain control by playing the ball directly is an intentional personal foul.
d. Grabbing, holding or pushing a player away from the ball is an intentional personal foul.
e. Undue roughness used to stop the game clock is an intentional personal foul and, if severe, should be called a flagrant personal foul.
f. It is an intentional personal foul when, while playing the ball, a player causes excessive contact with an opponent.

The intentional personal foul must be called within the spirit and intent of the intentional-foul rule.

WOMEN'S-ONLY GUIDELINES

SECTION 7. WOMEN'S POST PLAY

The post-play guidelines must be followed by all officials to have consistent foul calls in this important area. A post player is a player with or without the ball with her back to the basket inside the free-throw lane or just outside the lane. Once a player has established her position legally as a defender on an offensive post player, she can neither displace her opponent nor be displaced from that position. When either happens, the official shall call a foul immediately. Officials need to be more aware of offensive post players in the lane for more than three seconds. Making this call will help curtail rough post play.

The following guidelines must be followed by players and called by officials:
a. When an offensive player with or without the ball has her back to the basket, the defensive post player may place a forearm or one hand on the offensive player. The defensive player may place a leg against the offensive player; however, if that leg is raised off the floor, a personal foul shall be called immediately. The defender may not place two hands, two forearms, or a forearm and hand on the offensive post player. A forearm and leg or a hand and leg may be placed on the offensive player as long as there is no displacement.
b. When an offensive post player with the ball has her back to the basket, the defensive post player must have a bend in her elbow if one hand is placed on the offensive player.
c. When a defensive post player places one forearm on the offensive player, she may use this forearm only to maintain position. Neither the offensive post player nor the defensive post player may dislodge her opponent. The official shall call a foul when a player is dislodged from her established position rather than waiting to see if there is an advantage gained.
d. An offensive post player with the ball, facing the basket, may be defended only with a forearm (see hand-checking b-1 in this section) unless she has not dribbled yet. In that situation, the defender may measure up (see hand-checking "a" in Section 7 below). Once the post player with the ball turns and faces the basket, she is no longer a post player but a ball-handler. When the offensive post player has her back to the basket with the ball and turns suddenly to face the basket, the momentary touching of the hand shall not be called a foul, but if the hand remains for longer than a count of two, a personal foul shall be called.
e. Players may attain a position where their bodies are touching each other but only to maintain position. Any attempt to dislodge an opponent from a position she has legally obtained is a personal foul.
f. The offensive post player cannot "back-down" the defender, once that defender has established a legal guarding position. The offensive post player cannot grab the leg or body of the defender, hook or in any way displace or hold the defender while she is preparing for the entry pass or already has the ball with her back to the basket. Three seconds in the lane is a violation that must be called on the offensive post player. If this violation is not called, the offensive team gains an unfair advantage. CALL THREE SECONDS.
g. The offensive post player with the ball cannot initiate contact and displace the defensive post player who has established her legal defensive position. This includes a defender with her arms straight up above her shoulders. Once the defender has established this legal position,

if contact occurs, the official must decide whether the contact is incidental or a foul has been committed by the offensive post player with the ball.

Verbal warnings given to players have proven to be ineffective whether officiating on the ball or off the ball. Officials should not talk to the players to try to prevent a foul but should call a foul when one occurs.

SECTION 8. WOMEN'S HAND-CHECKING

Officials must continue to call hand-checking from the beginning of the season to the end of the season. These guidelines must be followed:

a. Hand-checking on the dribbler is not permitted; however, a defender may touch the ball-handler with her hand once to measure her distance away for defensive purposes when the ball-handler is standing still and not dribbling. Once the ball-handler has completed her dribble and is holding the ball, touching the stationary ball-handler is not permitted. The second time the hand touches a stationary ball-handler the official shall call a foul. Additionally, touching the stationary ball-handler longer than a count of two shall be called a foul.

b. The only contact permitted on the dribbler from end line to end line (other than a post player with her back to the basket with or without the ball) shall be with the forearm.

   1. The forearm cannot stay on the ball-handler nor can it be used to push or guide the ball-handler. Placing the forearm on longer than a count of two shall be a foul.

   2. The wrist, back of the hand and the palm of the hand are not part of the forearm. Making a fist is the ideal way to put the forearm on the ball-handler; however, an open hand is legal as long as the palm is facing down and is not touching the opponent.

   3. Any displacement by either the defender or the dribbler shall be a foul. Contact resulting in displacement either with the hands, forearm or body is a foul. The dribbler may not use her hand, forearm or body to dislodge the defender.

   4. A defender who has legally applied a forearm on her opponent who has the ball, only to have that player move away, has not committed an illegal contact if the wrist and/or hand momentarily contacts that player. If the defender's arm straightens and contact with the hand and/or wrist persists, it is a foul.

c. When the defensive player is beaten to the basket and she reaches out and puts a hand on the opponent to intentionally have a handchecking foul call made to stop the dribbler from scoring, officials should call an intentional personal foul since this is not a legitimate attempt to play the ball or the player.

d. A foul shall be called when a defender touches the dribbler with her hand.
Note: On a drive to the basket when the dribbler has a hand placed on her, officials need to be aware of whether the dribbler has one more dribble to take. If so, officials should have a patient whistle and call the hand-checking personal foul as the player shoots. If the dribbler has two or more dribbles to get to the basket, the official shall call the hand-checking personal foul immediately.

e. It is not a hand-checking personal foul when a cutter without the ball is pushed or held with the hands of a defensive player; it is a pushing or holding personal foul. Immediate blowing of the whistle for hand-checking pertains only to the dribbler.

SECTION 11. WOMEN'S PRINCIPLE OF VERTICALITY

Defensive post players guarding a post player with the ball and defenders involved in trapping an opponent with the ball are entitled to have an erect (vertical) position even to the extent of holding their arm(s) above their shoulders. The defender(s) is not required to maintain any specific distance from a player. Once the defender(s) has established this legal position, if contact occurs, the official must decide whether contact is incidental or if a foul has been committed by the defensive player.

SECTION 12. (WOMEN) LEGAL DEFENSE (BLOCK/CHARGE)

There has been a lack of consistency in foul calls in this area. The following information should be taken into consideration when making these calls:

a. The defender has legally established her position when she has put both feet down on the floor and is facing her opponent. Once she has done this, she may move backward or laterally.

b. The defender is entitled to any spot on the playing court she desires, provided that she gets to that spot first, without contact with an opponent. A defender who establishes a position directly under the cylinder or behind the backboard when a dribbler becomes an airborne shooter is not in a legal guarding position, regardless if she got to the spot first. If contact occurs, the official must decide whether the contact is incidental or a foul has been committed by the defender. *Exception:* When a dribbler takes a path to the basket parallel with the end line, the defender's position directly under the basket is a legal guarding position and, if contact occurs, the official must decide whether the contact is incidental or a foul has been committed by the dribbler or airborne shooter.

c. If contact occurs by the dribbler moving forward at a faster pace than the legal defender is retreating or if the dribbler drops her lead shoulder or uses her forearm to push into the defender, a player-control foul shall be called on the dribbler.

d. The dribbler shall not:
   1. Charge into an opponent who has established a legal guarding position;
   2. Attempt to dribble between two opponents; or
   3. Attempt to dribble between an opponent and a boundary where sufficient space is not available for illegal contact to be avoided.

e. If a defender is able to establish a legal position in the path of the dribbler, the dribbler must avoid contact by changing direction or ending her dribble.

f. The dribbler must be in control of her body at all times. If illegal contact occurs and the dribbler is not in control of her body, the responsibility for the contact belongs to the dribbler.

MAJOR RULES DIFFERENCES

ITEM	NFHS	NCAA
Airborne shooter	In air after release of try or tap	Men—No rule Women—Same as NFHS
Closely guarded	Holding or dribbling in front court at 6-foot distance	Men—Same as NFHS Women—Holding only, front/back court, 3-foot distance
Coaching box: Size	State option, 14-foot box maximum	Extends from 28-foot mark to end line
Loss of use	If coach is charged with a technical foul	No rule
Disqualification: Players	Fifth foul or second technical	Fifth personal and/or includes direct technical fouls. Men—Intentional technical fouls
Non-team bench Head coach	Second technical Third (direct or indirect) or second direct technical	Second direct technical foul Second direct technical foul or third combination of directs and bench.
Player Participants After DQ	Direct technical foul also charged to head coach	Indirect technical charged to head coach
Double fouls: Personal	Alternating-possession throw-in at nearest spot	Back to same team with no reset of the shot clock or alternating possession.
Technical	Alternating-possession throw-in at division line	Point of interruption
Fighting	Ejection	Ejection. One-game suspension followed by season suspension—team and coaches

ITEM	NFHS	NCAA
Free Throw:		
Players on lane	Maximum of 4 defensive and 2 offensive players, two spaces nearest shooter must be vacant	Men—Same as NFHS Women—Same as men, bottom two spaces must be vacant
Restrictions - Violations	Restrictions end when ball touches ring, backboard or free throw ends	Restrictions end on release of the ball
Delay	Technical after warning for huddles and contacting free-thrower	No rule
Headwear	State association may approve for medical, cosmetic, religious	No rule
Offensive Team Fouls	No rule	Ball awarded out of bounds (no bonus free throws) when foul committed by any player of team in control (offensive team)
Officials on court	Fifteen minutes before start	Men—One at 30 minutes Women—On floor at 15 minutes and must return at 3 minutes
Player-control foul	Includes airborne shooter	Men—No airborne shooter Women—Same as NFHS
Shot clock	No rule	Men—35 seconds Women—30 seconds
Stop clock	No rule	After made basket with 59.9 seconds or less in 2nd half or OT
Substitutions	No rule	Not permitted with 59.9 seconds or less remaining in the second half (or OT) when clock is stopped for a made basket, a timing error or an inadvertent whistle

ITEM	NFHS	NCAA
Technical fouls:		
Penalty	Two free throws and possession awarded to offended team	All—Two free throws
Resuming play	Throw-in opposite table	Point of interruption Women—Same, except excessive timeout, loss of ball
10-second rule	Must advance from back court	Men—Same as NFHS Women—No restriction
Timeout(s):		
Basic length and reduction	Basic 60-second, reduced if both teams are ready	Basic 75 seconds, reduced when calling team notifies official (non-media)
Excessive	Technical foul	Men—Two shots and point of interruption Women—Two shots and loss of ball
Number and length	Three 60-second timeouts per game and two 30-second timeouts per game	Four 30-second and one 60-second for media. Four full and two 30-second for non-media
TV replay monitor	Not allowed	Officials may use for a timer/scorer mistake, clock malfunction, to determine individuals in a fight, rectify a correctable error …, at or near end of any period may use to determine if game clock or shot clock expired before release of shot
Unconscious player	No return without physician's (M.D. or D.O.) authorization	No rule

ITEM	NFHS	NCAA
Uniforms:		
Same number style/color front and back	Required	Not required
Horizontal lettering	Plane of letters may not overlap with plane of numbers, must be 1" from outside edge of numbers at any point	Must be 1" from outside edge of numbers at any point
Shirts designed to be worn outside the game pants	Not prohibited	Prohibited
Undershirt	Individual player must have same length sleeves	No unaltered sleeves, no cut-off sleeves or necklines
Videotape	Illegal to use during the game or intermission for coaching	Illegal only at courtside

Note: These differences do not include court markings; equipment; length of periods, game and overtime; officials' signals and mechanics; etc.

Coaches and players are encouraged to order the NFHS rules. They can be obtained at the following address and phone number.

NFHS Order Department
National Federation of State High School Associations
P. O. Box 361246
Indianapolis, IN 46236-5324
Phone: 800-776-3462

Appendix 2
Definitions
and Terminology

Back court is the half of the court opposite to a team's basket.

Backdoor occurs when an offensive player cuts behind a defensive player to the basket.

Ball-you-person triangle refers to proper help-side defensive position.

Baseline runs along the short sides (ends) of the court, underneath the baskets.

Belly up is the position that a defender assumes when a ball handler picks up her dribble. The belly up is a signal for the rest of the defensive players to deny their opponents the ball.

Boxing out is making contact with and screening an opponent from the basket with one's body in anticipation of a rebound.

Clear out is when a player moves out of a certain area the court to allow room for another player to operate one-on-one.

Cut is a sharp change of direction; players make cuts in order to free themselves from defenders in order to receive a pass.

Dead ball is a ball that cannot be dribbled. A defender shouts "dead" to alert her teammates to a dead ball on the court. Dead balls also refer to balls before they have been inbounded.

Denial is the term used to describe the position that a defender assumes on the wing when she doesn't allow her opponent to catch the ball.

Double-team is when two defensive players guard one offensive player.

Drive is when an offensive player dribbles to the basket.

Fast-break is used on offense to move the ball quickly down the court in order to gain a numerical advantage on the defense (2 on 1, 3 on 2, etc.).

Filling the lanes describes how players should run the fast break. Players should move down the court in designated areas (the middle, right, and left). These areas are known as lanes.

Foul is an illegal contact or another infraction of the official rules.

Front court is the offensive end the court where a team's basket is located.

Full court press is a defensive strategy in which a defense applies pressure on the offensive team the entire length of the court (from baseline to baseline). A full-court press can be a zone or a man-to-man defense.

Give-and-go is an offensive play in which a player passes the ball to a teammate and immediately cuts toward the basket looking for a return pass from that player.

Help-side or **weak-side** defense is played on the opposite side of the court from the ball.

High post area of the court extends from just above the free throw line to just below it (the first hash mark in the lane).

Low post area of the court extends below the first hash mark and includes the rest of the lane and both blocks.

Man-to-man defense, each player is responsible for guarding one opposing player.

Mismatch is a situation in which an offensive or defensive player had a distinct advantage on her opponent (in terms of size or ability).

Outlet area extends from the free throw line to the wing. Guards line up in the outlet area on after rebounds in order to be in good position to catch the outlet pass.

Outlet pass is the name for a pass made by a defensive rebounder to a guard.

Passing lane is the path that the ball takes in flight to another player.

Pick or screen occurs when an offensive player uses her body to impede the motion of an offensive teammate's defender.

Post refers to the area of the court closest to the basket, around and in the lane. (See high post and low post.).

Posting up is the term used to describe the position that an offensive player assumes in the low post area, which involves having her back to the basket.

Reversing the ball describes the basketball's movement as it travels from the strong-side wing to the weak side wing via a series of passes.

Sagging off means playing loose defense on an offensive player. Often the defenders that sag off are in weak side defensive positions (two or more passes away from the ball).

Secondary fast break follows the regular break (in the case that the offense couldn't get a shot off).

Stealing is when a player takes the ball from a dribbling offensive player, or intercepts a pass meant for an opponent.

Switch indicates a change in defensive assignment (often used in the context of the pick and roll).

Technical foul signals unsportsmanlike conduct by a coach or player or a violation of certain game regulations. A technical foul gives the opponent two free throws and possession of the ball.

Trap is a form of high-pressure defense, set by two defensive players in the hopes of stopping the ball and forcing a turnover.

Triple-threat position is the stance that an offensive player assumes after receiving a pass.

Turnover signals a change of possession.

Weak-side is the side of the court opposite the ball.

Wings are the areas of the court outside the three-point line (above the foul line extended) on either side of the floor.

Zone defense, each player is responsible for guarding an area of the court.

Appendix 3
Basketball Books
and Web Sites

WOMEN'S BASKETBALL BOOKS

A Drive to Win: The Story of Nancy Lieberman-Cline, by Doreen Greenberg and Michael Greenberg

A History of Basketball for Girls and Women: From Bloomers to Big Leagues, by Joanne Lannin

Basketball for Women: Becoming a Complete Player, by Nancy Lieberman-Cline and Robin Roberts

Chamique Holdsclaw: My Story, by Chamique Holdsclaw and Jennifer Frey

Coaching Girls' Basketball Successfully, by Rhonda Farney

Competitive Basketball for Girls, by Elizabeth Gettelman

Developing a Successful Girls' and Women's Basketball Program, by Stephanie Jordan

Five-Star Girls' Basketball Drills, by Stephanie Gaitley

Girls' Basketball: Building a Winning Program, by Clay Kallam

Hoops With Swoopes: Picture Book, by Susan Kuklin

Nothin' But A Champion: The Story of Van Chancellor Three-Time WNBA Coach of the Year, by Tom A. Savage

Raise the Roof: The Inspiring Inside Story of the Tennessee Lady Vols' Undefeated 1997-98 Season, by Pat Summitt and Susan Jenkins (contributor)

Raising Our Athletic Daughters: How Sports Can Build Self-Esteem and Save Girls' Lives, by Jean Zimmerman

Reach for the Summit: The Definite Dozen System for Succeeding at Whatever You Do, by Pat Summitt

She's Got Game, by Michelle Smith

Teresa Weatherspoon's Basketball for Girls, by Teresa Weatherspoon

You Can Be a Woman Basketball Player, by Tamecka Dixon

WBCA's Defensive Basketball Drills, by Women's Basketball Coaches Association

WBCA's Offensive Basketball Drills, by Women's Basketball Coaches Association

Winning Basketball for Girls, by Faye Young Miller and Wayne R. Coffey

Winning Women in Basketball, by Marlene Targ Brill

Women's Basketball: Inside the Practice Court, by Paul Sanderford

Women's Basketball: The Post Player's Handbook, by Anne Donovan

BASKETBALL BOOKS—MEN AND WOMEN

Basketball: Multiple Offense and Defense, by Dean Smith

Basketball for Dummies, by Richard "Digger" Phelps

Basketball's 1-4 Motion Offenses for Men's and Women's Basketball, by Harry L. "Mike" Harkins and Jerry Krause

Be Quick-But Don't Hurry! Finding Success in the Teachings of a Lifetime, by Andrew Hill

Blackboard Strategies: Over 200 Favorite Plays From Successful Coaches For Nearly Every Possible Situation, by Eric Sacharski (editor)

Coaching Basketball, edited by Jerry Krause and Ralph Pim

Coaching Basketball Successfully, by Morgan Wootten

Common Basketball Rules and Violations Made Simple, by Fred Bies

Full Court Press, by Mike Lupica

Husky Mania: The Inside Story of the Rise of UConn's Men's and Women's Basketball Teams, by Jim Shea

Leading with the Heart: Coach K's Successful Strategies for Basketball, Business, and Life, by Mike Krzyzewski

More Five-Star Basketball Drills, by Howard Garfinkel and Will Klein

Practical Modern Basketball, Third Edition, by John R. Wooden

The Basketball Coach's Bible: A Comprehensive and Systematic Guide to Coaching, by Sidney Goldstein

They Call Me Coach, by John R. Wooden

Wooden, by John R. Wooden

YOUTH BASKETBALL BOOKS

101 Youth Basketball Drills and Games, by Bruce E. Brown

Coaching Youth Basketball, by John P. McCarthy, Jr.

Coaching Youth Basketball, by Gerald O'Shea

Coaching Youth Basketball: A Baffled Parent's Guide, by Bill Thurston

My Losing Season, by Pat Conroy

The Bobcat Way: Coaching a Successful Recreational Basketball Program, by Steven E. Little

The Complete Idiot's Guide to Coaching Youth Basketball, by Tom Finnegan, Ph.D. and Bill Gutman

Youth Basketball Drills: 110 basic to advanced drills, by Burrall Paye and Patrick Paye

Youth Basketball Skills and Drills, Second Edition, by Rich Grawer and Sally Tippet Rains

BASKETBALL WEB SITES

www.aaugirlsbasketball.org: Amateur Athletic Union

www.basketball.com: Basketball news, statistics, etc.

www.basketballproducts.com: Basketball products for sale

www.bbhighway.com: Instructional videos, books, and links to basketball web sites

www.bgca.org: Boys and Girls Clubs of America

www.cnnsi.com: CNN and *Sports Illustrated*

www.cyosports.org: Catholic Youth Organization

www.espn.go.com: ESPN

www.foxsports.com: Fox Sports

www.fullcourt.com: Women's basketball news—*Full Court Press*

www.nabc.com: National Association of Basketball Coaches

www.naia.org: National Association of Intercollegiate Athletics

www.nba.com: National Basketball Association

www.ncaa.org: National Collegiate Athletic Association

www.ncaasports.com: Official web site for NCAA sports

www.nfhs.org: National Federation of State High School Associations

www.njcaa.org: National Junior College Athletic Association

www.officiating.com: Refereeing

www.powerbasketball.com: Coaching youth basketball

www.rivals.com: Sports news

www.sportamerica.com: Resource library

www.thenccaa.org: National Christian College Athletic Association

www.thesportingnews.com: *The Sporting News*

www.usatoday.com/sports: *USA Today* sports

www.wbca.org: Women's Basketball Coaches Association

www.wnba.com: Women's National Basketball Association

www.yboa.org: Youth Basketball of America, Inc.

ABOUT THE AUTHOR

Michael D. Mullaney has coached hundreds of girls' basketball games. His teams have consistently won league championships, tournaments and finished in the final four in the AAU Potomac Valley Region (Division II). He is currently coaching AAU and high school girls' basketball teams in Maryland.

At Bishop Kenny High School in Jacksonville, Florida, he was named Most Valuable Player for the 1973–1974 season, was named to the All-City Basketball Team as a point guard, and was awarded the 1974 John Burke Award for being the top student-athlete in the school. He was All-State in the mile and two-mile runs. He is a graduate of Florida State University.

He has been married to his wife, Sue, for more than 20 years. They have two wonderful daughters, Melissa and Michele.